RURAL UNWED MOTHERS: AN AMERICAN EXPERIENCE, 1870–1950

PERSPECTIVES IN ECONOMIC AND SOCIAL HISTORY

Series Editors: *Andreas Gestrich*
Steven King
Robert E. Wright

TITLES IN THIS SERIES

FORTHCOMING TITLES

RURAL UNWED MOTHERS: AN AMERICAN EXPERIENCE, 1870–1950

BY

Mazie Hough

Routledge
Taylor & Francis Group

LONDON AND NEW YORK

First published 2010 by Pickering & Chatto (Publishers) Limited

Published 2016 by Routledge
2 Park Square, Milton Park, Abingdon, Oxfordshire OX14 4RN
711 Third Avenue, New York, NY 10017, USA

First issued in paperback 2015

Routledge is an imprint of the Taylor & Francis Group, an informa business

BRITISH LIBRARY CATALOGUING IN PUBLICATION DATA

Hough, Mazie.
Rural unwed mothers: an American experience, 1870–1950. – (Perspectives in economic and social history) 1. Unmarried mothers – Maine – History – 19th century. 2. Unmarried mothers – Tennessee – History – 19th century. 3. Unmarried mothers – Maine – History – 20th century. 4. Unmarried mothers – Tennessee – History – 20th century.
I. Title II. Series
306.8'7432'09741'09041–dc22

ISBN-13: 978-1-138-66507-1 (pbk)
ISBN-13: 978-1-8519-6400-0 (hbk)

Typeset by Pickering & Chatto (Publishers) Limited

CONTENTS

ACKNOWLEDGEMENTS

This book has been long in the making and I owe a great deal of thanks to many people. First and foremost are the archivists in the Tennessee State Library and Archives, the Sherrod Library of the University of Tennessee-Johnson City, and the Maine State Archives. They brought me old files with a slight smile, 'We thought you might find this interesting.' The Good Samaritan staff invited me into their conference room and brought out reams of old minutes and reports. They also generously copied case record files twice, to remove identifying information. I want to also thank my history buddies, Carol Toner and Betsy Beattie, who always invigorated my love for what we were doing – tracking down documents that brought the people's history to life. My writing group always asked me questions that invariably led me to greater clarity (or back to the drawing board). 'What do you mean by traditional? What about race?' Thanks to Pauleena Mac-Dougal, Amy Fried, Sue Estler and Elizabeth Allan, but most especially to Marli Weiner, my mentor and colleague, whom we will sorely miss. And an especial heart-felt thanks to Paul Schroeder, librarian, carpenter, inventor and partner extraordinaire who has made me comfortable (and content) in my work and life. And last but not least, our daughters Greta and Emma and my co-conspirator in Women's Studies, Ann Schonberger, who have always encouraged me in whatever I chose to do.

INTRODUCTION

This is the story of rural white unwed mothers from Maine and Tennessee who, beginning in the 1870s, took advantage of the increased access to urban areas to find opportunities and support not available in their own communities. Although Maine and Tennessee differed in their economic and political structures, the rural communities from which these women came were remarkably similar. Isolated, rural communities everywhere in the United States shared a reliance on family and community that required hard work and neighbourliness. While men were by custom and law the heads of their households, women and children were valued for their labour, without which the family could not survive.

Between 1870 and 1950 the support and control of unwed mothers in the United States shifted from local communities to a network of social work professionals who counselled single pregnant women in more than 200 unwed mothers homes. Where once young women were kept in line by the oversight of older women who offered assistance but who also paid attention to any form of deviant behaviour, by 1950 trained professionals met with young women under conditions of extreme privacy and offered them choice but also emphasized the best interest of the child. Women in the late nineteenth century were likely to live with, or in close proximity to, their children born out of wedlock; women in the mid-twentieth century were as likely to give their children up to adoption and renounce any attempt to contact them again. This shift happened as the United States moved from a collection of island communities to an integrated nation state and as the care and control of the young women shifted from their local communities, to their individual states, to the national social work network.

Between 1870 and the mid-1900s the United States was transformed by an expanding corporate economy and consumer culture. Regional and local studies have described the ways in which rural communities responded to these changes and have generally concluded that the rural response combined adaptation and resistance. All agree that rural values persisted in spite of the changes. As Jeannette Keith notes, of all the 'millions who migrated from the hinterlands to the cities in the nineteenth and twentieth centuries; it was places like Upper Cumberland (Tennessee) that their values were formed'. Rejecting the idea that urbanization was a 'one-way street' she calls for recognition of an 'urban and rural dialogue'. Richard Condon speaks of rural Maine communities in the 1930s living in two worlds – the rural and the urban.[1]

This work focuses on the young women who moved out of their rural communities but who brought with them their rural experiences and values. Those experiences and values worked 'in dialogue' with what they found in the cities and what they found shifted with the growing power and influence of the professional networks, first in the state and then in the nation. At the turn of the century reformers in the cities throughout the US opened over 150 homes for unwed mothers.[2] Historians have found that the majority of women served in these homes came from rural areas. I argue that it is not possible to understand the experiences of the women in these homes – and of other pregnant rural women who came to the cities in search of support – without understanding where they came from and the values and experiences they brought with them. By 1950, however, the transformation of American society was complete. A majority of Americans, no matter where they lived, considered themselves middle class. Where once urban middle class values were at odds with values in rural areas, by 1950 the majority (though not all) of those living in rural communities shared similar beliefs in progress and individual achievement built upon hard work, education and respectability.

By focusing on rural white unwed mothers in Maine and Tennessee as they negotiated the changing conditions, this work reveals the way the political economy – first of the rural community, then of the two states and finally of the nation – defined their options. These options, I suggest, had more to do with the priorities of those who defined them than of the unwed mothers themselves.

Numerous historians have analysed the social and political implications of the transformation of the American economy and culture that began at the end of the Civil War. The revolutions in communication and transportation as well as the growth of corporate capitalism and the rise of the professional middle class all changed the form and function of communities. Small communities, defined by geography, and marked by face-to-face interactions and an interchange of goods and services extended over time gave way to communities defined by common interests and education. In the more complex, inter-connected United States of the mid-twentieth century, communities were defined not by space but by the acceptance of abstract rules, and the use of hard currency due at the moment of exchange. Modernity, a separation of space from place and the past from the present as well as a belief in change and a commitment to efficiency, was replacing traditionalism.

This transformation was also a transformation of social control and it occurred in two phases. The first phase was initiated by social dislocation as rural people moved in great numbers into the cities from the rural countryside and from abroad. In 1800 there were three cities of 25,000 people. In 1880 there were seventy-seven. By then one in four Americans lived in communities of over 8,000. This sudden congregation of strangers in cities where there were limited social networks and a growing disparity of wealth brought with them the threat of violence and loss of control. It was the stakeholders in these growing cities that forced new forms of social control on the state. As Lawrence Friedman notes of this growing urbanization,

> The city is the heart of modern society; society is governed from the city; the econ-
> omy depends on city life. The city is the place where people confront strangers most
> continuously, where their lives, property, and health are most at hazard. A society that
> is heavily urban and industrial, with extreme division of labor, has little tolerance for
> violent crime. Crime is bad for business, and bad for the social order.[3]

In the cities strangers confronted one another. Crime could only be regulated by an enforcement of the law and a criminal justice system that was seen to be impartial. Those in power in the city sought to impose law in such a way that everyone would know what to expect. This called for a system in which strangers – not neighbours – would make decisions about each other. In small communities law enforcement had relied on 'a wise panel of neighbors who understood the context of the crime'. In the city, new criminal justice professionals sought to replace that panel of neighbours with people 'who knew nothing, had heard nothing, suspected nothing' and who could treat the accused as if he was a complete stranger'. In a similar move, city officials sought to replace the neighbourhood coroner with a professional medical examiner, trained in forensics. For both coroner and jury in traditional communities, the community context and knowledge of the actors was as important as the facts. Crimes could be dismissed if the community determined them to be an aberration for the individual. It was the person and his relation to others more than the crime that was on trial. In the cities, it was the crime that was most important. 'The common denominator' in regulating the cities, Roger Lane concluded, 'was regular, predictable behavior, the same thing that made the trains and trolleys run and kept great crowds of hundreds or even thousands of people moving peacefully to and from work every day, at the same hours'.[4]

Unwed mothers were not considered criminals but as women unsupervised by men they did threaten the social order. Doreen Massey notes that in small-scale areas where control by the community can be tight, 'women have presented little threat to men. The scale and the complexity of life in the big city, however, make such regulation and control more difficult' and, as a result, control and surveillance in the city has 'always been directed particularly at women'.[5]

When the city stakeholders turned to the law to control unwed mothers, they turned to two distinct legal traditions. State legislators, judges and lawyers in both Maine and Tennessee sought to create 'regular, predictable behavior' in the cities, but they did so in ways that reflected the two very different political economies of the two states. While both Maine and Tennessee were originally part of one of the first thirteen colonies and were both settled roughly at the same time by Anglo-Saxon Protestants, they were distinguished by two very different demographics, economies and political structures. These differences resulted in two very different experiences for the unwed mothers in the two states.

Tennessee was marked by diversity in agriculture, wealth and race. The western two-thirds of the state were suitable for cash crops and the development of a slave economy; the eastern third supported only subsistence farming. The diversity supported by a slave economy meant that Tennessee's population was marked by a great disparity in wealth and privilege. At one end were African-Americans who had extremely limited privileges, legal or otherwise, and at the other, white male plantation owners could operate almost without limitation. As a certain level of wealth was required for those who served in the government and as the wealth comprised only a minority of the population, the state legislators wrote and enforced laws in such a way as to maintain their control of the state. They did this by emphasizing the distinctions of race, class and gender, and by offering certain privileges to all white men. As Victoria Bynum notes in her study of social and sexual control in North Carolina, 'Maintaining a slave society based on racial distinctions necessitated control over women's sexual behavior and offspring'.[6]

In Maine the agricultural conditions were not conducive to large land-holdings. Those who worked the land generally farmed as much land as their family labour allowed. As a result, there was much less opportunity for accumulating great wealth and less encouragement for people to move into the rural areas of the state looking for economic gain. In Maine, representation to the governing bodies did not require a certain level of wealth. Representation in both bodies of the legislature, however, was by community, even when those communities were very small. As the state's pauper laws required every community to support those who had a settlement within them, the legislators worked to make sure economic responsibility was assumed by someone other than their own small communities.

The second phase in the transformation of the treatment of unwed mothers came with the growing strength of the federal government and the professional middle class. In the early twentieth century, organizations began to pressure federal and state governments to assume responsibility for what their professional expertise determined was best for society. Doctors pushed for anti-abortion laws; social reformers pushed for repression of information on birth control;

women's reformers pushed to end what they called white slavery and for regulation of the food and drug industries. In 1913 the United States ratified the sixteenth amendment that enabled the federal government to "lay and collect taxes on incomes, from whatever source derived." The federal government now had the funds necessary to support a growing bureaucracy which could be used to disburse funds for social programs and regulation of commerce and industry. Over the following decades the federal government grew slowly but steadily. In 1870 the government employed a little over 50,000 civil servants; by 1950 that number had grown to almost two million.

As the government grew, so did corporations. Both depended on increased efficiency and widespread acceptance of bureaucratic rules sought by the new managerial class. James R. Beniger has called this transformation a control revolution. He points out that bureaucrats, by increasing their capacity to process information and by standardizing the information gathered, are able to 'maintain large-scale social systems'. Noting that the values of a bureaucracy that promoted efficiency were the same as those required of large corporations, Olivier Zunz adds that 'empire building was dependent on bureaucracy building, and the ultimate success of bureaucratic rules depended on the imposition of new values'. Those values, he suggests, were the values of the 'middle class, influenced by the managerial class of the corporations that brought their values into the rural areas'.[7]

For almost a century professionals had moved slowly to solidify their positions of authority within the society at large by requiring specialized training and national standards and by insisting they be consulted on their area of expertise. Their advice, they argued, was based on sound scientific principles. Deferring to their expertise was best for the individual and society. By 1950 their influence and their values united the country as families and individuals adopted the middle-class dream of upward mobility, built upon individualism, education and a good reputation. Robert W. Weibe writes of the shift in relations that emerged with the rise of the cities in the new industrial economy. For the new professional middle class, he maintained, the

> new order promised ... release. At a minimum it provided outlets never before available for their talents. Usually it offered them respectable and profitable positions as well. In time, they became sufficiently secure to look beyond the day's work and try to locate themselves within a national system.[8]

For new professionals, he argued, their organizations provided new values and interests to unite them even as their occupational cohesion 'widened the gap between the major cities and rural small-town America'.[9] If the treatment of unwed mothers in the rural communities were a response to the needs of those communities for women's labour, and the response in both Maine and Tennessee

a response to the needs of those in power in the state, the response that succeeded both in the 1950s filled the needs of the managerial middle class

Each step in this societal transformation had a particular impact on rural
white unwed mothers. While many community members retained their distinct
set of values they nevertheless needed to respond to the changing social context.
Historians of rural life in late nineteenth¯ and early twentieth-century United
States have described lives that are remarkably similar in the north and south.[10]
The foundation of this life was the family farm where roles were strictly divided
by gender and where the work of both men and women was critical for survival.
The families were embedded in tight-knit communities in which neighbours
looked after each other and provided help when help was needed and who kept
an eye on each other to make sure everyone complied with community norms.
Men were in control of both the communities and the families and children contributed necessary labour as soon as they were able. These communities were
isolated, relatively egalitarian and markedly static. Community members relied
on each other for basic services and for assistance. The small amount of cash
needed for taxes and goods that had to be purchased were gained through seasonal or temporary labour.

There is a strong similarity between the rural culture in these two American
states and that in Europe prior to industrialization. There is also a strong similarity in the way all of these rural communities dealt with birth outside of marriage.
In her overview of *Gender and Poverty in Nineteenth-Century Europe* Rachel G.
Fuchs outlines how historians of the family in Europe have identified responses
to unwed mothers in rural communities. Pre-bridal pregnancy was not always
a stigma and did not preclude marriage. Many single pregnant women either
stayed with their families or with kin and eventually married. Even when they
had moved into the cities, she concludes, 'Poor women had their own codes of
conduct retained from their lives in rural areas, and expected men to marry them
after they consented to sexual relations.' The uniformity of this response was
not complete. In Russia, for example, marriage was reserved for the respectable
and unwed mothers did not usually marry. Nevertheless, the persistence of this
widespread acceptance of out of wedlock pregnancy in preindustrial European
communities suggests that it was the insular nature of the communities, not religion or ethnicity, that determined this response.[11]

As in nineteenth-century Maine and Tennessee, communities in Europe
prior to the industrial revolution 'tended toward self sufficiency and self-con-
tainment'. They were governed by an 'intricate web of loyalty and obligation'.
People defined themselves within those communities by their relationships to
one another. While there were social hierarchies, everyone was included in a system of mutual claims and responsibilities. People were expected to look after
one another and this included providing for each other in times of want and, by

keeping an eye on each other 'imposing a conformity that most modern people would find absolutely suffocating'.[12]

Communities organized in this way would have a particular response to unwed mothers. Understanding that a woman would provide support for them when it was needed, they would balance her willingness to work with her sexual impropriety. They would know that, as she wasn't going anywhere, they could always keep an eye on her and prevent her from other rash acts. In addition, they could probably identify the man responsible and make sure that he provided what was necessary. In addition, relying on one another, working side-by-side, they would have come to know the woman through her work. Daniel Kemmis, reflecting on rural American communities, describes the tolerance that might grow out of shared work. He writes of a barn-raising in Montana and how it influenced the relationship between his mother, a woman who did not approve of alcohol, and Albert, who drank prodigiously and was 'too fond of off-color stories'.

> Lilly and Albert didn't like each other much better at the end of the barn raising that at the beginning. But that day, and many others like it, taught them something important. They learned, whether they liked it or not, a certain tolerance for another slant on the world, another way of going at things that needed doing. They found in themselves an unsuspected capacity to accept one another. This acceptance, I believe, broadened them beyond the boundaries of their own likes and dislikes ... In addition they learned they could count on one another.[13]

There was another factor involved as well. As Nancy Cott found in her study of marriage in the United States, isolated communities, remote from official state bodies, 'exercised practical control of marriage formation, preservation, and termination'. In many rural communities, sexual activity before marriage was accepted as the first step in a process. In communities where everyone kept an eye on everyone else, neighbours could accept pre-bridal pregnancy because they could make sure that marriage followed. As late as 1911, a maternity home staff-member in the United States commented of women from non-industrialized communities in Europe,

> Among certain classes abroad premarital relations seem to be common, and not looked upon as objectionable ... the idea commonly accepted in Germany and Austria of regarding a betrothal as sufficient grounds for men and women to live together ... is undoubtedly reflected in the opinions commonly heard from our girls that there is no impropriety in sexual intercourse if a promise of marriage has been made or may be reasonably expected.[14]

Similar acceptance of pregnancy outside of marriage has been documented within the African-American community in the United States. This response must be understood in the historical context of slavery in the United States, but it was also reinforced by the isolation of the black community by race if not by geography.[15]

While traditional communities had a similar response to unwed mothers that extended across time and location, when rural white women entered the cities towards the end of the nineteenth century, they entered a community where different social and gender relations were the norm. The cities, in contrast to the rural communities, were filled with strangers. They were spaces where people recognized each other by dress and behaviour, not by longstanding experience.

In Tennessee following the Civil War the cities were flooded with freed men and women; in Maine, the French Canadians arrived with their families in great numbers to work in the mills. In both states the cities grew rapidly as immigrants from the countryside moved to where there were jobs and where goods and entertainment beckoned.

Threatened by the loss of means to control the fate of single women, men in both places turned to the state. In Tennessee, legislators rewrote the laws to pressure white women to protect their own reputations and their families' honour. In Maine, city managers sent women back to their hometowns. In both cases, the laws that were enforced reflected the interests of those in control of state government. Joan Jacobs Brumberg has pointed out that the late nineteenth century was a time when 'illegitimacy had become a traumatic event'. While a lack of systematic record keeping makes it hard to determine the extent of pregnancy outside of marriage, the public discourse exploded with discussion of the poor unfortunate, fallen or ruined single woman who became pregnant. Made thus visible in the public imagination, negotiating a whole new set of gender relations and expectations, the rural white women found support among the wives of those involved in the state's politics and economic activity who opened maternity homes. With the support of the privileged women they had an opportunity to learn how to navigate the new terrain of public and private spaces as defined within each state.[16]

Over the next half-century middle-class values permeated the American culture as the federal government increased its influence over the states, and professional organizations expanded their national networks. In the affluence that followed World War 2 many white families believed they could achieve middle-class status. In 1944 Congress passed the GI Bill of Rights which provided returning GIs with priority for jobs, loans to establish small businesses and farms, educational benefits and technical training, and mortgage assistance to buy homes. As one historian has noted, this was 'perhaps the most significant social legislation of the war years. Sociologists have identified occupation, place of residence, and level of education as three crucial determinants of social class. The GI Bill granted veterans the means to improve their status in these three areas and more'. Four years earlier a national poll estimated that almost 80 per cent of Americans considered themselves middle class. With a position in the middle class presumably within reach, white families strove to achieve it. What this meant for their daughters was that they had to maintain the family's reputation and accept a sexual propriety maintained by a vigilant and private family.[17]

The impact of this shift on unwed mothers was profound. Between 1945 and 1973 an estimated one-and-a-half-million unwed mothers relinquished their infants to strangers for adoption. In that time, there were as many as 25,000 women in more than 200 maternity homes that had to turn away as many as 35 per cent of their applicants for lack of room. Secrecy within the homes was essential and many travelled out of state to make sure their privacy would be protected. Ann Fessler interviewed as many of these women as she could find. She tells story after story of young women in small towns who were pressured by family members, social workers and priests to give up their babies. Said one, 'I remember being really afraid of how she [her mother] would act. I was the one child of her four who just might make it through school, might make it out of our little town'. Another commented 'I was from a small town, so I didn't tell anybody because in 1968 you were considered trash if you were pregnant. They symbol of being a good, white, middle class family was a lily-white daughter'. Still another acknowledged, 'It was weird because the purpose of sending me there was to hide it, but everybody in town already knew. You can't keep a secret like that in a town of 1,200, so I didn't get why I had to go away'. Noting studies that found those who placed their children for adoption 'generally ... had higher educational aspirations', Fessler concludes,

> For those families who were moving up, whether white or black, there was a tremendous fear of losing the ground they had gained. Conforming to the middle class values of the time was paramount. Many of the women I interviewed spoke about their parents' fears of being ruined if anyone learned they had an unmarried pregnant daughter.[18]

As with the rural communities, industrialized communities shared a similar response to unwed mothers in the last half of the twentieth century. Canada and Australia, for example, report similar stories of women being forced to give up their children to save their families' reputations. In the forefront of those advising the women and their families were professionals. The policies, Fessler concludes, 'were shaped by experts – primarily psychiatrists, social workers, and medical professionals – and promoted by social organizations that had the power and means to disseminate the ideas'. As one young mother noted, 'The message was this is the good thing to do for your baby. It would be really impossible to keep it'.[19] This message was very different from the one many rural women received only several decades earlier.

A Definition of Terms

The fact that so many unwed mothers interviewed by Fessler identified themselves as middle class even though many were from small towns and did not have a lot of money makes clear how slippery socioeconomic terms can be. The definition of rural is equally as slippery. The formal definition used by the US census is a town of 5,000 or less. Avis C. Wiggins, who studied 'the migrant girl' in Nashville in 1933 found that 57 per cent of the girls came from the open country, one to fifteen miles away from a community centre or post office. The majority came from centres with populations less than 2,000 and over a third came from communities of less than 500.[20] I am interested specifically in communities which are relatively isolated and in which community members rely upon one another for mutual assistance and support. The women who came to the Good Samaritan Home in Bangor had to have references from three people in their communities, so it is easy to identify their rural backgrounds. The women in Tennessee are less easy to trace, though the scattered evidence places them in small towns in Tennessee and the surrounding states. Whether they were pregnant when they came to the city (as I believe they were in the Maine cases) or became pregnant after they arrived in the city (as may have been the case for some in Tennessee) is less important than that they identify in some way with a non-urban locality – that they grew up in, and became familiar with the values of, the small communities. The relative isolation of the communities is important. It encouraged mutual aid. There were a few Franco-Americans who came to the Good Samaritan Home and often these women were from communities larger than 5,000. They were not directly from a rural community but their community was an isolated one. The Franco-American population in Maine came from the rural area of Quebec and settled in the cities to work at the mill. They were motivated by the idea of *Survivance* – that is, they wanted to retain their culture separate from the Protestant Anglo community in which they found themselves.

'Unwed mother' is an equally difficult term to define. Daniel Scott Smith concluded in his research on illegitimacy that the amount of births to unmarried women between the Civil War and World War 1 is extremely difficult to determine and that 'it is doubtful whether scholars will ever be very certain concerning the magnitude of the problem'. Protestant churches did not keep such records; many states did not require the registration of births until the second decade of the twentieth century; and the federal government did not include such statistics in its vital statistics until 1933.[21] Women who gave birth outside of marriage had a variety of options and were more often defined by others based on their class, race and location than by themselves. Women left babies in city streets; their families locked them in attics or paid institutions to rear their children; the courts found them to be 'in fear of falling' and committed them to industrial training schools. The term 'unwed mother' at the end of the nineteenth and beginning of the twentieth century was generally reserved for those who entered maternity homes or placed their children for adoption through social service agencies or the black market. Anecdotal evidence suggests that various ethnic groups kept 'illegitimate' pregnancies far from view. In Maine, one woman reported that her great-great-grandmother was an Irish Catholic immigrant who went to work in the mill and was 'taken advantage of'. Her parents locked her in the attic and her sister and brother-in-law took care of her baby. A court case initiated by an out-of-wedlock child makes clear that at least one wealthy Jewish family paid an orphanage to bring up a child. Immigrant women – not labelled as unwed mothers – gave birth in the poor farm. Others were committed to the Industrial training school where they gave birth. And still others stayed home and took care of their child as best they could. For the most part, those defined as unwed mothers had some claim on the dominant culture. They were generally white and native born.[22]

I have identified the rural communities as 'traditional' and the cities as 'modern' though both terms are complex and variously defined. By traditional I mean communities which remain relatively stable through generations. Darrett B. Rutman prefers the term 'small' to identify communities in which '"farm families faced the same essential problem: how to extract from what land they have the wherewithal to meet their needs and wants. And everywhere the relationships between families tend to form neighborhood networks'. These communities share a certain mutuality but differ in terms of their social stratification, demographic and connection to a larger world. I find his conceptualization useful but the term he uses too slippery for a larger work.[23]

Methodology

This is a comparative study of two states chosen because they represent two regional (and very different) responses to unwed mothers. Rachel G. Fuchs wrote that one could not understand the single pregnant women in Paris in the nineteenth century 'without first trying to fathom the world in which they lived. The attitudes that politicians, writers, and social commentators held about them in many ways circumscribed the women's lives ...' I would add that one also needs to understand the world (community) from which they came in order to understand the choices they made.[24]

In my analysis I draw on feminist geographers who reflect on the complexities of place. I agree with them that place matters and that the rural place and its impact on peoples' lives has not been investigated as it should. Doreen Massey argues that geography is instrumental in the construction of gender and that space must be 'conceptualized integrally with time'. Localities, she argues, 'are

not just about physical buildings, nor even about capital momentarily impris-
oned; they are about the intersection of social activities and social relations ...
which are necessarily, by definition, dynamic, changing'.[25] Reflecting on globalization she notes that it is not enough to 'talk of the collapse of time and distance,
or to see it in terms only of movement and flows ... what is at issue is the changing geography of (changing) social relations. And to analyse the impact of those
changes it is necessary to take account of both sides of the formulation'.[26]

Evidence of the lives of rural women at the turn of the nineteenth century
is scant given their lack of leisure time. Nevertheless, it is possible to recreate a
sense of how others viewed them and how they may have viewed themselves by
exploring the world in which they lived and the choices that they made. The two
states I have chosen not only developed two different legal responses to unwed
mothers, they also provide access to different kinds of sources. Though I had a
comparable resource in court records, the other sources were diverse. In Maine
I found a treasure trove of primary documents in the detailed minutes, case
reports and letters kept by the Good Samaritan Agency in Bangor. In Tennessee,
I found numerous historical studies of the political economy and its impact on
women, both those that looked at Tennessee specifically and those that looked at
the south as a region. Tennessee and the south also inspired a number of contemporary social investigations and oral histories while Maine and the Northeast
did not. By triangulating these diverse but rich materials I have uncovered a
story that deserves to be explored more fully. I have found that those who have
experienced rural communities find my explanations true to their experience. I
can only encourage more research in this area.

This work is divided into five chapters. The first explores the nature of the
rural communities in both the north and the south. It then outlines the two very
different legal traditions that developed in Maine and Tennessee.

In 1876 and 1877 privileged women opened five unwed mothers homes
in Tennessee. Chapter 2 tells the story of how the one opened by the Woman's
Christian Association attracted rural women because it helped them to negotiate the gendered terrain in Memphis. The opportunity that the WCA Home
offered women was short-lived as the white privileged women chose race over
gender and remodelled their home to fit with the prevailing legal tradition that
emphasized the importance of reputation for all white women and white men's
role in protecting it.

A rash of infanticides in the last two decades of the century alerted privileged
women in Maine to the desperate situation of unwed mothers in rural communities. Of the two homes that were opened for unwed mothers, one implemented
the rural practices and attracted both large numbers of rural women to the Home
and widespread support from the community. This is the story of Chapter 3.

Chapter 4 returns to Tennessee when the US Children's Bureau and other organizations staffed by the new professional social workers were pushing for national standards in the care of unwed mothers and their children. Georgia Tann, the director of the Memphis Tennessee Children's Home Society drew on both the authority of the developing social work field and on Tennessee's tradition of placing children in families of greater status than their own, to develop a large and notorious child adoption programme.

Chapter 5 explores how those same professional standards forced changes in the Good Samaritan Home that led to rural women rejecting its services.

1 RURAL COMMUNITIES AND REGIONAL DIFFERENCES: MAINE AND TENNESSEE

In 1870 the United States was a collection of island communities, rural places that were relatively isolated from one another and in which populations were stable over generations. These communities were similar to traditional communities in Europe where everyone within a family worked hard, where children were seen as assets (promising work now and in the future) and where neighbours both took care of each other and kept watch over each other. Over the next fifty years, those island communities would be drawn into a larger world as new technologies, a growing national economy and an expanding consumer culture penetrated their isolation. By 1920 more than half the country's population would live in the city and radios, automobiles and the post office would connect all but the most remote areas to the metropolitan world.

This transition would have a profound impact on single women who gave birth outside of marriage. As community isolation eroded so did the community's ability to control and watch over its members. When this happened, women were forced to turn to the state and to the laws developed by those in power. It was there that they met and had to deal with laws that were very different in Maine and Tennessee. This was true even though the two states were both once part of the original thirteen colonies and inherited the same British Common Law tradition.

In political, economic and demographic terms, Maine and Tennessee provided a stark contrast to each other. Although many Tennesseans fought to preserve the Union and a number of Maine men 'skedaddled' to Canada to avoid battle, the states opposed each other in the Civil War. Not only were some of the war's bloodiest battles fought in Tennessee, but federal forces occupied much of the state for much of the war. When President Andrew Johnson of Tennessee vetoed the civil rights bill that was to have protected freed slaves, Senator William Pitt Fessenden of Maine proclaimed that Johnson had 'broken the faith, betrayed his trust, and must sink from detestation to contempt'. Reconstruction marked the beginning of Republican Party dominance in Maine. Although it was contested, particularly by those in the eastern part of the state, the Democratic Party controlled much of Tennessee.[1]

Economically and demographically the two states were equally disparate. Tennessee is geographically divided into three distinct regions: the mountainous and rugged east, a more fertile and flat middle, and the western delta along the Mississippi River. The distinct regions attracted three distinct agricultures. Subsistence farms in the east, diverse crop production in the middle, and cotton in the west. Most of the west and much of the middle grew on slave labour. While the first settlers who moved into the east in the late 1700s were white pioneer Protestant families looking for land, the plantation economies of the other two regions drew an increasing numbers of slaves into the state. By 1870 almost a quarter of the population was black, and these recently freed slaves lived almost exclusively in the middle and the west.

The varied agriculture and access to forced labour led to a great disparity of wealth within the state. Some planters – a small portion of the population – benefited from the work of over 200 slaves. Meanwhile, the first settlers on mountainous terrain in the east, far from commercial centres, eked out a living. The majority of white farmers were middle level farmers who had been able to work towards owning their own farms over time. Following the Civil War, tenant farmers replaced the slaves in working the land. In exchange for the use of the land, they paid landowners cash or a share of the crop. This crop-lien system bound both freedmen and a number of poor white farmers in an endless cycle of debt and dependence.

The disparities in wealth were not as great in Maine as in Tennessee. Most farmers owned their own land. Those who gained great wealth were engaged in shipping, factory production or lumbering in the interior. While the wealth centred in the cities, political power was spread across the state as every town sent representatives to the state legislature on a rotating basis. Maine, then a region of Massachusetts, abolished slavery in 1783 and was admitted to the Union in 1820 as a free state. What few blacks there were in the state – never more than 1 per cent –congregated in the cities. Maine's diversity came from French Canadians who, beginning in the 1860s, came in family groups to work in the shoe and textile factories. They too primarily congregated in the cities.[2]

In spite of the political and economic differences, the rural white folk in both Maine and Tennessee lived remarkably similar lives. Most were Protestants. Many had ancestors who had come as pioneers to carve out lives for themselves in what they considered to be wilderness. Limited as they were by poor transportation and lack of communication with a larger world, they lived in very similar island communities. The essence of an island is that it is cut off from the mainland and is, by necessity, self-sufficient. While it would be an exaggeration to say that this isolation was absolute – in the course of the late nineteenth century an increasing number of farmers in Maine and Tennessee were drawn into the market economy – the communities remained relatively isolated and self sufficient. Resources were limited and valued. Barter prevailed and neighbours helped each other out in times of trouble or when extra work was required. H. Clay Stiner of Tennessee remembered the community in Norris Basin, where 'Everybody lived alike. If some of the neighbors got sick and had a crop out, the other neighbors would go in and work his crops or whatever else was needed ... [If] one had the sickness, if one didn't have food, they'd take the food into the home. If one died, they take care of the body'. In Maine, up to the turn of the century, communities hosted pound parties where people brought a pound of something to the party to support a widow or others in need.[3]

Even in areas where farmers were more mobile, community remained important. Tenant farmers of the south moved more often than other farmers. Nevertheless, Margaret Hagood who interviewed 254 tenant farm women, most of whom lived 'in the open country, rural farm area', found that few were 'more than three miles from a store' and that every woman interviewed referred to 'this neighborhood or this community'. They judged their communities, she noted, by the level of social interaction they found within it and by its 'cooperation, friendliness, and local customs'.[4]

This kind of mutuality relied on a stability that continued through time and generations. Community members could trust that if they provided services now they would be provided with similar or equal services in the future. Parents knew they would support their children while they were young and rely on the children to support them in the future. It also reinforced a notion of us, the community, against them, the outsiders. H. Clay Stiner suggested that 'Every community lived to support itself' and took pride in 'not having to go to them [other communities] for anything'. Vera Stiner recalled the local practice of 'rocking'. When a boy from another community took a girl out, 'her friends that didn't want him to come in would be along the road to throw rocks at him ... and sometimes they'd get hurt too'.[5]

Those within the community, though divided by levels of wealth, shared a certain equality. In Maine, every male participated in town meeting where 'the most elemental decisions' were made. The personal nature of exchanges in all rural communities mitigated against merchants or landowners abusing their economic power.[6] 'Everybody lived alike', H. Clay Stiner commented of his community in Tennessee, and Myers Hill agreed.

> Not because of being poor or anything like that they wasn't looked down on in the community I lived in, because there wasn't any what you say well-to-do people in the community where I lived. And poorer people, everybody respected them just as much as they did everybody else, just as long as their character was good. The only people who was maybe looked down on was the people who had poor characters ...[7]

The other side of mutual support was the fact that everyone in a small community knew what everyone else was doing. There was a purpose in this knowing – neighbours would know when someone was in need – but there was also, no doubt, recreation in it as well. People watched each other and talked about each other.

> Now I know that some folks back through here in Big Ivy will say Aunt Tobe McKinney is a gossip. Law ha' mercy, a gossip is a sharp-tongue woman and I'm not that. I never say a harm word of nobody unless I hear they done meanness of some kind. Well, I do scatter the news when news is to scatter. Somebody's got to do that or how is people going to know what's going on?

said one informant to James Axell in Big Ivy Tennessee in 1938 or 39. I. A. Newby who traced the rural roots of the early mill workers in the south interviewed Vinnie Partin who remembered, 'We knew everybody. Carrboro was a very small place and we knew everybody. And we would get caught up with our work and then we'd go around in each other's alley, you know, in the room, and talk'. The proximity of their work may have made it more possible for the mill people to talk together often, but the WPA interviewers in rural Tennessee record constant comings and goings of visitors from the community while the interviews were in session.[8]

Lura Beam recollecting the Maine hamlet of 227 where her grandparents lived at the turn of the last century commented,

> Most of the people of the hamlet lived together so closely that the collective feeling was like that of the tribal clan or the British regiment ... everyone knew everyone else: what he did, what he had, what he paid, what had happened to him, how he met good and ill. Older citizens knew the younger as the continuing story of their parents and grandparents.

Jeannette Keith in her study of the Upper Cumberland in Tennessee concluded that in those communities in 1890, 'Solitude was unusual, and privacy was unknown; everyone knew their neighbor's business.'[9]

Knowing everybody was only part of the equation, the other part was talking about what you knew. 'To be "talked about" amounted to a vote of censure'. Beam noted. 'It meant a thorough canvas of ancestral shortcomings and current misdeeds ... that could hardly be lived down in a life-time. Talk was an appalling weapon calculated to keep citizens toeing the straight and narrow'.[10]

The family as well as the community offered both support for and restrictions on women. The family was the foundation of the community and within the family there was a strong definition of gender roles. 'The modal pattern is for the woman to do everything inside the house, for the man to occupy himself on the farm, and for both to share the intermediate duties centring around the back yard and relating chiefly to the care of livestock', Hagood found. J. B. Killibrew who published a detailed study of the resources in Tennessee in 1874 noted, 'The women of the rural districts, it has been said, do their own household work. It is not considered a hardship by them to cook, wash, iron, milk, churn, clean, spin the "filling" and make the cloth for the entire family. They also make their bed-clothes'. Beam describes a similar kind of balance in the lives of her grand-parents.[11]

In both North and South, farm women also filled in for men in the fields when necessary. The superintendent of the Good Samaritan Home wrote of one Maine woman who was called home that her life was 'indescribably hard':

> She tells me that she has taken the place of a man in the fields for years; that in the spring of '27 she herself planted thirty acres of potatoes, with a potato planter, that she assisted her father and step-mother to cut them for that planter, that she and her father did the haying, and that she was all the assistance he had in harvesting the crops.[12]

This division of labour was required to keep a farm operating. As a result eve-ryone worked hard, everyone's labour was important, and everyone found it necessary to be married. It also meant, however, that the work was unrelenting. The Children's Bureau reported in its study of white farm women in the south, 'One mother prepared the family meals, did a big washing, and churned on the day her baby was born ... Another carried two gallons of water 100 yards uphill an hour before labor began. A third washed and scrubbed on the day of her confinement.'[13]

Men did not do women's work and women's labour was so important that young girls were required to fill in for their mothers when necessary.

As one southern daughter described it, 'Mammy died when I was twelve years old. She laid her burden down and I took it up'. Another older daughter detailed her days:

> I was hollered out of bed at 4 o'clock and after I'd got the house cleaned up if I didn't go to the branch to wash, I went to the field to hoe. When I seen the sun get to noon I went back to the house and cooked dinner. Then when I'd hung my dishrag on the plum bush outside the kitchen door I grabbed my split bonnet and took back to the cornfield[14]

There was plenty of work to go around and the children were expected to do their share. As one tenant mother explained it:

> They can begin toting in wood a stick at a time when they're two. Soon after I start 'em to drying knives and forks, because they can't break them, and when they're a little older, the other dishes. They can sweep by six and carry water in small buckets

and tend the baby. By ten they can clean house, make beds, and straighten up, and by twelve or thirteen can cook a meal if they have to.[15]

Children were assets. The number of acres apportioned to a farmer often depended on the number of children he had. As one Kentucky man, father of five, commented in 1938, 'What more could a man want? The more children I have the more land I can tend, the more money I can make'. Owners of the mills in rural areas in the south also gauged the work a family could perform by the number of children involved and gave preference to larger families. 'Always', Newby asserts, 'this emphasis on numbers appears. Mill officials, like rural landlords, were first concerned with the size of a man's force'. Jones I. Freeze remembered, 'When Mr. J. W. got ready to open up his mill back in '86 he didn't have but thirteen houses for his hands. Mr. J.W. figured if he hired big families, he could get enough hands in them thirteen houses to work his mill ...'[16]

The important role that children played in the rural family resulted in a certain acceptance of children born out of wedlock. Laurel Thatcher Ulrich who studied one rural Maine community in the late eighteenth and early nineteenth centuries, found 'There is no evidence in rural communities women who bore children out of wedlock were either ruined or abandoned ...' Instead, though the entire community kept a close eye on all young women, their sex outside of marriage was accepted as part of the gradual transition into adulthood and the women kept their children, remained with their families and eventually married.[17]

Scattered evidence suggests that this was true in rural communities in Maine and Tennessee a century later as well. Liston Pope commented in his study of rural workers in the mills in Gastonia in 1942, 'Sexual immorality is discounted to a greater extent among mill villagers and illegitimate children are generally accepted without serious penalty'. In the early 1900s a teacher in an Appalachian school wrote that one girl, who had never known a father, was 'never slighted by the others in work or play'.[18] Margaret Hagood in her study of tenant farmers during the Depression found parents anxious to control their daughters' sexuality, but she also found that children born out of wedlock 'were fully welcomed into the family and are objects of the devotion and petting usually accorded to the "baby" of the family by all its members'.[19] Lura Beam asserted of her rural community that 'a sexual experience before marriage was reprehensible in men, unpardonable in women. If it were followed by a forced marriage, the couple lost face. Since everyone knew, they might just as well have worn a letter'. Nevertheless, in her hamlet of 227 in one decade there were seven forced marriages and three births out of wedlock.[20]

We can understand this acceptance of children born out of wedlock when we consider the context. The importance of the family network and the willingness of neighbours to help out when necessary meant that a child without one or both parents could find a home with others. The oral histories from Maine and Tennessee are filled with references to children being taken into others' homes. One Tennessean noted that her husband's mother wasn't married and he 'was raised up by his kinfolks'. Another commented on the good-looking girl who threw herself away. Her daughter was 'the little girl that Miller and his wife took to raise. That's one thing about share-croppers. They never seem to have too many children to feed and clothe but what they can find a place for one more'.[21]

In closed communities, where children's work was important, infertile couples would take in children to help with the work and to take care of them in old age. As one Maine woman noted about the twelve-year-old daughter she adopted, 'I took her because we needed help'.[22]

As Beam acknowledged, community members paid attention to neighbours' sex lives and remembered their impropriety long after it was over. Nevertheless, the value of a woman's labour, the dependence of the family and the community on everyone's work, led to an evaluation of women that was based as much on what work they performed as on their reputation for chastity.

In addition, as Nancy Cott in her study of marriage points out, the close supervision that the community provided allowed the community to be more lenient of sex outside of marriage. Through the nineteenth century and even later in some rural areas, she noted, 'The most effective disciplining as well as honoring of marriage ... took place in the local community.' Where the population was spread out and far from state control, 'the state apparatus was not likely to enter the life of a couple unless they were reported to authorities by neighbors'. The informal public 'made up of family, kin, and neighbors exercised practical control of marriage formation, preservation, and termination ...'[23]

The mountains of Tennessee protected communities from the reach of the state and residents tended to ignore some state laws. As one historian pointed out, public documents for the Appalachian Highlands reveal virtually no divorce before World War II, although New Deal social workers found a substantial minority of single adult households that were created by separation as well as death. Lola Simmons, who moved directly from the mountains of Eastern Tennessee to Knoxville, described her reasons for failing to get married. She admitted that neighbours talked about her living with her partner and having a baby with him but, she said:

> I don't see no difference in the way me and Calvin feels about Cap (her child) because we never did have the time nor money to git a preacher or justice of peace to say a few words over us. It costs a lot of money to git married. More than five dollars some places. We never seen five dollars ahead till we come down here to Knoxville. They it seemed like a plumb fool waste of money. They tell me...common-law marriage is just as good as a church or court one any day. So I ain't noways ashamed that me and Calvin has never got around the regular kind.[24]

Men worked hard too and in many marriages the work of both balanced each other. But custom and law gave the advantage to the men. They moved in a larger circle. Their work took them away from the farm more often. In addition they were the ones who earned the cash through seasonal labour, and could vote and hold office. On the farm (and in the mill) they were the ones who controlled the labour of the others.

This constellation of values and practices led to a concept of young womanhood that was different from that in the developing middle class. The middle class concept of 'true womanhood' grew from the idea that men and women occupied different spheres. It called for families to be kept separate from the workplace and public view, and for families to pay attention to the family's respectability. For its daughters, it called for the protection of their reputation for chastity. Middle-class values were penetrating into the rural areas but recognition of this new standard depended, in part, on proximity to the aspiring middle class. Although Hagood found acceptance of children born out of wedlock among the tenant farmers, she also found that tenant mothers were strict with their daughters and would not let them go out of the house alone with a boy. She noted the fact that 'economic opportunity for climbing is so very slight leaves as the only way for the tenant to identify himself with the superior class, the clinging to the forms of middle class respectability'. [25]

Court records tell us more about the state apparatus and those who were attempting to make it work for them than the individuals caught up in it. Even so, appellate court records for Maine and Tennessee offer us a tantalizing look at the implications of the rural gender arrangements for young single women. In both Maine and Tennessee, rural women involved in bastardy and seduction suits appear to have had a certain freedom in unsupervised space, a knowledge of abortion, birth control and legal options, and a community that understood that sex might happen before marriage.[26]

In both states, young women seemed to have the freedom to move in a wide area without supervision. They got pregnant in their kitchens and bedrooms, at their next door neighbour's or sister's house, in the woods and on the way to church. A Tennessee judge chided a father for not showing 'the prudent care of the virtue of his daughter' when he 'habitually permitted her to go alone at night. Both on horseback and in a buggy ... to church, with young men and return between ten and twelve o'clock'. Another chided a stepmother for allowing her stepdaughter 'to go to (her brother-in-law's) house after she was a full grown woman'[27]

It was certainly in the best interest of a man accused in a breach of marriage case to claim that the woman in question was sexually aggressive. Nevertheless, the explicitness of some accusations sometimes even corroborated by the woman herself suggest at least some rural women had common knowledge about sexuality and its consequences. Men told of women refusing intimacy until they could be protected and of going on their own to obtain abortions. As one court noted,

> The plaintiff ... insists that she was as willing as he was to have sexual intercourse, but feared the consequences, to wit pregnancy ... He claims she yielded this objection on his telling her he could use an instrument for protection called a 'cundrum', and that he went to a neighboring village, on this understanding, and procured this article, and then went to see her, and she asked if he had it, expressed herself as very glad of it ... and when he adjusted it she promptly engaged in the sexual act with him'. In this he is corroborated to some extent by the girl's own statements'. [28]

In another case, a man who was struggling to convince the court that he was not the father admitted under cross examination that 'he had visited her as a suitor, and that he had taken various liberties with her person, which need not be stated here'.[29]

The attorney representing Delbert E. Maxwell asked Lula Mann of Maine if she had not kept company with Jones for about a year and if she had not asked Jones to come to her house and there asked him to marry her. Lula refused to answer, even though the court assured her it would not have any bearing on the case. Mrs Lillian Gould told the court that Luella Drew had confided in her when she had recovered from childbirth and gone home to get baby clothes, that John Byers was the father. 'I was going to lay it on John Byers', Gould reported Drew had said, 'but my father wouldn't let me'.[30]

Employers and married men took advantage of some women, but others were intimate with their partners for as many as four years before they got pregnant and brought a breach of marriage claim.[31] A number of the women in both Maine and Tennessee married other men before their breach of promise or bastardy suits had worked their way completely through the courts. Alice Messer's son was two when she married someone who was not his father. The affiliation with a birth outside of marriage did not stop her husband from holding important positions in their Maine community and running for state office.[32]

Juries agreed that women should get compensated in a breach of promise to get married. The Tennessee appellate courts records are filled with cases in which, in spite of accusations of a woman's promiscuity, the jury awarded as much as $5,000 to the woman for the injury she sustained. In their deliberations, jury members noted the traditional practice of engaging in sex before marriage. As one jury concluded in 1913,

> She makes out a case of deliberate seduction – the case of an old, experienced man, who insinuates himself into the affections of a young, ignorant, inexperienced country girl, and by instilling in her the hope of a marriage, overcomes all her scruples ...

It is the case of a widower inducing an unsophisticated female to believe that it is no harm to embrace, if the parties are engaged to be married.[33]

If communities, as represented by the juries, allowed women a certain amount of sexual freedom, once women entered the court system, they faced judges who had a different concept of appropriate womanly behaviour. This occurred increasingly towards the end of the century as the railroads and then automobiles brought the expanding consumer culture into the rural areas and at the same time made travel out of those communities desirable and possible.[34] In both Maine and Tennessee there was a general out-migration of the rural populations. In both states social commentators bemoaned the declining rural populations and pondered how to keep the young people on their farms. The census for both states confirms there was reason for concern.[35]

When, as a result of these changes, single women left the communities that had both controlled and protected them, they entered larger communities that were defined by state laws. It was here that Maine and Tennessee women faced very different options. This was true in spite of the fact that Maine and Tennessee at the end of the nineteenth century had much in common. Both states possessed large rural populations and small manufacturing bases. A large proportion of people in each state relied upon small farms and the extraction of natural resources. Congress had admitted Tennessee to the Union in 1796 and Maine in 1820 but each had been part of one of the original thirteen colonies and each was developed by land speculators and Protestant families looking for land. Both states incorporated the laws of the colonies of which they had been a part and quickly extended suffrage to every white male citizen.

As similar as the two states were their different geographies led to two very different demographics, settlement patterns, agricultural economies and political structures. These in turn led to two very different legal traditions for dealing with unwed mothers.

Maine did not have the conditions that would have supported a labour intensive crop such as cotton or tobacco. In addition, the majority of farmers owned their own land and cultivated as much as they could with the labour of their own families. Consequently Maine did not look for or attract agricultural labourers. Although French Canadians had begun to move into the state in search of jobs in the mills, they strove to retain their separate identity in the cities as Catholics and French speakers. The rural areas remained overwhelmingly white Anglo-Saxon and Protestant.

In contrast, Tennessee was a slave state until all southern slaves were freed by the thirteenth amendment in 1863. Thus a significant black population often lived and worked close to whites, but race marked all who had any black ancestors as different within the law. The slave system and the wealth it created both enabled a minority of the white population to gain considerable wealth and at the same time challenged that minority to retain its control over both blacks and less advantaged whites. Numerous historians have explored the ways in which a white elite appealed to other white males to support its political power and the role that gender played in that effort. As one noted, the 'South's peculiar racial caste system has shaped the lives of women in a myriad of ways'.[36] The power structure shifted over time but the white elite always emphasized race and gender in its effort to retain its control. It offered white men of all classes privileges of being male and white. It also encouraged them to adopt elite values and behaviours that protected the lineage of a family and the clear separation of the races. Honour, or reputation, was critical to the power elite in Tennessee. Every white person could benefit from it, but only if he or she abided by its rules.

The two states had different settlement patterns as well. Maine inherited the town governance structure from colonial Massachusetts. The towns held regular town meetings, sent representatives to the state legislature, organized and supported a militia, provided support for the poor, and collected taxes for education.[37] It was the support for the poor, required by Maine's settlement laws, that had the most significance for unwed mothers. For Maine's settlement laws placed the responsibility for the support of children born out of wedlock directly onto the town.

Maine, like every other state in the nineteenth century, had a poor-law which required every town or county to provide basic support for its residents. As Blackstone explained in outlining the British Common Law from which these laws came, 'there is no man so indigent or wretched, but he may demand a supply sufficient for all the necessaries of life from the more opulent of the community by the statutes enacted for the relief of the poor'.[38] Maine's law was unusual, however, in that it not only required a town to support any of its members in need but also allowed town members to provide that support and charge the town for the costs.[39]

To obtain a settlement in Maine one had to be born in the town or live in it continuously without receiving public support for five years. Once having gained a settlement, however, an individual did not lose it until she or he either moved out of state or gained a settlement elsewhere. A woman and her child had the settlement of her father until she married. While the law required towns to support everyone who had a settlement within them, towns did everything they could to make sure they only supported those they had to. In colonial times in Massachusetts, towns 'warned out' indigent strangers who threatened to remain within them. Cases in the nineteenth century, debating who was responsible for a particular pauper or family of paupers fill the Maine appellate court records. Maine towns sued relatives for not providing for their dependents and sued other towns for not taking care of those for whom they were legally responsible. 'A father may emancipate his children or transfer his parental rights to another', the court stated in 1840, 'but this does not relieve him from the obligation of furnishing them with necessary support if not otherwise provided'.[40]

Towns also regularly returned paupers to their place of settlement or charged their place of settlement for any support provided. Records of the overseers of the poor in Bangor suggest that every effort was made to send pregnant women back from whence they had come. In cases where women came to Bangor needing support, for example, the overseers of the poor of Bangor sent formal notice to the towns in which the women had settlements. The notice stated that an individual needed support:

> We give you this information that you may order removal or otherwise provide for him (her) as you may judge expedient. We shall charge the expense of his support to your town as long as we are obliged to furnish him with supplies.[41]

The overseers of the poor, elected annually, could provide supplies or auction the support of an individual to the lowest bidder. As towns erected poor farms in the mid-to-late nineteenth century, the practice of auctioning off the poor gave way to placing them in the farms. Whatever the solution, however, the town poor, concluded one historian 'for all their shame at being put on public display, were not anonymous. Poverty was not an abstraction'. Both those who determined what to do with a pauper and those who provided for her were one's neighbours.[42] Retaining power in Maine did not require political balancing between those who had and those who did not but instead involved protecting the resources of the rural areas.

In Tennessee it was the county rather than the town that sent representatives to the legislature, organized the militia, and arranged for the treatment of the poor. Every four years after 1834 county residents voted for such county officials as the justice of peace, sheriff and county trustee.[43] The county commissioners of the poor were responsible for maintaining the county poor farms where those who had gained a settlement by living in the county for one year might go. The commissioners thus served as intermediaries or buffers between the community and the poor. The absence of appeals with regard to care for paupers in the court records of Tennessee compared to the plethora of cases in Maine suggests the different degree of community involvement in providing support.[44]

Maine and Tennessee also differed in the productivity and diversity of their agriculture. Both states developed commercial agriculture in the nineteenth century. Maine farmers dealt with 'poor markets, poor transportation and a growing season filled with uncertainty'. A large percentage of Maine farmers owned their own land and followed a 'typically New England strategy of growing a broad range of subsistence crops to hedge against market or crop failure'.[45] The difficulties posed by the climate and soils limited how much any one farmer could accumulate. As a result the discrepancy between the rich and the poor was relatively small.

In Tennessee farmers who were well situated could take advantage of the favourable farming conditions and the availability of labour to accumulate large amounts of land and capital with cash crops. Young men often worked as labourers on their way to owning their own farm.

While Maine farmers faced common challenges in their efforts to make commercial agriculture benefit them, Tennessee farmers varied dramatically in their access to commercial markets. In East Tennessee the land was not suited to major cash crops and transportation was limited. Most farmers there relied on subsistence agriculture. In the more fertile middle and west Tennessee lands, some farmers could translate large landholdings and slaves into great wealth, while others were unable to afford land. As a result, there was a great discrepancy in wealth even within the white population. By 1860, 20 per cent of those who worked the land were tenant farmers; some owned less than twenty-five improved acres and a few owned plantations of more than one thousand acres. Farms ranged in value from a few hundred dollars to one-quarter million. Donald Winters in his study of ten representative counties throughout Tennessee found that the top 10 per cent of farmers owned a little more than half of the farm value by 1860 and the bottom 20 per cent held a 'minuscule portion of total value'. Upward mobility for whites, however, was possible. A large number of tenant farmers in his study succeeded in acquiring land in ten years and those who owned land increased their holdings. Some increased their holdings significantly. James Shirley, for example, who in 1850 worked fifteen improved acres, by 1860 owned a farm worth ten times the amount and had increased the number of slaves he owned from one to five.[46]

The different access to wealth led to different forms of political representation in Maine and Tennessee. Maine had no property requirements for members of the legislature or governor and every town, no matter how small, sent a representative to the legislature on a rotating basis. Maine representatives and senators, as a result, committed to protecting their towns from unnecessary financial burden. They did this by emphasizing everyone's responsibility for taking care of one's own.

Tennessee, on the other hand, required that members of the house and senate own at least 200 acres and the governor, at least 500.[47] As a result the Tennessee Legislature implemented laws that reflected the interests of a certain economic segment of the population. These interests included maintaining power and privilege. The elite did this, in part, by allowing all white men the privilege on controlling their families but only if they remained committed to protecting all white women's reputations and maintaining the state's racial caste system. In addition, while offering those with property special privileges, they encouraged the upward mobility of whites by linking class with behaviour and inviting others to adopt upper-class behaviour.[48]

The differential access to wealth in Maine and Tennessee had an additional consequence. The fact that most Maine farmers owned their own land may have led to out-migration, but it also offered little opportunity for newcomers to join the agricultural class. As a result, Maine communities, although losing populations, were otherwise stable and could count on one generation supporting another in due time. Maine communities relied on inter-generational systems of mutual obligation that extended from the family outward. Family farms passed through 'as many as four or five generations'. In return for the inheritance of the farm and the estate, title transfers obliged children to provide for their parents in their old age, with, as one title delineated, 'suitable meat, drink, lodging, and a horse and carriage to ride when they think proper ... and ... medicine ... and ... a decent burial'.[49]

In a similar fashion, the parents provided their minor children with 'care, nurture and support' in return for their correlative rights to the children's 'services and earnings'. Maine's first adoption law specifically excluded inheritance rights. It established instead that an adopted child 'be deemed the same rights as the child of the body, merely for the custody of the person and the right of obedience'. Adoptive parents could, and did, bring seduction suits against those who enticed their adopted daughters away, depriving them of the services that they had acquired through the adoption.[50]

Community members also participated in this set of mutual obligations. Laurel Ulrich, in her study of a Maine midwife's diary, noted how older women who no longer had children at home to perform certain necessary work would take neighbourhood girls into their homes. In exchange for training in household tasks, the young women would provide hard physical labour.[51]

The reciprocal obligations worked as long as people remained within the community. Maine's laws served to reinforce the status quo. The adoption law, for example, required only that an adopted child be maintained to 'the condition or degree' to which the child was accustomed.

In contrast, the communities in Tennessee where money was to be made by agriculture were more fluid and changing. While most Tennessee farmers did not own slaves, the majority of those who sat in the Legislature did. For them, the inter-generational continuation of family wealth was more important than inter-generational mutual obligations. In contrast to Maine, Tennessee's first adoption law focused on the right of inheritance.[52] Furthermore, the coerced labour of slaves (and later freedmen) undermined the assumption of mutual obligation based on work performed. Race automatically placed African-Americans in a category unto themselves.[53]

In short, the political and economic imperatives in Maine led to the development of laws which reflected the values and practices of its small communities – closed to outsiders, dependent upon an inter-generational system of mutual rights and responsibilities, and designed to encourage residents to remain within and contributing to the community. On the other hand, the political and economic imperatives of Tennessee led to the development of a statewide system of control that was hierarchical but expansive – open to outsiders, reliant upon coerced labour, and congenial to the upward mobility of whites and the accumulation of wealth.

For unwed mothers, these two different political economies translated into two very different bodies of law as both states modified the shared Common Law tradition with regard to bastardy and seduction. In Maine, the laws encouraged women to be independent by providing them with a certain autonomy, emphasized the importance of responsibility, and made clear distinctions between those who belonged and those who did not. In Tennessee, the laws gave men authority to protect women's reputations, emphasized the importance of a white woman's chastity, and were open to all whites who accepted the rules.

According to British common law the child born to an unwed mother had no legal standing. As Blackstone commented:

> The incapacity of a bastard consists principally in this, that he cannot be heir to anyone, neither can he have heirs, but of his own body; for being nullius filius, he is therefore kin to nobody.[54]

Having no kin posed two economic problems for children born out of wedlock. They could not look forward to inheriting from anyone and they had no one responsible for their support. Furthermore, common law included no provision for adoption and, therefore, no legal way for children to assume an inheritance. Common law, however, did provide for the support of children born outside of marriage. Though the English bastardy legislation of 1575–6 referred to 'an offence against God's law and man's', its import was exclusively economic. Making reference to the bastards 'being now left to be kept at the charges of the parish where they be born, to the great burden of the same parish', the law authorized two justices of the peace to order both the father and the mother to support a child born out of wedlock and to commit them to jail without bail until they provided enough surety to perform the order.[55]

In Maine, the settlement law that emphasized a community's responsibility was crucial. The local community controlled a woman's options but gave her autonomy to act within that community. It did not ostracize a woman who gave birth out of wedlock. Instead, its members joined together to ensure that the putative father provided sufficient support to the mother and her child for as long as was necessary. In order to gain such support, however, a woman had to reveal to the community at large the details of her pregnancy and remain within the community where everyone knew her story.

The Maine bastardy law of 1820 remained virtually unchanged for over 100 years. It gave a woman who gave birth to, or was pregnant with, a 'bastard' child the right to go before any justice of peace and ask that a prosecution be brought against the man she accused of being the father. The justice of peace 'taking her accusation and examination in writing, under oath' would then send out a warrant for the man and bind him with 'sufficient surety or sureties' to appear at the next court session, where the case would be tried by jury. At the trial the woman had to state the time and place where she conceived 'with all practicable precision' and, having been 'put upon the discovery of the truth during her travail', she had to have named the man and remained constant in her accusation.[56] If the man were found responsible he could be charged with the costs of the suit, the expenses of the delivery and regular payments for the support of the child. The court was to determine the amount of support and the length of time for which it was to be given based on the woman and the child's needs. The man found by the court to be the father of the child was required to give a bond to ensure that he would continue with his payments. If he could not give bond, he was jailed.

At the heart of the trial was the requirement that a woman name the father of her child as she was giving birth. While originally the law required this only if a woman wished to testify in her own trial, by 1835 it had become an essential element of the case. 'It was deemed', the court concluded:

> that in the hour of her agony and under the danger of immediate death, there would be little fear of the utterance of the falsehood or the concealment of truth on her part. Obligations equivalent to the sanctions of oath and securities for trustworthiness greater than any derivable from cross examination, result from the critical nature of her position.[57]

Once a woman had named a man during her labour and was constant in her accusation of him thereafter, there was little a man could do to defend himself. It did not matter if the woman had asked someone else to marry her, had named someone else before the birth or had intercourse with another a few days after conception. It was immaterial even that a woman had been a prostitute for the past three years. 'In this court', the court stated emphatically, 'the character of the complainant for chastity is not an issue.'[58]

Bastardy law in Maine gave standing to the unwed mother and placed her in her community context. Only the woman herself could initiate a bastardy suit, and once she had initiated it, the court could not dismiss the suit without her consent. This was true even when town officials, a guardian or the woman's father negotiated a settlement with the putative father.[59]

While the requirement that a woman state where and when she got pregnant required a woman to reveal intimate details in court, the information allowed the jury to consider the social relations that were involved. In 1841, for example, Emily Woodward accused John B. Shaw of getting her with child. At first Emily testified that conception occurred in her father's sitting room in May. When the doctor testified that the child was born full grown in October, Emily claimed she had been mistaken. She had conceived the child in February in the bedroom adjoining the kitchen. John claimed that Emily had not been constant in her accusation, but the court determined that the variance as to time and place did not matter as long as she continued to accuse the same man. The couple had been engaged; and John had asked Emily's brothers to publish their intentions to be married. The court concluded, 'We cannot fail to reflect that there may be facilities for association, in a continued courtship, which the jury could understand and appreciate'.[60]

In 1843, Ann Burgess accused Leonard Bosworth of getting her with child in Bosworth's kitchen just before bedtime. The jury found for Ann, but Leonard appealed. He argued that Ann had taken out a complaint against another man before giving birth and therefore she was not constant in her complaint. Ann's lawyer pointed out that Ann was in Leonard's employ and argued that it 'would be subversive of justice if compelled by threats from the father of the child in whose house she lived she accused another' and that this should furnish him means of escape. The court agreed.[61]

Almost 100 years later seventeen-year-old Annabelle Boisvert brought a bastardy suit against Leo Charest. Although Annabelle signed a statement that she did not know the paternity of her child and received fifty dollars from Leo, the jury found Leo guilty and the appeals court agreed. No doubt, the court argued, the jury thought the young French girl did not understand the meaning of paternity. No doubt too, the jury 'thought that he desired to get rid of her as easily and as quickly as possible at small expense'.[62]

The court acknowledged that the sight of a woman testifying in a bastardy suit tended to sway the jury but, as it concluded in the case of Emily Woodward who more than once had intercourse with her lover, the jury had gone far 'but probably not further than they should, in order to prevent an undue influence of sympathy with the deserted and unfortunate female'.[63]

The woman's community played an important role in the suit as well. Under Maine law, a woman had the settlement of her father and her child shared her settlement. The town had a vested interest in the outcome of the trial for it would have to support the mother and child if the father did not. The law was designed to 'relieve the town from burthen as well as to aid the mother in their support', and once a woman had initiated a suit, she could not reach a settlement outside of court without the agreement of the town. Officials of the town could, and did, track down a putative father and negotiate the terms of a settlement with him. They paid legal fees for a woman and encouraged her to bring suit.[64]

Perhaps on account of the town's vested interest in a suit, the settlements from a successful suit were often substantial. They included the cost of delivery as well as regular support of the child until it was eight years old or older. 'It is impossible precisely to foresee the period when charge ought to cease', the court determined. 'Much will depend on the health and capacity of the child'.[65] Furthermore, there was no statute of limitations. Even if the man went to jail for being unable to pay his debts and took the debtor's oath, he was still required to fulfil his obligations to his child. Due to the double nature of the suit – the responsibility to the town as well as the woman – the law required the man give assurance that he would fulfill his obligation in a bond to both, and even in the mid-1800s that bond was often as much as $1,000.[66]

As supportive of women as the Maine bastardy legislation was it did not support all women. It discriminated against those whose fathers had not lived in the state long enough to obtain a settlement and those who had not invited others to attend the births of their children. Settlement laws allowed towns to provide service to a woman and then send a bill to her town of settlement or to send the woman back to her town. Those from outside of the state were outside of this system. The records for the overseers of the poor in Bangor reveal that more than two-thirds of the women who gave birth in the city's poor farm between 1830 and 1925 were immigrant women from Europe. They came to the poor farm just before they delivered, stayed for four weeks, and disappeared from the record.[67]

Those who gave birth alone suffered an even worse fate. The requirement that a woman name the father of her child during labour not only gave importance to the woman's testimony but also required that she be with others when she gave birth, for she had to name the father to someone else.[68] Under a law adopted from a 1696 Massachusetts statute that began:

> Whereas many lewd women that have been delivered of bastard children to avoid their shame and to escape punishment, do secretly bury or conceal the death of their children, and after, if the child be found dead, the said woman do allege that the child was born dead, whereas it falleth out sometimes (although hardly it is proved) that the said child or children were murdered by the said woman, their lewd mothers, or by their assent or procurement ... [69]

Maine legislated that an unmarried woman whose infant died at birth should be punished as if she had committed murder unless she could prove by one witness at least that the child had been born dead. The law also incorporated the Massachusetts statute that punished any woman who concealed the birth of an illegitimate child by setting her on the gallows for half an hour with a rope around her neck. This section of the law made clear the distinction between those who delivered in secret, without even one witness, and those who did not. An 1841 Maine law emphasized this fact by stating that even if the woman were acquitted of murder under this statute, she would still be punished for concealment. Gradually the legislature diminished the punishment for both offences and, in 1869, the court determined that a woman should no longer be forced to make the birth public. Nevertheless, the case in which this decision was made reveals the continuing two-sided nature of the bastardy laws in Maine.[70]

Margaret Kirby was an immigrant woman who gave birth to a dead child and left it in someone else's – most likely an employer's – privy. A boy found the body and a coroner determined that the baby had been born dead. Neverthe-less, Margaret was brought to trial. Alone, dependent on others for her support, too far from her home to return to it, Margaret had few options. She was not punished and the court determined in the future that women in her position should not be required to make public the birth to 'the first over-curious med-dlesome, inquisitive scandal monger'. Nor, however, was she provided with any assistance.[71]

In contrast to Maine, Tennessee implemented laws that made clear distinc-tions by race and class rather than geography or settlement. These laws changed over time in response to changing political conditions.

Like Maine, Tennessee developed a dual system for the treatment of unwed mothers, one that distinguished not by community affiliation but by class and race. Poor women of both races were vulnerable to the state involving them in a bastardy suit while families of the upper class (or those successfully adopting upper-class behaviour) had the right to bring a seduction suit against any man who deprived a woman of her virginity.[72] While bastardy suits offered a woman only a small compensation and threatened her with the loss of her child, seduc-tion suits could result in substantial compensation. They required, however, that men step forward to protect women's reputations or (later) that women act with appropriate reticence. With this dual system, Tennessee courts encouraged white men to support the political system by offering to protect them from the petitions of poor women, by keeping control of children and inheritance in male hands, and by emphasizing the rewards of appropriate upper-class behaviour.

Tennessee's original bastardy legislation was adopted from North Carolina's law of 1741, and had much in common with Maine's law. As in Maine, the draft-ers of the original law intended to 'save the county harmless' from supporting the child of an unwed mother. Also as in Maine, they relied on a woman's word in court. Within several decades, however, the Tennessee Asembly passed laws which severely limited the autonomy allowed a woman and the amount of sup-port she was likely to gain.

The initial law empowered a justice of peace who had information that a sin-gle woman within his county was delivered of a child to cause such a woman to come before him and examine her on oath concerning the father. If she did not name the father, the justice could put her in jail until she did. While the woman could not escape going to court, the man could not escape the penalty. Once a woman had named a man upon oath before two justices, 'the person so charged is undeniably fixed. He can never be received to aver the contrary ... If an issue be made up, and the jury find he is not the father, still he is so in legal contemplation'. For if another court overturned the original decision, the court asked rhetorically, 'who then is to maintain the child? There is none left but the public, and thus the very object of the law is defeated'. The court required a man charged with bastardy to pay the physician, midwife, supplier of necessaries and the one who provided maintenance of the child.[73]

In 1822, when suffrage was extended to all white men, the Tennessee Assembly rewrote the law. The new law allowed any man to contest a paternity charge by submitting an affidavit in which he stated he was not the father and that the charge was without foundation and made out of malice towards him. Although the man did not have the right to a jury trial and although the court could not compel the woman to testify, the defendant could attempt to impeach the woman's moral character or show evidence of her general bad character in order to discredit her testimony. A man could, for example, bring in others to testify that they had had sex with her. 'It would be monstrous', the court determined in 1835, 'to fix a stigma on a man's character and a burden on his estate, upon the unsupported affidavit of a woman, whose character was so abandoned that no one would believe her on oath'.[74]

The new law went even further. It imposed a three year statute of limitation and ordered that the amount to be paid be limited to ninety dollars in total: forty dollars the first year, thirty dollars the second and twenty dollars the third. At the end of the three years the law determined that all 'allowances shall cease...and the County Court shall dispose of the bastard child as most conduce to its interest, either by giving it to the reputed father, or binding it out to some suitable person'. Furthermore, the law stipulated that the money was to be paid directly to the commissioners of the poor and not, as in Maine, to the woman herself.[75]

In 1871 the court made explicit what had been the practice for many years when it determined that the county court was forbidden 'from making any provision for a bastard' – that is, from taking actions against a putative father – except in cases in which the child was, or was likely to become, a county charge.[76]

Bastardy law in Tennessee was limited and punitive. It was not, however, the only recourse for an unwed mother. Unlike Maine, where bastardy law remained the major legal tradition related to illegitimacy, Tennessee developed two parallel traditions built on the legal concepts of legitimation and seduction. At the heart of the set of laws was differentiation. As sociologist Barbara F. Reskin asserts, 'Differentiation ... is the fundamental process in hierarchical systems, a logical necessity of differential evaluation and differential reward ...' It 'assumes, amplifies, and even creates psychological and behavioral differences in order to ensure that the subordinate group differs from the dominant group'. Tennessee laws distinguished between black and white, male and female, and the wealthy and non-wealthy.[77]

The most clear distinction was that of race. An 1870 law prohibited white persons from marrying or cohabitating with 'negroes, mulattoes, or persons of mixed blood descended from a negro to the third generation'.[78] Any child born to an interracial couple was automatically deemed illegitimate. While race and gender were fixed dichotomies in nineteenth-century Tennessee, wealth was not. The laws encouraged both white men and white women to aspire to the privileges inherent in a higher economic status by assuming the behaviour attributed to the wealthy. Court records refer to this behaviour as 'character' or 'honour'. It was different for men and women, and it was intimately connected to one's reputation.

Historian Bertram Wyatt-Brown in his study of the concept of honour in the Antebellum South asserts that 'family purity – in lineage and reputation – was the bedrock of personal and group honor'. He suggests that public rituals and gossip worked to ensure that family members acted so as to preserve the family's reputation and inviolability. Legitimation and seduction laws offered formal legal means by which men and women could guarantee purity in lineage and reputation. While men retained control of both well into the nineteenth century, the disruptions to the male hierarchy of the Civil War led to laws that allowed women to protect their own reputations without the assistance of a man.[79]

Tennessee law set a man firmly in charge of his family and his family lineage. The court continued to maintain the common-law assumption that the husband was the 'sole and absolute head of the family' and that in marriage 'the separate legal existence and authority of the wife (was) suspended and neither she nor the minor children, can do any act, except by his authority expressed or implied'. This exclusive authority of the husband to dispose of his children extended to the adoption and guardianship of his children over which his wife had no control.[80]

Male control of the family lineage and inheritance was further supported by the law which enabled men to legitimate their children born out of wedlock by petitioning the court. Once legitimated, the children were 'as if ... born in to the former in lawful wedlock'. The legitimation law inextricably linked legitimation to inheritance. To legitimate, a man had to name his child as heir.[81]

The appellate court records suggest that men of wealth turned to legitimation to appoint a male heir when they had no other children and when the mother was not from the same class. The children moved into the homes of their natural fathers and apparently suffered no discrimination. In 1801 Robert Searcy appeared before the Assembly to legitimate his son, whom he called Robert

Searcy Junior. The fact that Robert named his illegitimate son after himself and went before the assembly to legitimate him even when he had other children, suggests that for Robert senior the fact of having an illegitimate child was not a major embarrassment. Half a century later, the court commented with regard to J. C. McReynolds who was unmarried and had no other children, 'It was natural that he would thus legitimate his only child'. McReynolds took his son with him to Georgia where he 'ultimately taught him his profession', dentistry, and formed a partnership with him.[82]

While legitimation laws enabled wealthy men to ensure their lines of inheritance and bastardy laws protected those lines of inheritance from the appeals of poor women, seduction laws enabled men to protect the reputations of their families and to ensure the purity of the family lines. The common-law tradition of seduction reinforced the traditional mutual obligations within a family. Until they came of age daughters owed their parents obedience in return for support. Under the law, parents could sue any person(s) who 'seduced' their daughters away from the home and deprived them of their daughters' service. In Maine this remained the basis of the seduction law well into the twentieth century.[83] In contrast, Tennessee law very quickly transformed the concept of seduction from the theft of a woman's labour to the theft of her chastity or reputation. This change in the law eventually led to a woman being able to sue for her own seduction and, because it was no longer based on the loss of a woman's labour, allowed for much larger compensation. While black women were involved in bastardy suits, there is no evidence that they were involved in seduction suits.

In 1807 James Wallace of Tennessee brought a seduction suit against William Clark, charging Clark with breaking and entering his house and debauching his daughter. William, James maintained, had at diverse times 'with force and arms, to-wit swords, staves and other offensive weapons ... beat, wounded and evil treated' his daughter Jane, getting her with child. As a result, James claimed, he lost the comfort and service of his daughter and servant, and 'was forced to be at great labour and trouble, and to lay out a large sum of money ... in maintaining her and taking care of her in the lying-in'. But Jane, it so happened, had been living at her sister's when the child was conceived, and the attorney for William offered to show that Jane was a 'woman of easy virtue'. The court ruled, however, that this was immaterial. Every citizen was entitled to the benefit of the laws in the preservation of his reputation, as well as his life, liberty and property, the judges asserted. The court placed a high value on James's reputation. While the lying-in cost $200 and Jane, being in her sister's house, was not providing her father service, the appellate court ordered William to pay $1,000.[84]

The court in 1807 did not elaborate on what it meant by reputation. Future seduction cases made clear, however, that 'reputation'was another word for honour or character, that it meant different things for men and women, and that its value was determined by the status of the man bringing the suit. In Maine, a woman who got pregnant outside of marriage could bring a bastardy suit in which the major issue was who should support the child. In Tennessee, a woman in a similar condition, unless she were a pauper, could rely on her father to bring a seduction suit. Alternately, if the man had offered marriage the woman herself could bring a breach of promise suit on her own and claim seduction to increase the damages. In both cases the major issue was the woman's reputation. In Maine, the centre of the case was the birth and the woman's naming of the child's father. In Tennessee, the centre was the conception, or what led up to it, and the woman's reputation at that time. Before the Civil War a woman could not bring a seduction suit for herself on account of 'the appearance of indecorum ... from which an unprejudiced verdict could scarcely be expected'. She could only sue to protect her reputation in a breach of promise case, when the man had tricked her into giving up her virtue. 'A promise to marry is not unfrequently [*sic*] one of the base and wicked tricks of the wily seducer to accomplish his purposes, by overcoming that resistance which female virtue makes to his unholy designs'.[85]

The court made clear that a woman's reputation was dependent upon her sexual purity and was absolute. While reputation or honour for a man resided in his ability to defend his family from sexual violation and his ability to do this could be graded on a continuum (i.e. he could always retain some level of character), a woman's reputation depended on her chastity which once lost was almost impossible to regain.

The difference in the meaning of honour and reputation for men and women was based on the idea of difference in their sexual characters that required men to protect women. Noting in 1814 that a jury could award a woman more money in a breach of promise suit if she had been seduced, the court determined morality required such a decision:

> in order to repress the libidinous advances of the male sex ... Considering the character of the two sexes distinctly marked out by nature, little doubt can remain. The modest and retiring character of the female sex in general excludes the idea of seduction. Unsolicited, they are unobtrusive, and their chastity, so essential to the happiness of society, secure. For a man to court a young woman of good character, secure her attachment and her confidence, thus to break down the fences and remove the guards of virtue, a successful incursion follows almost of course, if he be without principles of honor.[86]

Without a good reputation, a woman had no standing in court. She could only bring her suit if the man had offered to marry her in order to seduce her and once she had charged a man with a breach of promise to marry he could impeach her testimony by calling other men to testify that they had prior sexual knowledge of her. Furthermore, if the man could prove that he had proposed supposing 'that the plaintiff was modest and chaste, and it turned out she was not', she lost her case.[87]

The antebellum court considered a woman's reputation important for keeping both the woman and the society in order. In 1825 the court determined that a woman should not be compelled to testify in court in a bastardy suit:

> It requires little knowledge of the female character, to predict that such an open exposure of the frailty and vice of the woman, would tend to tear away the film of modesty she had left, and turn her loose upon society profligate and shameless ... Hardly any situation can be conceived, better calculated to drive into desperate and abandoned profligacy a woman who has already departed from the path of virtue, than an open examination before a court and large crowd, in which she is compelled to expose her own abandonment.

Further, the court added, 'she would have almost irresistible temptations to commit perjury ... The best evidence of a return to a virtuous course is a denial of any departure therefrom'.[88]

When a father or husband sued for seduction, he was suing for reparation for the 'dishonor and suffering visited upon the family'. As the court pointed out in 1857 he could lose the comfort of his daughter 'in whose virtue he can feel no consolation' and experience anguish over 'the other children whose morality may be corrupted by her example'. Unlike the reputation of a woman which was absolute, a man's reputation was measured along a continuum. A tarnished reputation did not prevent a man from suing for some amount of money, but 'the general reputation and standing of the family' could be shown 'with a view to enhance, or by the defendant to diminish the damages'.[89]

The cost of a family's reputation was high. The most the court could order a man to pay to support his child in a bastardy suit was $90. In the first seduction suit to reach the appellate court James Wallace asked for and received $1,000. Later payments would range from several thousand to fifteen thousand dollars.[90]

The monetary value of a reputation depended upon a family's social standing. As the court stated in 1858:

> It will not do to permit juries to place all females upon the same common level, and to lose sight of all those just distinctions, founded upon conduct, character, and social positions of the parties, in view of which the damages, in each particular case, ought to be estimated.[91]

While the court considered the social standing of a family in determining the dollar amount value of the reputation, it, nevertheless, invited any man to bring a suit for seduction. For example, the court described Ellen Jonnard's stepfather as 'an obscure stranger in indigent circumstances, and standing alone in the community'. Julius Maguinay was a foreigner, a travelling salesman who spoke a foreign language. His wife took in boarders. When one of the boarders got Ellen, Maguinay's daugher, pregnant he offered her thirty-five dollars not to bring a seduction suit. When Maguinay brought suit anyway, the boarder tried to show that Maguinay had not acted as a husband and father should, that 'he was not the head or governor of the family, that he in fact exercised no authority government or control over it ... that instead of being served by the members of the family he became their servant'. But the court determined otherwise. It found that Maguinay and his family 'seemed to have preserved a reputation above all reproach, up to the time of Ellen's seduction', and it ordered a retrial. Maguinay won.[92]

In a similar fashion, over forty years later, the court listened to the argument of G. A. Jones whose daughter was a domestic at John Bradshaw's farm. One night when Bradshaw's wife was away, Bradshaw forced Jones's daughter to have sex with him. Bradshaw argued in his appeal that Jones 'made no physical resistance and uttered no outcry'. The court, however, pointed out that she was alone with him in a farmhouse, was in his employ, and might have thought such was useless:

> While a girl of more refinement and more education, and a keener sense of dignity of her womanhood, would have resisted, and would have screamed, and would not have submitted, except to overpowering force, she may have thought that such a course would be useless and perhaps endanger her life.

The court supported the award of $2,500 for Jones.[93]

The Civil War and its aftermath marked a watershed in seduction law in Tennessee. Prior to 1886 only a man could bring a seduction suit on the legally recognized fiction that the family had lost the service as well as the reputation of its daughter. The new interpretation of the law redefined seduction as simply 'the despoiling a woman of her virginity'. The court amplified:

> Today she is a virgin, she yields to the seducer, and she is no longer a virgin, but has lost this womanly treasure, and is degraded by the act into the ranks of the despoiled and unchaste, and no human power can restore her to what she was before the fatal error.

The new law conferred upon white women the unprecedented authority to negotiate a compensation for the loss of their own reputations without a breach of promise to marry, but the new law had its price. At the same time as women were empowered to bring suit for their own seductions, they were obliged to internalize the required standards of sexual behaviour. Prior to this time, a father could win a seduction case even if his daughter had had sexual intercourse previously with another man. All that mattered to the court was that her reputation had remained intact. Nancy Cruze, for example, may or may not have been a virgin, the court concluded, but in all events the community thought she was one. The fact that she had had a previous affair did not mitigate the damages for, as the court pointed out, 'the reputation of the female seduced, in the estimation of the public, could not possibly have been prejudiced by the existence of a secret locked up in the bosom of immediate parties'.[94]

By the 1880s the court regularly enquired into a woman's sexual behaviour before and during the seduction and its findings were critical to the suit. While the earlier body of law assumed that a woman was sexually passive, the new law required that she be so. It cannot be, the court maintained:

> that a man who prevails by arts, persuasion, and entreaties upon a woman who has yielded before to such appliances should be held equally guilty and equally responsible with him who by flattery or false promises has first robbed the virgin of her chastity.[95]

Not only was the woman's previous experience held to be relevant but also her willingness to participate in the seduction itself was crucial. In 1886 McCorkle escorted Franklin to church. When Franklin became pregnant, she charged McCorkle with seduction, but the court disagreed. The testimony showed that Franklin had engaged in sexual connection with McCorkle on several occasions – one night twice before ten o'clock, once in going to church and once on the return. 'The idea of a woman thus engaged in sexual indulgence at every opportunity being seduced at every act of intercourse is to our minds absurd', the court ruled. In addition, it pointed out, the record suggested that the sexual desire was dominant in the girl, herself, and that there was 'no evidence that she ever had a virtuous impulse after the first act'. The crucial question in a seduction case, the court affirmed, was, 'does the willingness arise out of the sexual desires or curiosity of the female, so that she only needs opportunity for the commission of the act, or is that willingness induced by some act, representation or statement of the man?'[96]

With the 1888 law a woman's chastity, once the property of her father, now became her own. As a result, single white women of limited means could take advantage of the law to gain a certain economic independence even though they had no standing or position in the community. However, the price was high. In order to benefit from the opportunity a woman had to live up to the social prescriptions that the suits made clear. Two examples of white women of limited means who operated independently suggest the possibilities and dangers inherent in the law.

Bertie Fye was one of the growing number of young women who left their families to find work and support themselves at the end of the nineteenth-century in Tennessee. Bertie, a German immigrant, joined McDonald's Matrimonial Agency of Chicago when she was twenty-one 'with the view of forming an acquaintance suitable for marriage'. Through the agency she met and began writing letters to William P. Kaufman, a farmer and stave and lumber mill man of Tennessee. She admitted to him that she could have stayed home with her stepmother, but she would rather not. Bertie eventually came to Pine Bluff, Arkansas, to explore the possibility of marriage with William. In spite of the fact that she stayed with William in his house for several weeks at a time and in spite of the fact that he claimed she had 'lewd and unchaste conduct' before and after their engagement, she successfully sued William for breach of contract and seduction when he broke off their marriage engagement. Bertie won her suit in part because she had kept letters which detailed her continuing resistance to William's advances. William remarked in one how she 'knocked fire out of his eyes like electric wheels' when he caught her by the ankle. In another he excused himself for trying to take advantage of her by explaining that he had the right to try her virtue. After a lengthy hearing the court concluded:

> While the fact that a woman, accompanied by no one visited a man that had made her a proposition of marriage, and remained several weeks in a house maintained by himself alone, indicates great imprudence on her part, it does not show her to be of questionable virtue, in view of the fact that improper proposals made by him to her during the visit were always indignantly rejected.

Furthermore, because William accused her of lewd behaviour and then failed to prove the charge, the damages were aggravated. Bertie won $3,000. She had won a substantial sum but only by being virtuous. 'It must be admitted', the court stated, 'that the test to which the plaintiff was subjected during her courtship was a very severe one'.[97]

Twenty years later Alma Gibson faced similar tests and was found wanting. She had left her family home in Parsons to get a job as a night-time telephone operator in Lexington. W. L. Finch called one night shortly after she began work. The other operator told her who it was and told her she was all right and to go ahead and talk to him. Finch wanted to come to see her where she worked, but she refused, telling him it was against the rules. They talked every night or two for several months and finally she agreed to have him come up. When he took hold of her hand and started to kiss her, she said, 'I told him turn me loose or I would knock him down'. He said other girls do and kept on pleading and then finally, she testified, he 'threw me across the table and I yielded to him, but I didn't willingly consent'. He returned several times after that and each time 'promised that he would see that I was not thrown aside, and he would protect me, and I trusted him and was looking for protection if anything happened'.[98]

Alma testified that she had never had intercourse with anyone else, but her actions were questioned in two ways. Finch brought in letters she had written to another man at the same time that he was having relations with her; and he offered the testimony of a third who was prepared to testify that Alma had 'permitted him to take unwomanly liberties with her' the first time she met him. The court agreed this testimony was important:

> It is highly improbable that a woman who would have the conversation and submit to the familiarities of a perfect stranger as claimed by Sellers in June or July was a pure and virtuous person in December, especially when the correspondence with Tucker ... is taken into view.

Equally as damaging were Alma's actions the night of the seduction. Under cross-examination she claimed that she understood him to have assured her that she wouldn't get pregnant and that he loved her. The lawyer commented that it was a 'mighty short acquaintance to be in love'. She answered that they had been talking over the phone and the lawyer asked, 'You got in love with him over the phone?' 'He just overpowered me some way, caused me to think so much of him'. Alma, in other words, had shown herself sexually responsive. The court concluded:

> if the female surrenders her virtue upon a representation of the man which all know is contrary to the laws of nature, such a representation cannot be deemed to be the inducing cause for her willingness to indulge in the act, and her indulgence will be ascribed to sexual desire, or curiosity, or previous sexual experience, rather than to artifice, deception or promises.

The court ruled in this case that the chastity of the female before and after the seduction was material. It therefore ordered a new trial in which Finch's witness could testify and asked the jury to decide whether Alma surrendered out of sexual desire or curiosity (in which case she could not sue for seduction) or whether she was induced by Finch (in which case he was liable).[99]

Over the course of the nineteenth century Maine and Tennessee developed two very different legal responses to unwed motherhood. At the end of the century white rural women in both states would have cause to become acquainted with those different legal traditions.

2 TENNESSEE: MAINTAINING HIERARCHIES OF RACE AND CLASS

The economic conditions generated by the Civil War and Reconstruction drove rural white pregnant women out of their isolated communities and enabled privileged white women in the cities to assume responsibility for them. United with the rural women by race but divided from them by class, the privileged women challenged the white male prerogative to protect white women and to determine the absolute importance of their chastity. In doing so, they created a space in which the rural women could adapt to city life and be trained in the middle-class standards so necessary to upward mobility in the city. Although the privileged women asserted their right to redefine honour for themselves and their white sisters, they did not challenge the racial hierarchy. Facing an increasingly militarized and masculinized racism and unable or unwilling to confront it, within little more than a decade the privileged women dropped their challenge to male authority and, with it, the opportunity they had offered to pregnant rural women.

The Civil War brought devastation to much of the Tennessee countryside and decimated Tennessee's male population. Close to 200,000 Tennesseans fought on one side or the other during the war. The casualties were so high that according to one historian, 'a large percentage of families (were) without men, or at least without men able to work'. Even where men were available, the war disrupted their planting and harvesting or destroyed their crops. 'In many parts of the state', one historian has noted, 'men returned to a land of waste and barrenness'. A newspaperman commented,

> Go from Memphis to Chattanooga and it is like the march of Moscow in olden times ... Whether you go on the Salem, the Shelbyville, the Manchester or any other pike [from Murfreesboro] for a distance of thirty miles either way, what do we behold? One wide wild, and dreary waste ...[1]

Under such conditions families would find it hard to support any additional member and single pregnant women would be less likely to be able to rely on a father or brother to help negotiate a marriage.

The first recourse for many rural white women who needed support was the male-defined legal system where their gender and their out-of-wedlock pregnancy made it difficult for them to succeed. Washington County, home of the Tri-City area of Johnson City, Kingsport and Bristol, is in the far eastern corner of Tennessee at the edge of the Appalachian Mountains. A sample of the bastardy suits contested in Washington County District court from 1869 to 1886 suggests that, while this eastern Tennessee community turned to bastardy suits in much the same way as did the communities of Maine, the laws governing bastardy suits defined a woman's options in an entirely different way.[2] As in Maine, the bastardy suits were public, requiring the woman to testify and involving a large number of community members. In Maine, however, if a woman named the father of the child as she was giving birth, she was almost certain to win her suit. In Tennessee, a woman won if the man did not contest the issue. If he contested, she almost certainly lost and, even if she did not, faced the likelihood of losing her child in three years.

Tennessee law automatically determined a man charged with bastardy as the father of the child unless he contested the accusation. In the forty bastardy suits identified in the sample, every man made oath that he had 'at no time had sexual intercourse (with the defendant) from the first of the tenth to the first of the sixth month before the birth of the child' and that the charge was 'wholly without foundation made out of malice to him'.[3] In every case, the judge ordered the case to trial.

The fact that in every case in which the witnesses were listed, there were at least six witnesses and that the trials lasted as long as several days suggests the public nature of the trial. Both men and women testified. Often the witnesses included family members or several members of one family who were possibly friends of the litigants, but they also included community members who claimed their disinterest in the case. When Elizabeth Ames, for example, argued that she could not appear in court as she was too sick, Catharine Deal, fifty-eight years old, signed with her mark a statement that she had overheard Elizabeth say she was not going to attend the trial, and John Grisham testified that Elizabeth had spent two hours recently in the store where he worked.[4]

Family members participated in the trials in many ways. Fathers or brothers went surety for the man accused – that is, they promised the court they would pay a fine if the man did not appear for his trial. And family members at various times assured the court that they would 'save the county ... and all other counties in the state harmless from the maintenance of said bastard child'.[5]

Because the state had an interest in assigning responsibility for the support of a child to someone else and because only women who were unable to provide support were allowed to bring suit, one would assume that the trial would be weighted in defence of the woman. In some respects this was true. The court automatically judged a man responsible for the child unless he contested the charge and it immediately assessed those who contested with a $250 surety. If the man absconded, as did John Sliger, the men who went surety for him had to pay the full price of the required support for three years. If he showed up again, as Sliger did, the state could keep $180 of the paid-over surety to ensure that Sliger saved the county from all charges of maintenance. In addition, the *in forma pauperis* law of the state allowed paupers to bring suit without having to pay court costs. After 1871, only women who were paupers were allowed to bring a suit and they could therefore appeal the verdict at no cost to themselves.[6]

In spite of this weight in favour of the woman, it is striking in this sample of cases how often the men won. The reasons for this were embedded in Tennessee law. In the first place, the rules of evidence made it extremely difficult for a woman to prove her case. The frustration of Millie Bolen can be imagined when she asked the magistrate 'who [*sic*] she could prove it by'.[7] While there was no way for a woman to prove the paternity of her child unless the father confessed, a man could win his argument by raising questions about the woman's character. The handwritten notes on the court docket in the case of Sarah Hampton suggest the difficulty this created for women. Sarah's only 'proof' that Baxter Little impregnated her was the evidence given by her father or brother that Sarah and Baxter Little had gone out of the house together one night for a few minutes and, the implication was, that Baxter had had the opportunity to get Sarah pregnant. But Baxter brought Baberl Little (who may have been his brother) in to testify that while he had seen Baxter at Sarah's one time, he had heard Sarah speak of other men as being the father. James Clayell agreed. He had heard Sarah say that the young one was someone else's. 'I do not know whether she was joking', he added, but 'her character is bad'. Sarah countered that she never said it was someone else's in earnest, she had only been joking. She had said that it might be someone else's and wouldn't they have been a little pleased. Sarah's argument was to no avail. The court concluded:

> The testimony conflicting between the parties and the plaintiff in this case being proved to be a notorious whore, leaves the mind of the chairman protem in doubt who might be the rightful father of said child and therefore gives the defendant the benefit of the doubt.[8]

In contrast to Maine, the decisions in bastardy suits in Tennessee were made by judges, not juries. This may have also had an impact on the outcome. Several comments by the Washington County Tennessee women suggest that they considered sexual intercourse as but a step in the process of getting married. As Elizabeth Ames claimed, Nelson Mohler wronged her by violation of a marriage contract 'which was first to have been consummated'.[9] Historians have noted the pre-modern view of marriage that considered sexual intercourse the first step in a union that was finalized in an official ceremony. The high rate of pre-bridal pregnancy in rural areas raises the possibility that this view lasted well into the nineteenth century. While Tennessee juries understood such community values or practices, judges, better educated, perhaps aspiring to or having achieved middle-class status, would be more likely to apply the developing middle-class standard of chastity before marriage no matter what.[10]

The fact that the law required a woman to be a pauper before she brought suit added a further imbalance, for the man often had more money with which to pay for expert counsel or witnesses. Ellen Hurley's trial is indicative of the power this gave to the man. According to Ellen, Henry O'Brien threatened to kill her if she did not swear the child to Nathan Mitchell. She then brought a suit against Nathan but 'it appearing from the testimony' that Henry was the father, the case was dismissed. She then brought suit against Henry. Henry hired a lawyer who engaged the expert testimony of a doctor to discuss whether or not Ellen's baby might have been premature. The lawyer also, most likely, counselled Henry to use his most successful argument: that the offence occurred in Green county, not in Washington county, and therefore was outside the jurisdiction of the Washington county court.[11]

At the heart of these suits, however, was the question of who would support the child. Even if a woman won a bastardy suit, she stood to lose her child at the end of three years if not before. A man involved in a case could take his child at any time. George H. Crosswhite, Esq., for example, whose surety was also an attorney, petitioned the court as soon as his child was born for her care, custody, and control. He also requested that he be relieved of 'all fines, or penalties for support of the child and that he be bound to support her only as a member of the family'. He charged his daughter's mother, Jennie Tapp, 'as not a suitable person to have charge and control of said child as she is a woman of bad moral character as to virtue'. And he asked that he be given permission to adopt the child and to change its name from Lucretia Tapp to Sophrone Alethe Crosswhite. His petitions were granted, though there is no evidence of Jennie's agreement or position one way or another on the issue.[12]

John Bacon petitioned the court when his child was three years old and the court concluded, 'seeing that the father is willing to take and raise the child and see that it does not become a county charge ... was pleased to order that the said child be delivered to the defendant'.[13] Elizabeth Arounstrout understood this potential loss of her child when she stated, 'being both able and desiring to maintain the child recently born to me, I hereby (request) that the bastardy proceedings now pending against John McCracken be dismissed'.[14]

Even if a woman won a bastardy suit, she only obtained the minimum support of ninety dollars total for three years. As Edward Clopper noted in 1920, 'Ninety dollars at most! One could hardly keep a mule colt for three years in

Tennessee for ninety dollars. A child has to be supported for five times three years and more'.[15]

White women from the countryside, who could not find the support they needed from the courts, turned to the cities to find it. In 1875 the Catholic Church organized the first unwed mothers home in Tennessee. That year and the next white Protestant women opened three more homes in Tennessee's three major cities.[16] In each case the women claimed they had gone into the city to volunteer in charity efforts and had found young pregnant women who had nowhere to go. A Nashville group of church women went 'into the homes of the very poor on volunteer relief missions' during a severe cold wave and found 'a distressing number of unmarried mothers' who 'had been driven from their homes by the censure of their families'.[17]

The Chattanooga women went with their minister to bring the Gospel into the licensed districts of the city. 'The most startling fact revealed to them', they noted later, 'was that young girls, expectant mothers yet unmarried, had found this district their only harbor'. In a similar scenario, the Woman's Christian Association in Memphis found when it opened a lunchroom and temporary lodging for working women, that 'something must be done for a class of women who timidly sought those doors, one after another, but whose moral leprosy barred them from entrance'.[18]

The privileged Christian women who opened the homes joined numerous other white, mostly Protestant, women who responded in cities across the country to the needs of what they termed 'fallen women'. Some of these began as a refuge for prostitutes, others as temporary homes for homeless women and children. Most turned quickly to serving young single pregnant women. By 1946 the Children's Bureau estimated that there were 200 maternity homes nationwide, and two-thirds of those whose founding dates could be identified opened their doors before 1900.[19]

The Tennessee women had much in common with these other Protestant women. Like them, they volunteered their work to set up and run the homes and offered 'sympathy, sisterhood, and piety'. They referred to the pregnant women as 'fallen women' and assumed they had fallen because men had taken advantage of them. They encouraged the women to keep their babies and offered them salvation through Christianity. Often they required a six-month stay in the home.[20]

The Chattanooga and Nashville homes aimed to rescue young women from the 'tiger clutches of utter degradation', by offering them shelter and redemptive Christianity. Both homes accepted any woman who applied as long as she agreed to reform, and their reports make clear that they housed women from diverse backgrounds. The Chattanooga Board claimed that its home sheltered 'school teachers, saleswomen, actresses, servant girls, dressmakers, deserted wives, girls born and bred in the slums, and girls of respectable parentage'. 'One of the few simple rules that the poor creatures are asked to obey', the press noted in 1898, 'is not to talk even to each other of what has been. All that is asked of each one desiring to enter is, "Are you repentant?"'[21]

Two homes opened in Memphis in 1875 and 1876. One, sponsored by the Catholic Church, supported the white male power structure in every way. The other, organized by the Woman's Christian Association (WCA), challenged male authority and as a result assisted white rural women in finding their way in the city. The last quarter of the nineteenth century in the south saw decades of great turmoil as white men of privilege sought to regain control in the state and in the home. The extent to which some white women took the opportunity of this turmoil to challenge male authority and, for a brief time, offer a unique opportunity to the pregnant rural women is made clear only with a comparison of the two homes in Memphis. The challenge, however, was short-lived as the white women could not ignore, or counter, the increasing pressure to support white privilege and the defining value of race.

Peter Bardaglio identifies the end of the nineteenth century as a period of transition in the south when 'the demise of slavery and the emergence of new social relations during the post-war years necessitated the development of alternative forms of social control'. He traces the shift from one source of authority and order (the family) to another (the state). In the time of this transition, he concludes, 'neither worked well when it came to enforcing racial and gender norms'. It was a time when alternatives were possible and white privileged women in Memphis, like other privileged women in the other parts of the South, took advantage of this transition time.[22]

Tennessee law and tradition placed great importance on a man's ability to protect the women in his care and emphasized the importance of chastity for white women. Both made clear distinctions in the way they treated women whose reputations were intact and those whose reputations were not. Acting with virtue, however, was a symbol of class and the sexuality of poor white women was often considered suspect. Prior to the Civil War white men jealously protected their prerogatives as white men to control the actions, and the reputations, of those within their domain without outside interference. The emancipation of the slaves and the resulting loss of authority led these same men to gradually embrace the actions of the state in support of their authority. They rewrote the laws to emphasize the importance of reputation to all white women and to enable women to protect their own chastity. At the same time they had to contend with others challenging white men's sole prerogative to determine the meaning of chastity.[23]

The Catholic Church opened the first home for unwed mothers in Tennessee and this home was the only one of the early homes that thrived. Not coincidentally, it was the only one that unreservedly supported the authority of men.

In 1875 the Bishop of Nashville invited nuns from the Convent of the Good Shepherd to come to Memphis to establish a home for women. The Order of Our Lady of Charity of the Good Shepherd, established in 1639 for 'repentant women, desirous of abandoning the paths of sin', embodied the idea that 'only the highest type of religious woman could succor the ... penitent'.[24]

The convent was a total institution, removed from the influences of the outside world. As late as 1963 the Convent stressed to the *Commercial Appeal* that all the pets – six dogs and a parakeet – were female and that newly arriving girls would remain for at least a year, under the twenty-four hour supervision of the nuns. Once the girls entered, 'All reference to previous habit or conduct ... is strictly prohibited. Evil is never discussed nor referred to. Virtue is made attractive by precept and example'.[25]

The Convent provided for Catholics and non-Catholics alike. Unwed mothers were strictly separated from the rest of the women served. As the nuns noted in 1916:

> There are practically three large institutions under one roof, with separate kitchens, dining room, dormitories, work and school rooms and regulation recreation halls. One home is for the preservation of very young girls who might be exposed to immoral influences; one for the Magdalenes, and one for the reformatory work. The buildings are so constructed that the juveniles ... never come in contact with those in the reformatory ...

The Convent made it its policy 'never to advertise nor to solicit girls to enter'. Instead, it took referrals from parents, guardians and the municipal court.[26]

While the girls could never become members of the Order of Our Lady of Charity of the Good Shepherd, they could enter a penitent order, the Order of the Magdalene, in another city. Alternatively, they could become consecrates and remain in the home performing various domestic duties but taking no vows. At least some residents did, in fact, take advantage of this limited opportunity.[27]

By 1925, the Convent of the Good Shepherd had served close to 8,000 young women. It reinforced white male authority by only accepting referrals from authorities, emphasizing and maintaining the distinction between chaste and unchaste women, and offering opportunities, albeit limited ones, to those who conformed.[28]

Elite Protestant women opened the second home a year later at a time when Memphis was in demographic and political turmoil. Established as a riverboat town in 1840, the city had grown rapidly as it took advantage of its location as one of the few sites above the flood plain on the Mississippi River and as a crossroads of railroad lines. Before the war it was recognized as the 'largest inland cotton market in the country' and, after, as a depot for goods shipped across the country. It was the fastest growing city in the nation in the 1850s and, by 1860, had become the sixth largest city in the south. Between 1864 and 1866 alone its population doubled; by 1890 it was to double again to 102,320.[29]

Numbers tell only part of the story. Union troops controlled the city from 1862 to the end of the War. Former slave men and women poured into the city, first seeking refuge in the Union army, later seeking jobs and a new life. Tension over the arrival of a large free black population erupted in a riot in 1866 which killed forty-six African-Americans. In 1867, 1873 and 1878, successive yellow fever epidemics decimated the city's population. In the last and worst epidemic more than half of the population left the city. The epidemics brought a major shift in demographics as many of the recent German and Irish immigrants left the city never to return. By 1900 the city was 49 per cent African-American and virtually devoid of foreign-born. The immigrants who continued to pour into the city came from the surrounding countryside.[30]

Simultaneously, the white elite of Memphis lost control of the city twice in two decades. In 1862 the Union army took control of the city and ruled under federal mandate until 1870 when locally-elected officials regained control. When the city was devastated by yellow fever three years later officials surrendered the city's charter again, this time to the state.[31]

As a result of the rapid population expansion, social fragmentation and confusion over municipal authority, the city failed to provide even minimal services for the rural immigrants who continued to pour into Memphis. Statistics from the end of the century suggest the level of social disorder that had grown over several decades. By then the murder rate in Memphis was the highest in the country and the suicide rate was far above the national average.[32]

Beginning almost immediately after the war, white women of Memphis began to respond to the social chaos by creating a number of organizations that gave them a voice and a role in the running of the city. The women who organized were white and well off. They organized on the basis of gender and were not timid in their demands. They got involved in politics, commercial development, criminal justice and education, among other things. Sometimes, but not always, they claimed the special prerogatives of women as they took advantage of the uncertain governance of the times to assert their right to participate in the reordering of the society.

In 1872, for example, women organized to protest wage reductions for female teachers, called for a female principal and demanded equal gender representation on the school board. Men, one outspoken critic charged, 'are by virtue of their sex not competent to preside over children'.[33]

While the women committed to educational reform claimed they were only acting to protect 'the natural place of women', other women organized to gain entry to the male world of politics. Elizabeth Avery Meriwether, for example, published a journal advocating for women's rights. In 1876 she cast a ballot in the presidential election and then gave an address in a local theater explaining why women should have the right to vote. She became a long-time member of the National Woman's Suffrage Association.[34] Elizabeth's sister-in-law and suffrage activist who accompanied her on speaking tours across the state was Lide Meriwether, one of the organizers of the unwed mother's home. Lide was active in the Woman's Christian Temperance Union (WCTU). She lobbied for prohibition, for raising the legal age of consent, for a police matron in Memphis, and for women's rights. At the WCTU's National Convention held in Nashville, as president of the state WCTU, she exhorted: 'On Tennessee soil you are to think and speak and act precisely as seemeth good in your own sight ... our state needs a good shaking up and don't be afraid to give it'.[35] Women responded to her call. By 1895 the Memphis Woman's Council – a citywide network of women's organizations – boasted a membership of forty-eight organizations and over 3,000 women.[36]

The Woman's Christian Association (WCA), founder of the Memphis home for unwed mothers, was one of the oldest of these women's organizations. Organized 'for the good of women carried on wholly by women' in 1875, it developed a wide array of programmes that included a women's hospital, a women's exchange (cooperative) and a prison visiting programme. Many of these lasted well into the twentieth century.[37]

The WCA started as an interdenominational sewing circle of 'prominent citizens', twenty 'Christian ladies', who taught sewing to poor scholars and, 'by force of example', taught them 'the way, the truth and the light'. In this way the women 'relieved a family of ... deserving poor' whose children now had suitable clothes in which to go to school.[38]

The WCA's first two concerns were to systematize charity and develop a source of adequate domestic help. Their idea, the *Commercial Appeal* explained, was to bring together 'a body of Christian workers from all denominations' so they might 'cordially unite in their labors' and 'impart and receive information as to the best methods of carrying on their work'. The Association planned to divide the city into seven districts. A board of visitors for each district would then visit each family in the district to find out which children failed to attend Sunday school and which families needed relief. The Association also planned to open an employment agency 'to procure good homes for worthy applicants without charge to them, and to furnish employers with reliable help at the moderate charge of one dollar'. Membership was set at 'only two dollars' per year and, the women noted in their newspaper appeal, if ladies would only join 'we could establish the employment agency on a permanent basis'.[39]

Training good domestic servants was in the personal interest of the privileged women in Memphis who often bemoaned the difficulties of getting good help. Another aim of the WCA was closely related to the interests of their families.

The early WCA members were associated with the rising business class that had a vested interest in the growing city.[40] Historian Marsha Wedell was able to identify the profession of the husbands of four of the ten founding members. These were a bank president, a plantation and cottonseed-oil mill owner, a lawyer and investor, and a clergyman of independent means who made his money largely through real estate. Soon the Association also included women who were married to eight men prominent in the cotton business, five lawyers, four of whom later became judges, railroad board members, physicians and wholesalers of groceries and chemicals. Two of their husbands were officers in the Taxing District, two had been mayors, and one was a state legislator.[41] In a city which relied upon private donors to provide for the needs of an increasing and potentially disruptive poor population, the WCA's proposal to systematize public charity 'so that unworthy parties may not be draining the treasury of each at the same time' would have held special appeal for those donors.

While the finding domestic servants and overseeing the distribution of charity supported the interests of their class, within a year these women of means attempted to reach across class lines. To support the working women who came to the employment agency, the WCA opened a lunch room with several rooms for temporary lodgings on the second floor. 'Presently', a historian of the WCA reported in 1894, so many with 'moral leprosy' sought help there that in January 1876, the WCA opened the Navy Yard Mission in the Commandant's House on Promenade Street for 'fallen women'. In 1880, noting that there were more applicants than could be provided for, the WCA moved the Mission to larger quarters on Alabama Street.[42]

Lide Meriwether, one of the WCA members who was instrumental in organizing and finding support for the Mission, explained her philosophy in *Soundings*, a journal she published in 1872. In it, she exhorted women to find connection with and protect their fallen sisters. Dedicating *Soundings* to the Sisters of the Good Shepherd for their commitment to 'THE GREATEST OF ALL CHARITIES' she called upon Protestant women for similar self-sacrificing and untiring efforts. 'I cast out a plummet line to 'take soundings' of the deep heart of women', Meriwether commented in her dedication. 'God grant it may bring up gleaming pearls and shining sands of gold'.[43]

Soundings was a collection of stories about fallen women, all of whom were innocent until seduced and abandoned; all of whom died. The problem was not men, Meiwether suggested, but women. In every story she emphasized the fact that the women died not because men seduced them, but because women accepted the sexual double standard. One woman could not find work because 'the fiends pursued me: they whispered in the ears of those who gave me work that I was an outcast, with the leprosy of sin; that my baby was a plague-spot'. Society women shunned another woman while they welcomed her lover; they refused to provide work to a girl born of a prostitute and thereby forced the girl to steal; they jumped to the wrong conclusion and caused another woman to die of sorrow when they assumed her brother was her lover. Women, in short, were responsible for destroying other women's lives. They accepted the double standard, allowed a woman's reputation to determine her life, and withheld the economic support they could provide her by offering work. Meriwether questioned:

> Where can be the influence for good, in this crushing burden of shame, that curls and freezes the blood, even in the 'holy of holies' a mother's hearts, and forces her even to hate the innocent, unborn child, for the shame it is to bring upon her; and thus deafens our ears with the horrors of infanticide, and fills our streets with nameless and friendless children, abandoned and cast away.[44]

She castigated the double standard that led society to condemn a fallen woman but to accept the man who had seduced her. She did not ask society to 'anathematize man', she stated, but to accept woman. 'I have but little faith in the good effects of threat, denunciation, and anathema', she commented. For Meriwether, religion demanded that women acknowledge their responsibility to and provide support for their fallen sisters, and she suggested that failure to do so was as evil in God's eyes as sexual impropriety. 'I arraign you before the bar of your own soul, to answer solemnly and truthfully – Guilty, or not guilty – concerning your sister?'[45]

In her journal and in later editorials, Meriwether challenged women to recognize the role they played in other women's lives. She called on women to recognize their own passionate natures, to acknowledge that they too felt desire, and to recognize that what separated them from fallen women was only good fortune. Women should judge each other not on their past sexual conduct but on their present commitment to religion, she suggested. Unfailing virtue was not as important to God as faith.[46]

Meriwether called for women to end their discrimination against fallen women. 'No need telling me', she wrote, 'that because a woman takes one wrong step she must needs take two'. She called on women to stop discriminating against the 'girl who overtaken by strong temptation, has taken the first fallen step'. Society women, she suggested, literally had the power of life and death over women. They could offer social acceptance and jobs, or they could ostracize them. Her own experience proved that these steps could make a difference. For the past forty years, she asserted, 'I have taken young girls with their children into my home and there cared for them and they have gone out and led good, pure, clean lives and died triumphant deaths'.[47]

Perhaps even more radically, she suggested that all women understood sexual passion. She consistently pointed out that she was a happy woman and that her happiness came as much from being a wife as from being a mother. Calling for other women to share in her imaginative understanding of the fallen woman, she suggested that they recognize the attraction of sex.

> I ask, not of the 'lilies' and 'angels'; neither of the clods and icebergs that are formed and fashioned as women; but of every honest, candid, true woman, with a warm, impassioned heart beating in her bosom. Is the power of the master-passion of humanity a less temptation than the sparkle of the wine cup or the rattle of the dice?[48]

She suggested that the women of Memphis should recognize the fact that they came from sheltered lives, 'shielded in happy homes by loving mothers'. The women of the home, she suggested, 'motherless and friendless, were sent out among the ravening wolves of starvation wages and strong temptations'. It was economic circumstances that forced them to turn to prostitution, not a lack of moral fibre. Unlike the women of the WCA, they had not had the advantages of education, the access to 'wholesome truths contained in great thoughts'. As a result, they were not 'given the means of self control that only thought and study can impart'.[49]

In spite of her call for women of the middle class to embrace women from other backgrounds, Meriwether acknowledged that they would find themselves separated from these women by a huge divide. Warning the Christian women of the numerous difficulties they would face in working with fallen women, she counted among them 'the thousand obstacles that are to be encountered in the nature, education, and surrounding of the women with whom they have to deal'. Within the last few decades, she suggested, other women have called for sympathy for 'this class of unfortunates', but those writers spoke without experience. 'They honestly believe that in ten cases out of twelve these women were either lured on to their destruction by a self-sacrificing love, or driven by the demon of starvation', Meriwether commented. On the contrary, Meriwether pointed out, the majority of them have been brought up in shame and degradation, not even one-half of them can read or write. 'All ideas of virtue, chastity, religion, moral responsibility, or rectitude, are as far from their knowledge as from than of any wild beast of the forest'. If they could be reclaimed only by opening a way for their return to the good and virtuous, how easy, she suggests, the task would be. But they are 'more heathen than the Congo or South Sea Islander'.[50]

Meriwether was referring to 'fallen women', a term that many people have associated with prostitutes. But the reforming women of Chattanooga and Nashville spoke of 'young girls, expectant mothers yet unmarried' and 'unmarried mothers ... driven from their homes'.[51] Memphis at this time was devoid of foreigners and its population was rapidly increasing with immigrants from the rural countryside. Beginning with Reconstruction and increasing steadily into the 1920s the rural whites of Tennessee moved out of their communities and into the cities. This out-migration was primarily young and, increasingly, female.

By 1930 the US census recorded an excess of over 22,000 white women over white men in Tennessee's urban areas.[52]

The large cultural gap that Meriwether identified was as much a gap between rural poor and urban middle class as it was between chaste and unchaste. The availability of consumer goods, reflected in and encouraged by the growing newspaper culture, separated urban from rural women at a time when there were no phones, radios or cars to help bridge the distance between them. In addition, there was a growing disparity between the birth rate within the city and without as children remained critical to agricultural communities but became an economic drain especially to the middle class in the cities. Others growing up in Tennessee at that time have noted the wide cultural gap that existed within Tennessee. Evelyn Scott described the poor whites who arrived in Clarksville at court time as 'Curious people ... A race apart. Unknown. Incomprehensible'. A WPA narrator who worked in a clothing factory as a youth commented,

> I'll tell you I never before knew that such people existed. Most of them had come in off of the mountains somewhere and they had such a funny way of talking that plenty of times I wouldn't know what they were saying. The girls were usually either sloppy fat or thin and dried up. Their hair all hung in strings and a good many of them dipped snuff and spit all the time. They wore the doggonedest clothes I ever saw ... [53]

The class and urban rural divide were in some respects more profound that the racial divide. Ida B. Wells, a black teacher, writer and social activist in Memphis who was born a slave had much in common with Meriwether. Like Meriwether she was well educated, wore fashionable clothes, attended the city's concerts and was committed to reform. Wells attended a Knights of Labor gathering which Meriwether addressed and both – Meriwether as a member of the WCA and Wells as a teacher – were required to be of 'good moral character'. Like Meriwether, she responded by asserting her right and need to protect women. Confronting a minister who had hinted to her friends that she had lost her position as a teacher for sexual impropriety, Wells demanded his apology and made clear that she would accept it only if he announced it from his pulpit on Sunday 'in case anyone else in town had heard of his remarks'. 'I told him', she wrote in her autobiography, 'that my good name was all that I had in the world, that I was bound to protect it from attack by those who felt that they could do so with impunity because I had no brother or father to protect me.'[54]

In spite of the attributes she shared with Wells, Meriwether did not cross racial lines when she opened the Mission. She did, however, deliberately blur other lines, most specifically those drawn between classes and between women with their reputations for chastity intact and those without. She did so by establishing a home that brought white women from different backgrounds to live or to worship together.

The Home was open to women 'steeped in sin' and those seeking employment, those deserted by their husbands and those like Mary Love, member of Lauderdaid Presbyterian Church who 'being unable to support herself was placed here by friends. Humble, loving child of God, Bible her constant companion'.[55]

Unlike the Convent, the Mission encouraged white women to apply on their own and accepted all who did. Meriwether reminded readers that 'reformation of women thoroughly steeped in sin is only an occasional chapter in the great volume of reform recorded in houses like this'. Members of the WCA's Mission committee were particularly interested in helping young women from the countryside. 'First, young girls often come in from the country or small towns in the vicinity seeking work and finding none. Meantime, money is gone and temptation meets them on every side', Meriwether noted in a report on the Mission to the public. 'But any kind man or woman finding her in such peril can direct her to the home. There she is safely sheltered till she finds employment'. The Mission also, she noted, took in young girls whose parents or guardians found them hard to control or who 'being wage earners, are compelled to spend most of their time away from them'.[56] A report from the Mission in 1884 noted, 'We can only tell you of the homeless, friendless women, sometimes deserted wives, coming to us for protection and shelter until some way may be open by which they may honestly earn their daily bread'. Included among those in the Mission were those 'without any means of support or friends to provide for daily wants, whose constitutional infirmities render them incapable of fighting life's battle'.[57]

At the same time, the members of the board encouraged all middle class women to actively participate in the activities of the Home. The WCA was open to 'any woman of good moral character'. Members of the WCA Mission committee urged other members to volunteer their services in the Home or to help run its weekly all-women prayer sessions. They invited the female public to visit during the weekly afternoon social hour, to attend the bi-weekly religious services, and to come to lectures in the Home. The residents did all the work of taking care of the Home under the supervision of a matron and her assistant, but volunteers provided training in all the household duties.[58]

The Mission relied on religion to overcome class divides. It offered 'moral and religious instruction with training in every department of household labor'. By 1884, it was providing regular Sunday church services conducted by local ministers, Thursday services conducted by the women of the WCA, and the word of God taught morning and evening. Each 'inmate' was required to learn a portion of the scripture for daily recitation.[59] One visitor commented in 1881:

> Each hour of the day is set apart for particular duties. There are so many hours set apart for devotional service, so many for labor and so many for recreation. No noise or confusion of any character ever mars the quietude of the establishment or its

surroundings and morning, noon and night witnesses the observance of the most perfect discipline.[60]

Religion enabled the WCA women to mix with the women in the Mission and thus stand against society's norms. Acknowledging the 'difficulties were great', the women exhorted one another, 'For comfort and encouragement we have admonition. 'Let us not be weary in well doing for in due season we will reap if we faint not'. The reaping may not be till hereafter but we know the sewing must be now".[61]

Their faith urged the women to find a connection with the fallen woman. In 1884, the Reverend N. M. Long called upon those who attended the annual service at the Mission to 'have faith in those for whom you work'. Though one had fallen to the depths, still, he claimed, 'there are principles in him on which God is building and on them we may build with confidence'. Long suggested that all humanity held in common a sense of justice, a consciousness of right and wrong, and sympathy that 'links us in fellowship with all our kind'. 'I say there-fore', he urged, 'have faith in those for whom you work; judge them by yourself, not by the meanness simply but by the good if you have a sense of right and desires for better life and longings after purer states of being'. The WCA women in the *Gleaner* spoke of the importance of sympathy. 'Sympathy means like suf-fering', they claimed, 'therefore those who have had sorrows and suffering can come nearer to the heart of the creature in distress'.[62]

The WCA relied on religion to redeem what appeared to be an 'irrevocably ruined life'. A fallen woman might in fact, it argued, be 'made a source of power in the salvation of others'. 'Thankful to be allowed to walk in the footsteps of their blessed Lord', she might be a more successful missionary than those who had never fallen.[63]

That this worked to the advantage of at least one resident is suggested in the 1904 Annual Report which pictured a woman standing on a parquet floor beside a potted plant, her hand on a carved wooden table. The Report thus intro-duced Louemma Angel who 'after years of training in the Vanguard Training School of St Louis, felt called to go as a missionary to India, and is now doing splendid work in that field'. Though appearing to be a model of middle-class decorum, Louemma had delivered a child in the WCA Home. She left her child in the Vanguard School also to be trained as a missionary.[64]

If the Home encouraged cross-class interaction, it did not encourage dia-logue. The women of the WCA were not there to learn about poor women, they were there to instil in poor women the values of the middle class. Nevertheless women sought out the Mission's services in great numbers. The letters they later sent as well as an analysis of the services the Mission provided suggest the ways in which the women who sought the services of the home benefited from them.

Most important, perhaps, was the shelter and medical support the Mission provided. Women could come and deliver their babies in the Mission at no charge (but hard work, see below) to themselves. The WCA's journal, *The Gleaner*, regularly published letters of appreciation for the Home from poor, (always) rural, women. The WCA women might have reflected as did the Chattanooga Board that it was 'true that some have gone back to the old life. That was to be expected. Some have pretended to reform, just for the use of the home until it suited them to take up again the dance of death ... ' Nevertheless, they admitted all women and noted with pride that at least some showed their appreciation by supporting the home from their limited means. In 1892 the *Gleaner* reported donations from 'a grateful though heartbroken mother in Mississippi' who sent $50 'wrung out, no doubt, in toil, self-sacrifice and tears, as some acknowledgement of what had been done for her erring daughter', from a domestic in a Memphis family who sent $20 'to defray part of the expense of another girl, an old friend brought there in deepest trouble from Arkansas', and from a 'humble, grateful woman' dismissed several years ago, 'never forgetful of the hands that rescued her' who sent '$4 of her earnings in the kitchen toward payment of her debt of love'.[65]

Whether or not the women who came to the Home acceded to the ideas or values of the WCA they could take advantage of this free care. As the *Memphis Ledger* reported:

> If Lillie Bailey, a rather pretty white girl, seventeen years of age now at the city hospital, would be somewhat less reserved about her disgrace there would be some very nauseating details in the story of her life. She is the mother of a little coon.

According to the *Ledger*, Lillie was a 'country girl' from Hernando, Mississippi, where her father had a farm. She came to Memphis to go to the home, where she remained almost three months before the child was born. At its birth, 'the ladies in charge of the Refuge were horrified' and sent her immediately to the City Hospital.[66]

Lillie obtained shelter by revealing as little as possible about her story. She claimed at first to be from Arkansas and in spite of her three-month stay the women of the home learned little about her for 'she would not tell much'. When 'an attempt was made to get the girl to reveal the name of the Negro who had disgraced her, she obstinately refused and it was impossible to elicit any information from her on the subject'. When the women tried to get her to name the man she replied that it was 'a matter in which there can be no interest to the outside world'. What happened to Lillie, thereafter, is unknown. With courage and persistent silence, however, she managed to gain three months of support.

The women who managed the Mission clearly wanted to transform the residents by teaching them cleanliness, industry, order and religion. At the same time, they provided the residents with training in middle-class culture. The order and work required in the home could provide them with training in middle-class values and practices that would enable them to find a job (or a husband) in the middle-class society of the city. The home provided – under strict supervision – what one anonymous writer warned others to watch out for: domestic servants who used their positions to learn how to become ladies and then left.[67]

The WCA in the Mission attempted to mould women into the appropriate middle-class image through discipline and order. The original stated purpose of the WCA was to 'work for the moral, social and intellectual condition of women and children' and the WCA often reiterated the importance of cleanliness, order, and industry. Meriwether called the Mission a place where women were transformed, 'fit for the world's work and God's service'. As one visitor described the home:

> No noise or confusion of any character ever mars the quietude of the establishment or its surroundings and morning, noon and night witnesses the observance of the most perfect discipline ... The building and premises are kept constantly in the most perfect condition of cleanliness.[68]

In addition to training in middle-class values and lifestyles, the home offered women an opportunity to find acceptance in a community where faith worked to counterbalance past conduct or social status. The head of the Mission committee noted with pride a card found in one resident's Bible after her death. The card stated, 'I the undersigned believe to have found Jesus to be my precious Savior, and I promise with his help to live as his loving child and faithful servant all my life'. This particular woman was dependent, not fallen, but the committee for the Mission regularly reported on letters from past residents claiming, 'I would like to be a Christian', or 'I hope, with God's help, to live the life of a Christian'.[69]

The strict discipline may have been onerous, but for some who had led a chaotic life, it may also have been compelling. As one former resident wrote, 'I would like to be back in the Home, if only for one evening, and hear the same voices in the chapel, and go over the lessons once again. There I received so much help and so much strength'. The religion and acceptance that the wealthy WCA members offered the residents may have been predicated upon acceptance of middle-class values and behaviour, but it was acceptance. Another resident wrote, 'I was bitter against the world when I came here, but I have learned in a measure to understand God's love and kindness ... I know he is my friend and has given me friends here'.[70]

For many rural women, however, the Mission also offered an opportunity to learn skills that they could use to help support themselves in the city. The WCA reported that it considered industry as 'one of the greatest helps in forming or remodeling character' and consequently kept the women in the Mission working at various jobs. The industry was not only good for the women, it was also necessary for the home which was constantly struggling for funds. In 1881, the managers reported that they had been planning to open a laundry but, due to lack of water and conveniences, the severe winter, and want of means to fix it up, they had not yet succeeded. The Board, they stated to the press, had 'found considerable difficulty in obtaining remunerative employment owing to the inexperience of their workers and the low prices paid but it was hoped that, as the interest in these matters becomes more general, this difficulty will disappear'. Three years later the Mission opened a laundry which brought in $242. That year the residents also sewed for local establishments, made a silk quilt which they sold for fifty dollars and, as sewing 'brought in less money as profitable work could not be obtained', considered opening a rug industry.[71]

The income from all of these, however, was not enough to support the Home. In 1880, the WCA began to board poor children who had at least one parent living. In addition to providing a necessary income, the boarding children provided good public relations. The WCA pointed out that the parents of the children would not give them up for others to raise more properly but would board them at the Mission where the WCA could provide them with religious instruction. They made the best use of their time, the WCA stated to the press, 'hoping to plant seeds that may bring forth fruit in eternal life'. They invited the parents to join in the regular religious services as well.[72]

The WCA provided for the children physically as well as spiritually. They came, noted the WCA, 'poorly clad and poorly fed and are to be cleansed and nourished and made comfortable'. Reports of the WCA at this period stressed what the home provided for these 'waifs', suggesting that the WCA was fully aware of the good public relations that this service to young children provided. Not coincidentally, the practice of taking in other children enabled the women who delivered in the Home to have their children taken care of with the rest.[73]

That training in jobs that might earn them a livelihood was important is suggested by the struggles that the WCA's first endeavour, the employment agency. The employment agency was started in 1876 to provide employment for the women coming in from the country and at the same time provide domestics for the WCA women. It foundered from the beginning. Mrs M. E. Mills stated that applicants 'were generally not very well qualified (for position as domestics) and could not conscientiously be recommended to employers'. As a consequence, the employment agency was not as promising as desired.[74] In 1899, the WCA established a school of domestic science for the women in the boarding school, having found that 'the most disheartening feature, incompetency, of the majority of those applying for domestic work, and the consequent disgust of those in need of trained service'. They rented a room and hired a teacher but after 'three months' experience and heavy expense' they found they could not generate enough interest among the young women to justify such an outlay'.[75]

In 1891, the WCA opened a second boarding home in Fort Pickering at the invitation of the Bluff City Cotton Mill Company. The Mill wanted to secure a class of operatives 'free from reproach, morally, and to keep them so' and the WCA wished 'to secure employment for the many unskilled young women applying to us for work and home'. This endeavour also lasted only three months as the workingwomen found they were not content with factory work.[76]

A year later the superintendent for the boarding home noted that in addition to dress-makers, seamstresses, telephone operators and clerks they had residents who were 'not skilled in any special line of industry of whom we are proud, but who want to learn something'.[77]

The women came in part because they had no other choice economically or socially, but the home also offered them some distinct advantages. In addition to food, shelter and healthcare during delivery, it offered them a certain political leverage. In a world where reputation mattered and where social status brought different treatment under the law, poor rural women could also benefit from the WCA women's prominent social position.

The WCA members were part of the privileged ruling class even as they challenged it. As a result, their interactions with women whose reputations were tarnished were not unequivocally in support of these young women. Nevertheless, the WCA women could provide an important counterbalance to the white privileged men who were jockeying to maintain their social control.

A good example of the ways in which different people got involved in a white woman's reputation and life is provided by Maud Stafford, who came to the home in 1881. Maud Stafford was a 'young country woman' from Greenville, Mississippi, and the daughter of a judge. She had relations with a young bookkeeper and, when her affair became known, she fled to Memphis in 1881. The unfolding drama, covered in great detail by the city paper, reveals how the Mission cooperated in protecting a wealthy white woman's reputation and thus helped to reinforce the status quo.[78]

Judge Stafford of Greenville, Mississippi, adopted Maud in 1864 in St Louis when she was nine weeks old. She was, her adoptive father asserted, born in wedlock, a posthumous child of an 'honorable confederate officer'. Her new parents gave her 'every advantage of education', including a year of college in Detroit. When Maud, 'a young country woman', was fourteen years old her adoptive mother died. A year later Maud began an acquaintance with H. W. Meisner, a bookkeeper at Goldsmith's grocery. The acquaintance, Maud told a reporter who interviewed her in the Mission, 'ripened into an intimate friendship'. H. W. escorted her to public assemblages and on evening walks. When he made an improper proposal, she 'promptly and positively resented' it. H. W. nevertheless caught hold of her and 'by superior forces overpowered her, pushed her down and gratified his lustful passions'. There being no friend near at hand, 'she was powerless to do more than weep over the accomplishment of her ruin'. For almost a year she brooded over her misfortune, fearing to divulge it to anyone 'she could not say why'. H.W. had initially left town, afraid she would expose him, but he came back later and promised to marry her, so she kept the matter secret. Up until that time she had been virtuous. When the matter 'by some means unknown to her ... became public and her ruined character became the theme of gossips to the extent she could face it no longer' she consulted with friends, 'some of whom were married ladies'. One friend advised her she had but one alternative: to go to Memphis and enter upon a life of pleasure. This woman assisted her in getting her clothes out of the house and in catching the train.[79]

According to the landlady 'at a well-known up-town house of ill fame', two men came seeking admission for Maud. At first the brothel keeper refused, but when they told her that the girl had been seduced and had expressed a desire to enter a house of prostitution and warned her that if she didn't take the girl, others would, she relented. Before she accepted Maud, however, she made it clear that she would not take a virtuous girl.

It was soon obvious, the landlady claimed, that the girl was 'green', so she turned her over to another girl 'who would instruct her in the ways of her new life'. Maud soon had a constant stream of visitors, many from the 'best class of people'. While she was there she wrote a letter to 'Darling William' (her seducer) and appealed to him to come and get her as he had promised.

Captain Haver of the police force told his story to the paper. As soon as he received intelligence on late Sunday evening that a girl had been brought to the city for the purpose of prostitution, he set out to find her. It was not difficult as her arrival was well known to the 'sporting element'. When he told the proprietor of the brothel that he would take the girl or arrest the brothel keeper, the brothel keeper offered him Maud. Maud, however, 'most positively objected at first'. She said she had come by her own choice and was determined to remain, that she was of age, free to do as she pleased and guilty of nothing. Captain Haver explained that as she had left home without the knowledge of her parents and had declared her intention of becoming a prostitute, he was justified in making the arrest. He also 'supplemented the plain talk with pictures of misery and unhappiness she was plunging into'. So effective was he, she changed her mind and agreed to go to the Mission Home. That night at the station house, she 'had as comfortable quarters as could be provided', but couldn't sleep, 'mainly because of remorse at her miserable condition'. Young men crowded to the station house – even offered to go bail – but the police captain refused to let Maud go. He instead wired her father, Judge Stafford, who answered: 'Put Maud in safe hands. I will come immediately'.

Judge Stafford, in a letter to the *Daily Memphis Commercial* wrote his thanks to the good people of Memphis and Greenville who had rendered him assistance 'in my effort to save my daughter from a fate ten thousand times more terrible than death, and with a good prospect of success'. 'Beware', he wrote,

> of the prowling wolves of society, who are all about you, seeking an opportunity to slake their thirst in the blood of the fairest lambs of your flock. You cannot be too watchful. If it is my lamb that is the victim today, it may be yours tomorrow. Remember your towns and cities are full of H. W. Meisners ... who perch themselves on the most conspicuous seats in your fashionable churches.

It might have been Maud who later wrote a letter to the WCA. There was one, the WCA noted, who had a strange commingling of temptation and triumph and who had been snatched, as it were, from destruction. 'As I leave now, for my home, I cannot but return thanks to the Christian ladies ... I hope to prove to them that it has not all been in vain as I hope, with God's help, to live the life of a Christian', this resident wrote.[80]

Maud's story reveals how reputation governed her life and determined the actions of the public towards her, from law enforcement to the demi-monde. Maud left only when 'gossips got wind of the scandal' to 'avoid public shame'. Her female friends, 'some of whom were married' did not pressure her lover to marry her but, instead, advised her to become a prostitute because she had no alternative. The brothel keeper accepted her even though she was 'green' on the assurance that she was 'not virtuous'. Men's actions towards her were also determined by her reputation for chastity. Men of the 'sporting world' flocked to the brothel and to the police station to see her. Captain Haver went into the brothel to rescue her with the help of the law and the 'pictures of misery and unhappiness she was plunging into'. Maud's father broadened Maud's story into a morality tale, one that was useful for the society at large. This might have been your daughter, he emphasized.

With her father, the police and the Mission pressuring her, Maud recanted. She had initially refused to leave the brothel and had written Meisner to come and get her. She ended by calling her lover a brute who 'gratified his lustful passions' and describing herself a passive victim in need of protection. She went home with her father 'who drank a good deal occasionally, in which condition he was unkind'.[81]

In the 1880s legislators and the courts began to rewrite and reinterpret the laws to enable white women – as long as they acknowledged the supreme importance of chastity to a woman's reputation – to bring seduction suits on their own. Women who knew how to take advantage of this law could gain a certain economic benefit if the man identified as the father were a man of means. At the same time, men who understood the workings of the law could protect them-

selves by undermining the women's efforts. The seduction laws were in this sense
a contestation of power and those with little power were likely to lose.

Savvy women appealed to the public as well as participating in seduction
suits to gain support. For example, Lucy Walton Rhett Horton of Tennessee
attempted to shoot her lover, John Morgan, son of a US Senator. Lucy's father
had been the law partner of Senator Morgan, which suggests that Lucy and her
lover were of a similar social status and of a similar age. Lucy's father, however,
had died and had left Lucy without a male to represent her interests in the court.
Lucy had already initiated a seduction suit against John for $20,000 under
breach of promise of marriage. The newspaper noted that she was 'a cultivated
and well-educated woman, of more than average good looks'. Lucy also had several letters from John Morgan which proved his conduct with regard to her. She
shot John and then, in the public attention that followed the shooting, appealed
to the public even as she appealed to John's father. 'This is such a terrible wrong,
and I am so helpless, and I appeal to your honour and manhood to let me see him
and plead with him for the innocence he has taken from me'.[82]

Lucy's friends argued that she had been temporarily insane when she shot
John, but her actions – keeping the letters, shooting her lover to bring public
attention, and appealing to John's father – all suggest she knew how to play the
system to her advantage. She might have even considered the possibility that
Senator Morgan, a public figure, would pay her off to keep her quiet if John did
not marry her.

Unlike Lucy, poor women were disadvantaged by their lack of education as
well as their gender and could not often stand up to a man higher in the social
hierarchy. The women who managed the WCA, however, wielded considerable
power by virtue of their social position. They could share with the women in the
WCA home their knowledge on how to take advantage of the laws.[83] In addition, they provided a place where women might be protected from the influence
of the more powerful white men. Poor white women and their families took
advantage of the opportunity offered by the WCA and other homes to wrest
control away from wealthier men. At the same time, however, more prominent
families could use the leverage of the WCA to reinforce the status quo – even
against the wishes of their daughters.

The power of privileged white men was clear in the story reported by the
Appeal in 1882. A girl and her mother, the paper reported, had been expelled
from a mill in Brownsville where they both worked. The girl, 'of prepossessing appearance' and 'unblemished reputation', left her job to have a baby. Her
mother, a widow who worked for sixty cents a day at the factory and the girl,
not knowing where to turn, brought a charge of bastardy against the son of
her supervisor. Claiming he was responding to a petition circulated among the
workers, the supervisor fired the widow and her daughter and 'sent them adrift

on a pitiless world'. The only reason for this action, the paper reported, was that the father 'thought to starve Mrs. Glass and daughter into a life of shame and save his son from prosecution'. What happened to the mother and her daughter is not known. Another young woman, however, in similar circumstances, suggested the advantages of what the WCA had to offer.[84]

In June 1882, the *Memphis Appeal* reported 'about as dirty a piece of work as ever came to light in this city'. According to the *Appeal,* the Chief of Police of Oxford, Mississippi had sought entrance to the Mission for 'a young lady who had been ruined and cruelly deserted by a prominent citizen of that town'. The town authorities had brought the unnamed young lady to the Mission to protect her from any attempts the prominent citizen might make to contact her and the WCA gave 'rigid orders that no one be allowed to hold conversation with her'.[85]

The prominent citizen made several attempts through intermediaries to contact her to no avail. And then at two one morning, a young man called upon Mrs Clarence Hall, one of the managers of the WCA Mission, and asked her to give a note to the matron to admit a young lady from Little Rock. The young man told Mrs Hall that they had started to walk to the Mission but the young lady had fainted, and so he had hired a hack. Mrs Hall questioned the couple and became suspicious. She told them to take the woman to a hotel where the ladies of the Mission would visit her in the morning. Although the couple claimed they had no money, the lady was firm. The next morning the WCA discovered that the 'prominent citizen' from Oxford had been one of the party. It was clear, the paper reported, that the man wanted to get the young woman into the Mission so that she could arrange a compromise or intimidate the pregnant woman into a withdrawal of her seduction suit. Perhaps he was even arranging 'to kidnap her and put her where she would be no further annoyance to the gentleman of prominence who had wrought her ruin'.[86]

The young country women who came to Memphis seeking jobs chose for themselves from the selection of services that the WCA women offered them. The young women, for example, refused to take advantage of a Home at Fort Pickering that was to provide a moral environment and failed to respond to the school of domestic science that was to improve their eligibility as domestic servants.

Those women who arrived pregnant had fewer options, but they made choices as well. For almost three decades the WCA reported that the Mission was overcrowded. All the women who came, however, did not stay. The WCA regularly reported that about one-third of those women who came left before they were dismissed. The reports don't include the length of stay, so it is impossible to know at what point the women left without approval. It may have been that they, like the women in Nashville, pretended to reform, using the home until it suited them to take up again the 'dance of death'[87] or stayed at least until they had medical attention for the delivery.

The Mission was flawed in the way that it provided for the women who sought its services. At the same time, it challenged the male hierarchy in important ways. The radical challenge to the patriarchy, however, was short-lived. The same forces that created a space for privileged white women to challenge male authority also led to an end to the challenge. At the turn of the century Memphis, like the rest of the South, was a battleground where the meaning of race and the power of the white elites were being contested. Between 1882 and 1930, 3,315 blacks in the United States died as a result of lynching by whites.[88] Lynchings were both a means of wresting control and a sign of the power struggle for white supremacy which was underway.

The 1870s and 80s were a period of sharp racial conflict in Tennessee as white legislators attempted to limit black participation in government and to ensure racial separation in the society at large. In 1875, the Tennessee Assembly passed the first Jim Crow law of the South when it prohibited blacks from travelling in first class accommodations on the railroad and allowed innkeepers and recreational establishments to exclude blacks. Blacks contested this law in the legislature and in public. Lynching – the extralegal murder of those charged with crimes – and the narrative that reinforced and excused it – played a critical role in this conflict over citizenship and civil rights. And white women's reputations for chastity were central to the lynching narrative.

Between 1882 and 1930 4,498 people died as a result of lynching in the United States 3,315 of whom were Black. The time of greatest lynching activity was between 1886 and 1896 when 82 per cent of all lynchings occurred in the South. In one year alone, 1892, 230 people were murdered. Although both men and women, whites and black, were lynched a great majority of those lynched were black males.[89]

The practice of lynching threatened African-Americans with violence if they assumed their rights as male citizens. The narrative of lynching – propounded in political spaces, churches and the newspapers – justified the murders and reinforced the practice. It built on the white southern expectation that white men would protect white women. Lynchings, the narrative suggested, were necessary because black men could not control their lust for white females, all of whom were innately virtuous. White men needed to protect all white women from sexual assault at whatever cost. As Robin Wiegman notes,

> [the] white woman serves as a pivotal rhetorical figure for shaping the mythology of the black rapist. Using her emblem as the keeper of the purity of the race, white men cast themselves as protectors of civilization, reaffirming not only their role as social and familial heads but their paternal property rights as well.

While prior to the Civil War the importance of a white woman's chastity depended in part on her class, the lynching narrative reinforced the importance of chastity for all white women regardless of class.[90]

The narrative worked locally to urge whites to adopt appropriate behaviour and to bond with whites over blacks. It also operated at a national level to justify the lynchings in the South. In 1894, the editor of the Methodist Church South journal suggested that more than 300 women in the South had been assaulted by Negro men within three months, and the US Speaker of the House of Representatives, formerly a judge of the Supreme Court of Georgia, declared that lynching 'seldom or never took place save for vile crime against women and children'. Ida Wells-Barnett investigated the charges that led to lynching and found that in almost every case they were false. This lynching narrative, she concluded, made lynching, a means of dominating through violence, acceptable throughout the country. 'Humanity abhors the assailant of womanhood, and this charge upon the Negro at once placed him beyond the pale of sympathy', she wrote.[91]

While the WCA Mission did not violate racial sanctions by admitting black women, it undermined the lynching narrative when it attempted to minimize the importance of a white woman's chastity and welcomed single pregnant women into the Home along with virtuous women. For the defence of lynching rested upon the assumption that white men had to protect white women because all white women were innocent and virtuous, all white men were the natural protectors of white women, and all black men would stop at nothing to rape a white woman. It is possible that cross-race solidarity might have blossomed earlier between women, but the increasing politicization of sexual propriety undermined such a possibility. In 1881 a Memphis newspaper noted that a 'colored woman' had objected to being thrown out of the first-class railroad car. The conductor claimed that he had not thrown her off on account of her race but that she was a 'notorious courtesan, addicted to the use of profane language and improper conduct in public places'. As historian Nell Painter has pointed out, there was a great deal of anger released in the post-war years and much of this 'came from women'. It is possible, she suggests that black and white women together might have articulated another kind of society had they been given a chance, but by the end of the century this possibility was foreclosed by the racial divide inflamed by the lynching narrative.[92]

For white women, innocence was innate and in need of protection. As the *Appeal* commented in its condemnation of a nationally popular song about a woman who 'had quaffed to the lips the unholy chalice of sin', the song expressed a 'tardy admission of the fact that virtue with women is innate, and that her degradation comes from contact with masculine turpitude'.[93]

If women were by nature innocent, men were by nature sexually aggressive. In answer to a citizen petition to 'abate nuisances of bawdy houses', the Legislative Council determined that to regulate houses of prostitution would be unwise 'because the question will never be satisfactorily solved until men have their passions under perfect control'. They haven't yet, the *Appeal* concluded, and to close the houses 'would result in more evil than good'.[94]

Men's sexual nature, if uncontrolled, was damaging to women. Emma Meyer in New York, the *Appeal* reported in 1881, was misled and deserted. She 'then gave herself up entirely to evil ways'. At fourteen, afraid to go home to her mother who was a respectable widow, she drank a bottle of poison and lay down on the sidewalk to die.[95]

While men were the seducers, they were also the protectors. When an unnamed 'young lady' was induced by a state legislator to stay on a train until Memphis, it was the conductor who intervened, convinced her to take the next train home, and saved her 'from a fate of which we will not speak'. When Maud Stafford entered a house of prostitution in Memphis because her lover had ruined her reputation, it was the police who encouraged her to come with them to the police station. When the young men crowded to the station house and offered to go bail for her, it was the police again who kept the young men at bay. When her father came to get her he warned 'you who are the heads of families ... beware of the prowling wolves of society, who are all about you, seeking an opportunity to slake their thirst ... You cannot be too watchful'.[96]

The narrative called on all white men, not just the elite, to protect white women. 'There never was a time', the *Commercial Appeal* noted in 1904, 'unless it was immediately after the war, when the carrying of arms was so prevalent as now'. And a visitor to Memphis cautioned fellow visitors, 'what passes for a jest in other parts of the country does not pass for jest here. A man must be careful of his language. You cannot impugn a man's honor and not fight'. That honour was connected closely to the reputation of white women is suggested by historian William D. Miller who noted that horsewhipping was still used in retaliation when a woman's name was handled too cavalierly and that men were exhorted to 'protect female virtue at all hazards'. The *Appeal* concluded:

> Today after centuries of progress we have reached a plane where there are other things dearer than life, and chief among these is female virtue. When this is slain ... the avenger has the right to go forth in quest of blood-atonement ... There is a higher law ... and that law readeth 'Thou shalt protect female virtue at all hazards'.[97]

While society could appeal to white men's sense of chivalry to curb their natural sexual aggression, there was nothing short of violence, this narrative suggested, that would control the lust of black men. The *Appeal* commented that in the decades following the war the ex-slaves had 'lost in large measure the traditional and wholesome awe of the white race which kept the Negroes in subjection even when their masters were in the army'. It warned that there was no longer any restraints upon the 'brute passion of the Negro', and added:

> The 'Southern barbarism' which deserves the serious attention of all people north and south ... is the barbarism which preys upon weak and defenseless women. Nothing but the most prompt, speedy and extreme punishment can hold in check the horrible and beastial propensities of the Negro race.[98]

In proof, the Memphis papers printed story after story of the rapes that led to lynchings throughout the South. According to the stories, the rapists paid no attention to the victims' status, age or decorum. 'ANOTHER SENSATION', the *Avalanche* reported in 1878, 'Negro committed outrage on ... girl 15 years of age' and in 1881, '19 year old colored boy, lived with sheriff's family for 14 years, accosted 11 year old daughter in the outhouse'.[99]

The WCA had challenged this construction in a number of ways. It argued that women could protect women, was a visible presence in the community that not all white women were virtuous and innocent, and suggested that the loss of virtue was not the worst thing that could happen to a white woman.

When the WCA women moved the Mission from the Navy Yard to Alabama Street, they brought the Home into the heart of the city. They also invited the public into the Home to share the regular Thursday services and to attend talks. By keeping women and children together in the Home, the Mission offered single mothers an opportunity to keep their children and to support themselves through the various industries that the Home engaged in. This included caring for their own as well as others' children. In addition, it offered some women an opportunity to achieve at least an appearance of a middle-class existence

With such a radical message, it is not surprising that the WCA found it difficult to garner support for the Mission. Meriwether had warned that even 'best friends', those who were 'kind hearted and liberal handed in every other cause, will fail you in this', and her prediction proved true.[100]

From its beginning the Mission suffered from lack of support. The WCA sponsored a wide array of programmes in addition to the Home and while over 300 women volunteered their services and gave money to the WCA annually, only a few of those chose to donate their time and money to the Mission. In 1881, WCA secretary Mrs. T.A. Fisher reported that although there were over 100 inmates in the Mission, the entire expense was supported by one individual. Necessity, she stated, compelled this one-sided support: 'Others would not, or did not give and what we feel to be an unjust proportion of the burden was cheerfully assumed by one'. Mrs J. C. Johnson, president of the WCA, 'made an eloquent appeal for aid' for the mission.[101]

Lack of support for fallen women was apparently widespread throughout the South. Later that year, Johnson gave a talk in St Louis to the International Conference of Woman's Christian Association in which she called for the WCA to support reformatory work. In her talk she pointed out how WCAs were establishing boarding homes, Bible classes, mothers meetings and the like, but 'how few report any efforts made or work done in' the direction of the sinful and erring. She pointed out that only once did a WCA national meeting address the subject of reformatory work. 'We acknowledge, dear friends, it is not pleasant work, but we think it necessary work and Christ like work'. The Refuge, the WCA leadership conceded in 1892, was 'never very popular work'.[102]

In spite of Meriwether's call to all Christian women to hire the fallen women, few did. Although the WCA enthusiastically announced that its employment agency would provide Memphis families with appropriate domestic help, and although domestic work was the work that might accomodate a woman with a child, there is no indication that the Mission placed women with children in families as domestic workers. Instead it trained inmates as seamstresses and laundry workers because this work taught the inmates the independence of being self-reliant and *partly* self-sustaining. (emphasis added)[103]

While the Mission suffered from lack of funds and lack of opportunities for its inmates, it suffered even more from overt community hostility. In 1881, neighbours complained to the Shelby County Grand Jury that the Mission was a 'nuisance to the neighborhood'. The Grand jury concluded that they were 'fully impressed with the fact that institutions of this class are detrimental to any thickly settled neighbourhood, by depreciating the value of property and detracting from its desirability as a place of family residence'. The Jury therefore recommended that the 'lady managers' as 'early as practicable' move the department devoted to fallen women to 'a more suitable locality outside of the city limits'.[104]

The WCA instead increased its campaign to present the Home as a worthy cause and forestalled the move for seven more years. Finally in 1888, suffering from lack of funds, community pressure, and an ideological war that made white women's chastity essential, the WCA voted to 'divide the dual work carried on by the Mission' and 'establish a separate home for women in a retired place'. It moved the 'magdalenes', as they were now referred to, out to 'a most eligible place' near Fort Pickering, but left the children in the Alabama Street home. A year later it opened a boarding home for women. Finally, when it had created three separate boards for three separate missions – children, working women and fallen women – and changed the name of the home for 'fallen' women from the Mission to the Refuge, the WCA abandoned its radical challenge to the society. Fallen women, this new structure suggested, were unredeemable and threatened to contaminate other women. In addition, they were not morally capable of taking care of children – including their own.

The distinction thus made between the magdalenes and the working women was profound. From its inception the boarding home for working women received substantial support from the community. 'Perhaps no other call ... to philanthropic work met with such hearty and enthusiastic response by the women of our city as this', the president of the WCA reported in 1893. The distinction between the two homes, between the independent and dependent, worthy and unworthy, was deliberate and pronounced and served to isolate and stigmatize the 'magdalenes' even more.[105]

While evidence suggests the women who filled to overflowing both homes came from the same rural backgrounds, the community lavished support and respect on the working women and offered little but sympathy and a place to hide to the fallen women. The WCA consistently made it clear that the boarding home women were self-supporting. The boarding home, the *Gleaner* emphasized,

> is not to be considered in the same light as our eleemosynary institutions – the Children's Home and the Refuge. To allow this is surely to defeat our own purpose of real helpfulness towards these brave bread winning girls.

While acknowledging that the Refuge was 'in some respects the most needy' perhaps the most dependent department, the WCA devoted more resources to encourage boarding (but virtuous) women's independence. When unskilled women arrived at the boarding home, the WCA taught them how to make bed-comforts and coin racks and to do 'just plain sewing'. By providing them immediately with this in-house work, it simultaneously trained them and enabled them to earn a living immediately. Occasionally the WCA paid for training in a business college. 'Each season developing noble self-sustaining women who go out to open business for themselves are employed by our best business houses', the Annual Report boasted in 1892.[106]

In contrast, the women at the Refuge were now increasingly described in abject terms as those unable to help themselves. They were 'homeless and friendless', 'penitent and unfortunate girls', 'those in whom all the light and love of life has been crushed', 'poor erring creatures' and 'sin stricken, helpless souls'. The purpose of the Refuge was to lift up these fallen creatures. What more pressing work, the WCA urged, than the 'building up of poor, weak bodies in broken lives, establishing habits of righteousness in those ... having lost their moorings, are seemingly inevitably drifting into eternal ruin?'[107]

As the boarding home for poor but chaste women continued to enjoy widespread economic support from the community, the Refuge struggled from the lack of funds. In order to open the home for working women, the WCA lined up 250 people who subscribed three dollars per year. A private donor, Mr Hu Brinkley, donated $64,000 for the home. By 1906 the WCA was able to build its own home at Second and Pontotoc. By 1926, it had accumulated more than $49,000 for a two story annex, a swimming pool and a decorative garden plot; by 1956, it had reserves of $72,000, enough for a complete remodelling and refurnishing. In stark contrast the Refuge, unable to attract enough support, closed in 1937.[108]

The separation between the women of the boarding home and the Refuge was so complete that in 1895 even Lide Meriwether who had written so force-fully against allowing reputation to ruin a woman was calling for a temporary home for working women who were awaiting admittance to the boarding home. 'They should not be sent to the Refuge', she insisted, 'for a nameless cloud will rest upon them, however innocent they may be, if they are seen going and com-ing, even for a few days, in search of work'.[109]

1888 marked the end of a radical experiment. As the Home changed its name from Mission to Refuge, as it separated out the self-supporting from the charity women, those with their reputations intact and those without, it dropped its challenge to the dominant ideology. No longer did the WCA urge its members to use their sympathy to connect with the fallen women, but suggested instead that they undertake the work as 'a cross and self-denial'. Where once they called for recognition of the common humanity that linked WCA members with fallen women, they now called for the godliness of self-sacrifice.

As a result, the WCA could report by 1901 that the public sentiment was growing for this work. No longer did the Refuge challenge men's authority to protect women or question the importance of a reputation. Instead, it worked to enforce the current structure. Reports of the Refuge after the turn of the century suggest that the institution had become a place of punishment and a means to force young women to comply with the society norms. Fathers brought their daughters to the Home; the matron expected women to give up their children to save their reputations and if they tried to do otherwise, punished them.[110]

In the early years, the demand for shelter at the Mission outstripped what the Mission, with its meager resources, was able to supply. As the WCA commit-tee shifted its focus in response to social pressure, its organization and purposes shifted as well. As a result, it lost its appeal to the women it planned to serve. Gradually the number of applicants declined until, in the midst of the Depres-sion, many rooms remained empty.

3 MAINE: PRESERVING RESOURCES: HARD WORK AND RESPONSIBILITY

Between 1877 and 1883 Maine judges sentenced five women to the State Prison for life for infanticide.[1] In every one of these infanticide cases, the evidence suggests, the women turned to infanticide out of economic desperation. Although every child murdered was born out of wedlock, in every case but one it was a month old or older and a number of people had involved themselves in caring for it. In every case but one as well, the mother did not kill the child on her own. She was assisted either by her relatives or her boyfriend. Four out of the five women came from small Maine towns. The fifth, an Irish immigrant living in Portland, was the anomaly in every case.

These convictions, an unparalleled event in the history of the state prison. In the previous fifty years only one woman had been committed for a life sentence. When he opened the first infanticide trial Supreme Court Justice William G. Barrows called for strict punishment:

> This is a case of highest importance. If these prisoners can escape by the stupidity or indifference of the community then our government is a failure. We have nothing but the laws which savages have, and the care of the weak must be left with God.

The local newspaper agreed. Commenting on the 'atmospheric wave of immorality around – exerting its baleful influence on our community', the *Oxford Democrat* called for the people of Oxford to mend their ways and to be vigilant. Convicting the women was not enough, the paper stated. 'Every community should drive all evil doers from their midst'.[2]

But the communities from which the women came responded in a different fashion. They called for sympathy not punishment for the women involved. In each of the four rural communities 100 people or more signed petitions requesting the governor pardon the women. As the clerk of the court wrote in the case of Sarah Whitten, he believed the people of Alfred would approve of the 'poor girl's pardon' because they were aware of the facts of the case. Sarah and her boyfriend had chloroformed their one-month-old child and thrown it into the river but, as her petition stated, 'she has the sympathy of the community'.[3]

These infanticides make clear the challenges Maine towns faced following the Civil War. Major economic changes increased geographic mobility, drained the small towns of their populations and undermined each town's ability to control and support its members. The war itself caused a major disruption of the population. Maine sent more soldiers in proportion to its population to fight in the war than any other northern state and suffered a greater loss than any but Vermont.[4] Many surviving Maine recruits took advantage of the lands opening in the west and their soldiers' bounties and never returned home. In addition, the growing national economy consolidated production in fewer hands and made goods produced in Maine vulnerable to national competition. Reliance on specialized crops for commercial markets led to an exhaustion of already thin soils. After 1880 both the number of farms and the amount of acreage under cultivation declined. What followed was a dramatic out-migration as many rural young people left to find opportunities elsewhere. Maine's small towns faced a steady decrease in their populations and a dramatic rise in their costs as they continued to provide support for the families of soldiers who had died or were disabled in the War.[5]

As native sons and daughters moved out of their hometowns and, often, their states, immigrants moved into the cities to work in the mills. French Canada provided the greatest number of immigrants. The Quebecois came in family groups and kept close ties with their home country. Not only did they speak another language, but they also followed another religion. Their Catholic churches and schools followed them into the predominantly Protestant state.[6]

As Maine's population grew more urban and more diverse, its population grew increasingly mobile. For the expanding working-class in the cities, faced with periodic unemployment and seasonal work, mobility became an important part of life. Every three years from 1870–90 50 per cent of the Franco population in Biddeford turned over. In Old Town and Lewiston the population turnover was over 60 per cent.[7]

These profound economic and demographic changes undermined the traditional community control that had provided support for unwed mothers. Maine's settlement laws required communities to support unwed mothers when their fathers had settlement in those communities – but the laws also required five years of continuous residence in one town without seeking support before one could claim a settlement. Bastardy suits required men to support children on the mother's word that they were the fathers – but the developing rail network required by the growing national economy made it relatively easy for a man to disappear. Tradition encouraged members within a community to watch over the relationships developing within them and to persuade young people who engaged in sex with each other to marry – but communities could not watch over women who left and marriage with a stranger, possibly of another religion, might not be a solution that the family or community wanted.

If traditional practices could no longer provide the support women needed, they were unlikely to find it within the growing cities. Confined as they were to jobs that paid substantially less than those for men and often called upon to help support their families, they had limited ability to support themselves let alone a child.[8]

A sample of stories in the *Daily Eastern Argus*, in January 1882, suggests the public awareness of and concern for the women released from parental or community control – both the dangers they faced as well as the dangers they embodied. All of the women in the stories act independently. They all have lost their chastity, but it is not their chastity but their freedom from control which is at issue. 'Lewiston is wild again over a case of abortion', the *Argus* reported in a front-page story on 14 January 1882. The young woman was eighteen, 'of an excellent family' and had 'always borne a good reputation'. Nevertheless, she left home one day having told her mother she was visiting two friends. Her mother, becoming suspicious and finding the girl at neither place, asked the police to help her find her daughter. They found her at the residence of Mrs M. Rose, 'a well-known trance medium'. The mother brought her daughter home in a 'precarious condition' and the police arrested Mrs Rose for committing an abortion.[9]

A week later the *Argus* told another story, this one of 'domestic intrigue, duplicity and wrong'. This young woman did not trick her parents, but was herself tricked by a man from outside of the community. Two years previously a salesman for a large wholesale firm in New York visited Skowhegan. 'He was an accomplished pianist and vocalist, with dark, curling hair and good presence … ingratiated himself without much trouble into the family … and soon won the affections of a daughter of the family'. After several months of courtship, the couple wed. Mr Rarick took his new wife to Montreal where he assumed another name and then left his wife 'to the miseries of a private boarding home'. When the girl's father learned that Rarick had deserted his daughter and that she had tried to kill herself, he went to get her. Mr Rarick, alias Mr Romayn, confessed that he had a wife and three children in Plainfield, New Jersey. 'Having heard from his own lips the story of his duplicity, his victim turned from him in loathing'.[10]

That same month another young woman revealed how a young woman with no family to protect her might still retain control of her life. Mrs Elizabeth Russell was only fourteen when the court charged her with bigamy. She was, the paper noted, of prepossessing appearance and seemed to enjoy the attention that brought her. When Elizabeth was eleven she was obliged to work for a living. Her mother had abandoned the family to travel with Silas J. Hurd, a man of poor circumstances who did odd jobs wherever he could find them. Elizabeth's mother returned several times to the family, but when she returned with an infant her husband refused to take her back. She left and took Elizabeth with her. One evening when the mother and daughter went walking, they met Hurd, who wanted the mother to go away with him again. She refused on account of the infant but pushed her daughter to go in her stead. Elizabeth 'was horrified at the idea'. At last, however, she 'was induced to leave her friends and make her home with Hurd'. Three months later she returned and a young man fell in love with her. 'He was not the sort of man she wanted', but she accepted his help in finding her a job. At this new job she met and then married the brother of the man who owned the farm. The rejected suitor, in a fit of jealousy, informed Elizabeth's new family that Elizabeth had been previously married; Elizabeth's new brother-in-law obtained a warrant against her. 'The girl-wife strongly asserts her innocence', the *Argus* concluded. 'She says the records ... have been searched in vain for a marriage'.[11]

What is striking in these stories is the autonomy that all three women managed to obtain. Forced to work at an early age, Elizabeth moved from place to place as duty or opportunity beckoned. Two men proposed to her even after she had travelled with an older man and Elizabeth chose what she wanted and rejected what she did not. The young women in the other two stories were not as successful, but the first managed to arrange for an abortion even while she was living within a vigilant family, and the second was able to walk away from her betrayer and return to her family.

As the stories suggest, young women outside of their families' or communities' control posed a threat to society and to themselves. They could use their sexuality to gain what they wanted and thus disrupt social stability or they could have a baby for whom no man could be held responsible and who would thus need to be supported by the society. Women in Maine responded by opening three institutions for sexually active young women between 1872 and 1902. The first, the industrial training school, sought to discipline young women. The second, the Temporary Home for Women and Children in Portland, provided support for women and their children as it sought to transform them. The third, the Good Samaritan Home in Bangor, provided support but only in exchange for hard work and the acceptance of personal responsibility.

The Industrial Training School was ostensibly different from the Temporary Home and the Good Samaritan Home in that it was not for pregnant women. In actuality, the courts could and did commit young pregnant women to the training school and, occasionally, young women who were not pregnant entered the unwed mothers home. The distinction between the two groups of young women was more cultural than biological. It marked those who belonged (those for whom towns accepted responsibility and who themselves accepted responsibility to maintain the status quo) and those who did not. The courts committed young women to the training school who were 'found in circum-stances of manifest danger of falling into habits of vice or immorality', those who were not willing to submit to community regulation. These were primarily from urban areas – young women who worked in the mills and whose families had recently migrated into the state. The training school took such women out of their families and communities and worked to transform them into 'law-abid-ing, self-respecting young women'. In contrast, young women applied on their own to the Good Samaritan Home, but were required to provide three refer-ences. These references ensured that the women belonged in, and would abide by the rules of, Maine's small towns. In the home, employees and volunteers offered the young women sympathy and care and demanded that they work hard, be responsible and remain self-sufficient.[12]

The Industrial Training School in Hallowell opened in 1875, three years after 'nearly a thousand ladies of Portland' signed a petition requesting the state establish such an institution.[13] The school rapidly expanded. By 1914 it housed approximately 120 girls who were on average fifteen-and-a-half-years old. Once a girl was committed, her parents lost all parental rights over her until she was twenty-one. It is clear from the school's descriptions and practices that there was a difference in values between the women who ran the school and the families from which its residents came. In many cases the residents were French-Cana-dian immigrants.[14]

Matrons of the school referred to their charges as 'wild and uncultivated' and 'not from pleasant and refined homes'. In 1914 the school report commented, 'nine times out of ten this type of girl will go down, if she returns to her former environment ... SHE is the only one who has developed; the home is the same and provides no strength or stability for her at the time she needs it most'. The school regularly placed the girls in other families and in other communities when it released them.[15]

Girls in the Industrial Training School could and did get pregnant. As one worker wrote of her charge in 1923, when the girl had become pregnant by her employer, 'If one could only escape pregnancies how much it would simplify our work'.[16] Young pregnant women in the Industrial Training School were either released to the community for their confinements or transferred to the Women's Reformatory in Skowhegan.[17]

The young women who applied to the Good Samaritan Home challenged the state by having children outside of the community's system for securing care for them. If the birth father could not be charged for the child's support the com-munity had few options. Given the high value placed on accepting responsibility for one's own and the concomitant distrust of strangers, families rarely agreed to place infants for adoption in the homes of strangers.[18] When extended families could not support a child, the town could apprentice the child to another family, but infants were too young to be apprenticed.[19]

If there was no accepted way to give an infant away to a stranger, there were few options for placing it in an institution that provided adequate care. By the mid-nineteenth century, many Maine towns had poor-farms, but an infant's chance of surviving in one without the care of its mother was slight.[20] Private families might take in a boarding infant, but a mother or her family or the community had to have the money to pay for the board.

By 1880 in Maine there were only three homes for orphans, and all of them refused to accept children under three. When the Female Orphan Asylum experimented with taking very young children in 1881, it concluded that, although this move had a positive effect on the older children, it 'added greatly to our work and to the care of the assistants'. The Asylum did not continue the experiment.[21]

In spite of the need to provide for an infant, community members were surprisingly supportive of young women. Eighteen-year-old Rose Dolley's trial for the murder of her two-week-old child highlights the way in which small town communities in Maine responded to women who had a child outside of marriage but who in other ways complied with community standards. On 30 January 1896, Rose appeared in Cumberland County Superior Court. As the newspapers later reported, Rose, from Windham, was a 'country girl born and bred' who kept company with a young man 'in the country where chaperones are practically unknown'. Rose testified that she had met James Libby four years previously and that 'he was my beau and I never had another'. She and James became engaged two years earlier but Rose 'being a poor girl and not at that time feeling that she possessed the necessary means to take such a step urged that the marriage be postponed'. Her beau, however, 'was taken sick and died', and shortly thereafter, Rose discovered that she was pregnant.[22]

With the help of her employer, Rose found a place at the Temporary Home of Portland but when the Home closed suddenly on account of scarlet fever Rose told the court she had half an hour in which to find an alternative placement for her child before she caught the last line stage to her home. The woman Rose asked to board her baby later testified that her husband had objected but, when Rose cried and said she was unmarried, 'I pitied her'.

Rose went to her own home but missed her child and persuaded her mother to go with her to pick it up. The next day a young boy found its battered body frozen in the woods. In spite of the gruesome details of the case, the paper noted at the end of the first day that Rose 'in her present friendless and perilous condition' had 'won the sympathy of scores of people'. 'Scarcely had the crowd begun to disperse than she was surrounded by a group of ladies, each of whom tried to outdo the others in speaking kind words of encouragement to the unfortunate girl'. Accosted with sympathy, Rose burst into tears.

The next day, Rose broke down in the witness stand and revealed that it was her mother, not she, who had murdered the child. Her mother, she explained, had tried to get the Catholic Home to take her son and, when the Home refused, took the child from Rose and carried it into the woods. The court sentenced Rose's mother to life imprisonment; the court officers collected a purse of over fifty dollars for Rose; and Deputy Sheriff Dresser took her home until she 'could recover from the effects of the awful physical and mental strains she had undergone and plan for the future'.

The *Argus*, which covered the trial in great detail, emphasized the economic motives for the murder even as it acknowledged Mrs Dolley's concerns for propriety. Mrs Dolley was a widow with three children who took in boarding babies and 'had a hard struggle for existence'. She also had among her neighbours a reputation for great religious fervour. Rose, the paper stated, could not support the child by herself. 'Mrs. Dolley felt that she had all she could do to care for her present family, and beyond all this Rose's child had no father and to have it in the family, from her point of view, would be a disgrace'. Nevertheless, the *Argus* proposed no sympathy for Rose's mother. Instead, emphasizing the importance of sympathy for the unwed mother, the newspaper concluded that had Mrs Dolley been more intelligent and had 'proper moral tendencies', she would have found some way to overcome the difficulty. Rose's situation had not appealed to her as it would have to a 'more enlightened woman'.[23]

Rose's story highlights the ways in which traditional Maine communities responded to unwed mothers in a way that emphasized community as well as individual responsibility. It is important to note that Rose was a young woman from a small town who wished to take responsibility for her baby and who appealed to the public with full details of her story. Not only did the women of her community show sympathy for Rose even when they thought she had killed her child, but both men and women also felt compelled to help her in some way when the trial was over. The newspaper took her mother to task for being 'unenlightened', for not helping and supporting her daughter when she had had a child out of wedlock.

In the wake of the very public infanticide trials at the end of the century, Protestant women organized the Temporary Home for Women and Children in Portland in 1881 and the Good Samaritan Home in Bangor in 1902. For the next forty years these two homes were the only homes for unwed mothers in the state.[24] While they both provided childcare as well as obstetrical care, required women to remain in the home for many months, and pressured women to keep their children, the Good Samaritan Home thrived while the Temporary Home did not. An examination of the history of the two homes suggests that the

Temporary Home in Portland, the largest and most ethnically diverse city in the state, tried to combine practices that both helped to control a potentially disruptive urban population of independent women and at the same time to support young, pregnant, rural women. The Good Samaritan Home, on the other hand, quickly limited its goals to providing support for the young rural women who agreed to follow its rules. Emphasizing the traditional small-town Maine values and practices, it garnered widespread support from the community.

The Temporary Home for Women and Children in Portland made clear from the beginning that it aimed to reform as well as to protect the women in its care. Its goals were to provide 'shelter and employment for the women and children of the State ... who ... are reduced to dependence upon public charity and who need to be protected from temptation to vice'. The Home was open to all women who applied, but by 1899 the Annual Report had more narrowly defined its mission to care for young women 'who have fallen through ignorance or unguarded surroundings, or who have been deceived through their affections and are in need of help for the first time'. By 1913 the Annual Report referred to its residents as 'girls' rather than women. The Board of Managers, all women, recommended the residents remain several months after delivery and encouraged them to care for their children as 'the strongest possibilities for the future lies along the line of mother love and mother responsibilities'. It also encouraged a woman 'to take a place for housework at low wages, where she can keep her little one with her, or if that is not possible we care for the baby in our nursery, requiring her to pay us its board'.[25]

The managers maintained that they admitted only young girls 'who have fallen through ignorance or unguarded surroundings, or who have been deceived and seduced'. They admitted everyone who applied, however, and their annual reports made clear that those who ran the Home saw their charges in need of reform in dress and habits as well as morality. The work of the matron, the Annual Report of 1899 asserted, was to instil proper work and moral practices. 'The chains of habit are not easily broken, and the work we have undertaken is not as a rule followed by speedy results', it pointed out. By 1913 the managers claimed that with instruction in housework, sewing and care of children, 'the rude speech, careless dress, bad temper and idle habits that they bring with them are often changed and the neat, gentle, obedient girl turns to us with gratitude when she leaves'.[26]

The Good Samaritan Home of Bangor, in contrast, after its first four years, operated exclusively as a home for young women who had recommendations from their communities and who agreed to take responsibility for themselves and their children. Unlike the Temporary Home, which struggled to attract young women, the Good Samaritan Home always had more applicants than it could provide for.[27] In addition, as Gertrude Atwood, a guiding force in the

Home for over thirty years, repeatedly emphasized, it succeeded in its mission. In the annual report for 1919, for example, she noted that invariably the women who gave birth in the Home kept their children. Pointing out that the courts had sentenced four other young unwed mothers to prison that year for having killed their babies, she concluded, 'we may feel that our efforts have not been in vain'.[28]

Following in the footsteps of the women who surrounded Rose Dolley at her trial – and in contrast to her 'unenlightened' mother – the women of the Good Samaritan Home board provided sympathy and practical aid to young women from rural towns who found themselves pregnant and were willing to take responsibility for the consequences. Many of the women who served on the board in its formative years were themselves from Maine's rural communities. They had moved to the city where their husbands gradually accumulated money and prestige. The institution that they built drew upon the values and practices of the small communities from which they came. At the same time, board members encouraged the rural women that they served to take advantage of the opportunities in the city. They sought to make the women independent and encouraged them to educate themselves and move beyond their hometowns.

The Good Samaritan Home began in May of 1901 when Robert Jordan, secretary of the Bangor YMCA, called for a meeting of women and 300 women from churches throughout the city came. Jordan had just become the first probation officer of the county. 'Many a young man in difficulty', the *Bangor Daily Commercial* commented in his obituary, 'through Mr. Jordan's efforts in his behalf, received aid and advice that placed him facing in the right direction after his lapse in complying with the rules'. On this spring day Jordan was calling on women to do the same for girls. The 300 women chose two women from each church, a total of forty, to formulate plans to shelter young women.[29]

At first the women rented a room on Hammond Street and solicited food and money on a daily basis. Within two years they had purchased a small house and, in 1905, a larger one. In 1913 they collected $416 in subscriptions and donations and held a heavily mortgaged home with only one hundred dollars in an endowment fund. It was uncertain, the General Secretary said much later of that time, 'whether or not the family would be fed'. 1913, however, marked the beginning of a phenomenal growth. That year James F. Parker left a bequest to an unspecified charity. Court referees determined that the money should be divided between Eastern Maine General Hospital and the Good Samaritan Home, two institutions 'doing the most for suffering humanity'.[30]

The annual report for the following year included a list four pages long of individuals who contributed to the Home. In addition, the report noted, the hospital sent nurses free of charge; coal dealers contributed coal; Bangor Gas and Light made no charge for gas; and the water board provided water for free.

Charles S. Jones provided fish for every Friday dinner; Caldwell Sweet Company provided all medical supplies; the Bangor creamery provided milk; Fred Crowell provided oranges and fresh fruit; and the Bangor newspaper provided free subscriptions. It was with just cause that the secretary could claim that the 'work of the Association is now recognized as a power for good in the community, and has gained respect and confidence of the people throughout the state'. A decade later the Good Samaritan Home board members collected $3,000 in subscriptions, had paid off their mortgage and accumulated $12,476 in a trust fund. Bequests to the Agency continued to come from a wide variety of Bangor citizens.[31]

The evidence suggests that this widespread support for the Home marked a shift in the organization from a religious orientation to a more secular one. Only a few annual reports and newspaper accounts of the Home survive prior to 1920. Nevertheless, it is possible to reconstruct the religious orientation of its early years. Board members named their organization the Deaconess Home Association and hired a deaconess to manage the Home. Its purpose, as stated in the incorporation, was 'to train and utilize Christian women in active evangelistic, philanthropic and charitable work, to provide a home for those needing refuge ... to devise and carry out plans for the protection, relief and training of neglected, poor, sick and unfortunate persons'.[32]

The first board members reflected this religious orientation. Rev. Leon Higgins and Robert Jordan served on the all-male board of trustees and several ministers' wives on the all-female board of directors. Early board member Mrs Robert Jordan provides an example of the Christian orientation of the board. She was born in Nova Scotia in 1870, began teaching at fourteen, and came to Bangor as a church assistant in special summer work. Her obituary noted that she was 'one of the city's greatest leaders in religious life', having taught interdenominational Bible class for twenty-two years and carried on work at the jail that was sponsored by the Women's Crusade. She was, among other things, a member of the Christian and Missionary Alliance, the Moody Bible Institute, the Bangor Gospel Mission and the Woman's Christian Temperance Union.[33]

At first the Home provided shelter to a wide variety of women from a wide variety of places. The first sixty-six residents listed in the admissions book ranged in age from fourteen to forty-seven and stayed anywhere from five days to almost a year. Almost a quarter came from Bangor and an equal number came from Massachusetts and Canada. The first twenty-five entries noted the women's occupations and they included waitresses, factory workers and a nurse as well as domestic servants. Some were married (perhaps abandoned); and there is no way of telling how many were pregnant. While most were Protestant, there were also a number of Catholics.[34]

In 1907, the structure and orientation of the Home began to change. From that time forward all the residents remained in the Home seven months or longer and the matron carefully noted the town in which they had settlement. That year too the Home opened its 'nursery department' for boarding babies and became the only non-denominational institution that provided for children under three in the state. By 1920, secretary Alice Harden claimed that appeals to board babies came in almost daily, sometimes as many as twenty-five a week. 'These are not illegitimate children', she made it clear, 'but children who have lost either father or mother or both parents, or who have been abandoned by heartless parents'. The Home charged for boarding these babies; the matron of the Home and her assistant supervised the residents in caring for them.[35]

In 1907 also the Board changed its name to the Good Samaritan Home Agency and replaced the deaconess with Miss Frances P. Scoboria, who would serve as matron for the next seventeen years. While the new name was religious, it reflected a shift toward practical humanism. It suggested that young women needed to be understood and helped to help themselves. As a later report explained, the name was 'significant of our purpose. Christ not only gave Himself but His intelligent sympathy and understanding'. The Good Samaritan, 'after investigating carefully the needs of the unfortunate wayfarer, supplied them, but in such a way as to not demean him'.[36]

By 1907 the Home had developed a structure that would remain intact for the next forty years. The residents applied most often by letter to the Home. They were almost exclusively from Maine and were generally under twenty. To be admitted they had to provide three references and proof that they were free of venereal disease. They had to also guarantee that this was the first time they were pregnant outside of marriage. When they entered they had to sign an agreement to abide by the rules of the Home. Among other things, each young woman agreed to 'perform her share of household duties', provide 'obedience to those in authority', not go out unless accompanied or receive visitors without permission, and allow inspection of all her correspondence. In addition, she had to pay an entrance fee of $50 and agree to stay six months after the delivery of her child. If she were unable to pay the fee, she could stay beyond her six months and work off her debt at three dollars per week if the Board gave her its permission.[37]

In the Home, the residents wore striped uniforms similar to those worn by nurses in training. Under the supervision of the matron and her housekeeper, they did all the work of the Home. In addition to caring for the children, they assisted the doctors in their deliveries, baked bread, grew and preserved produce from the garden, and worked overtime for the annual spring cleaning.

The hard work left little time for recreation, but in 1931 Superintendent Gertrude Atwood urged the Board to provide the girls with a little more entertainment, 'especially during the long evening hours'.

> Shall I be called a revolutionist if I suggest that we give some thought to allowing them the privilege of playing whist or hearts or some card game if they are happy in so doing and do not quarrel with their partners? Can we not also provide them with some old fashioned songs, not omitting the old love songs ... It is fine for them to sing familiar hymns, but we might all become fed up on the same ones ...[38]

The Board adopted her proposal and in the evening the women ate popcorn, sang around the piano, listened to the phonograph and, occasionally, danced. When they had time they made outfits for their babies. Occasionally, Atwood or another member of the board invited the young women into their home for dinner or a picnic.

When a resident's time was up, the board had to vote to dismiss her before she was able to leave. Board members would not dismiss a woman unless they were convinced that she was being placed in some 'suitable employment' or 'in charge of responsible relatives'. A 'suitable' placement was often a position in the home of one of the board members or of another Bangor family. Domestic service offered the dual advantages of allowing a woman to keep her child with her and reassuring the Board that she was being supervised. Women were also placed as nurses, teachers or clerks, and were encouraged to continue their educations at night if they were not able to continue them during the day.

The Home offered to board a woman's child until the child was three years old at the nominal fee of $1.50 per week. In order to encourage a woman to visit her child regularly, the board charged more to board a baby when its mother did not remain in the city. At least once a week, the women who left their children in the Home, returned to have tea or dinner in the Home and to see their children. Sometimes the women returned for holiday celebrations and, occasionally, to help with the spring cleaning. If a former resident lost her job or her employers failed to pay her adequately, she could return to the Home while the Board helped her to find another placement.

By 1920 all the women with a clearly identified religious orientation had left the Board. Those who remained were Catholic as well as Protestant, Episcopalians as well as Christian Scientists. What they shared aside from their interest in the Good Samaritan Home was their place in their community. All but one were married and many came originally from small towns. Most were married to men of moderate means who had worked or were working their way up the social ladder. In many cases they served alongside their husbands on the boards of such organizations as the Eastern Maine General Hospital, Community Chest and Bangor Savings Bank. In addition, although they were all involved in their churches, they were not active in larger religious organizations.[39]

For the most part, their husbands were not men of inherited wealth or position. Although their husbands eventually achieved such positions as newspaper editors, mayor and town council members, lawyers and bank presidents and joined the prestigious Penobscot Valley Country Club and the Conduskeag Canoe and Country Club, they had worked hard to obtain these positions. Many had come to the city to find opportunity. One was a travelling representative for a dry-goods firm; one was an insurance agent; one was a clerk in a bank; and another was a baseball player. Two attended small seminaries and worked their way up in business. Most had little formal education beyond high school.[40]

Norris E. Bragg, for example, whose wife was the first president of the association, was born in Dixmont. His father was a blacksmith who had moved to Bangor in 1854 to set up a supply house for other blacksmiths. Norris joined his father in the firm in 1864. By 1928 N. H. Bragg & Sons employed twenty-four people and was the largest jobber of iron, steel and heavy hardware in Bangor. Norris's nephew could afford to go to MIT.[41]

Ellis Y. Ellis, whose wife served on the board for well over twenty years, was born in Surrey in 1881. He attended public schools and then took a commercial course at Shaw's Business School (now Husson College). He was a bookkeeper in Armour Company and later worked for the American Railway Express Company and the Second National Bank of Bangor. It wasn't until 1912 that he became manager of the Bangor Motor Company and there 'found the interest and line of business which appeal(ed) most to his taste and his special abilities'. In 1925 he organized the E. Y. Eldridge Company. Within three years he had twenty-five employees and was the distributor for Studebaker, Cadillac, LaSalle and Erskine.[42]

If the husbands of the women on the board were marked by humble origins and upward mobility, they also evidenced a sense of responsibility to others in their community. As the *Bangor Daily Commercial* said of Arthur Chapin, 'His own early struggles made him peculiarly sympathetic, especially with young men beginning to make their way in the business world, his counsel was often sought and liberally given'.[43] Charles Wood, the paper noted, lived and worked for his family and that family included 'everyone in any way connected with him or dependent upon him for assistance and advice'. Many were active in the Bangor Building and Loan, which provided affordable loans for working men, and in the Bangor Mechanics Association and its offshoot, the Bangor Public Library.[44]

What is striking is that the whole family was involved in charitable and civic work. Married couples served together on the boards of the Homes for Aged Men and Aged Women, and of the Bangor Fuel Society. Husbands, wives and grown children worked together to manage the Good Samaritan Home. Most of the all-male board of trustees were the husbands of the members of the board and many of the doctors who volunteered their services to the Home had wives who served on the Board. Sisters-in-law joined the board together and children followed in their parents' footsteps as members of the board of directors or of the board of trustees.

For over forty years the women of the board were, with only one exception, married women, and they carried out the role that their gender, age and marital status would have carved out for them in the small town communities of their births. Together they supervised, trained and protected young women. They met monthly and, as members of the committee of the month, visited the Home several times each a year. Their husbands who served on the board of trustees advised them on financial and legal matters, but the women collected money, appealed to the legislature for aid and made policy decisions for the Home. Most of all, however, they involved themselves in the lives of the young women who came to the Home.

Each month they heard in detail about the women in the Home in reports from the matron, the general secretary and the case committee chair. They also listened to the letters sent by parents and former residents. From this detailed information they learned where young women who applied to the Home came from, how they cooperated in the Home, when they gave birth and who would supervise them when they left. Collectively board members arranged marriages, attended births, taught the meaning of work and cooperation and handed on responsibility for supervision of a resident to other married women when the resident left. While much of this work was carried on by one member of the board, the board members approved her actions at every meeting and formally voted to dismiss every resident whose time was up.

For over three decades Gertrude Atwood was the voice and driving force of the Good Samaritan Home. She joined the board in 1907 and assumed the roles of third vice-president, secretary, general secretary, purchasing agent, admissions and case committee chair, and superintendent in quick succession. She shared with many other members of the board a small-town background combined with upward mobility and a commitment to education.

Gertrude Atwood was born into a large family in Bradford in 1873. She attended schools in Bradford and Bangor and married William Atwood in 1901. Both Gertrude and William came from old Maine families, Gertrude from a family of reformers. Her great-grandmother was a sister of Anson P. and Lot M. Morrill, distinguished state legislators.[45]

William, four years older than Gertrude, came to Bangor looking for opportunity. For several years he managed the Bangor Exchange with a partner. He then sold his interests and began to work for a dried-goods company where he remained until his death in 1941. He was the store's representative in the Piscataquis and northern Penobscot counties and, according to the *Bangor Daily News*, 'became one of the best known and best liked traveling men in this part of Maine'. The largest part of the inheritance that he left his wife was stock in the company for which he worked.[46]

Gertrude was active in a large number of city and state organizations, most having to do with health and education. She was chair of the health committee of the Maine State Federation of Women's Clubs and actively involved in the Bangor Anti-TB Association, the Anti-TB Sanatorium, the Fresh Air School, the Bangor District Nursing Association and the York Street Clinic. She was also a member of the board of the Maine Public Health Association and the Penobscot County Chapter of the American Red Cross.

Her work was not limited to health projects, however. She was president of the Nineteenth Century Club and vice-president of the Maine Peace Society. 'Possessing a keen business brain', she was a trustee of the Bangor Savings Bank and director of the Community Chest in its first year. When her son and only surviving child was born in 1910 she resigned from her position of vice-president of the State Federation of Women's Clubs. Increasingly, her obituary stated, she devoted herself to the Good Samaritan Home. 'She lived for this institution', the *Bangor Daily News* commented, 'worked and planned for its good'. Sometimes, when necessary, she went before the Maine Legislature.[47]

Between 1908 and 1941 only six of the 500 women who entered the Good Samaritan Home came from out of state.[48] Under Gertrude Atwood's direction, the Home implemented policies and practices with which the residents' home communities would have been familiar. Within Maine's small communities married women traditionally trained young women in household duties, assisted them in childbirth and helped them negotiate marriages or obtain bastardy settlements. The Good Samaritan Board women did all of these things. Alice Harden, Secretary, reported in 1920 that, 'a great many girls who applied for admission to the home have, through the assistance of the home, been married to the men responsible for their condition'. Two years later then-secretary Gertrude Atwood reported that twelve of the women who had applied that year, upon investigation of their cases, were advised to marry and did so and never, therefore, entered the Home. When marriage was not possible, the Good Samaritan Board often succeeded in obtaining some sort of financial settlement from the father of the child 'for the young girl who has no one to depend upon but herself'.[49]

Supporting young women in childbirth was a central concern of the board. The Home had always relied upon doctors who volunteered their time to come to the Home to deliver the babies. Under Atwood's supervision, however, implementing additional measures that would ensure a safe delivery became a priority of the Home. Atwood was perhaps influenced by her early experience with the Home. In 1911, a few years after she had joined the board, Atwood took into her home a twenty-one-year-old waitress from Sherman Station. The young woman had given birth in the Home but had lost her baby when it was six weeks old.

A quick look at the ledger for the Good Samaritan Home would have told Atwood that in the previous three years, eleven babies – more than one third of those born in the Home – had died.[50] Atwood herself had lost two babies and, as she became increasingly involved with the Good Samaritan Home, she made it clear that medical care was a priority. By 1920 Maine General Hospital recognized the Good Samaritan Home as a hospital and placed several student nurses for training there. In 1923 the Board rewrote its bylaws to emphasize that its first purpose was to 'maintain a nonsectarian institution for the physical care of young unfortunate girls'. In 1925, Atwood reported that the Home had established its medical care on a hospital basis and, in 1926, she concluded that the women who entered the Good Samaritan Home received better pre-natal, natal and post-natal care than most married women.[51] In 1931, in the midst of the Depression when many organizations were cutting back on their services, the Good Samaritan board expanded the Home's hospital facilities. The Home ensured that the women were 'hospitalized' for two weeks following their delivery and enjoyed a two-week convalescent period after that. Of the hundreds of girls who have 'passed through the dark shadows of motherhood' in the Home, Atwood proudly announced in 1929 and every year thereafter, 'not one life among them has been sacrificed'.[52]

Childbirth was an event in which all the women connected to the Good Samaritan Home participated, if only by proxy. In spite of the fact that a doctor attended each birth, Atwood, the matron and at least some of the residents attended as well. Atwood regularly assured the mothers of the young women that the Home would serve in their stead during the delivery. As she wrote to the mother of one resident in 1931, 'We realize your anxiety regarding her, and wish to assure you that we will do everything possible to take your place when the time of her labor comes. She is a very sweet little girl and we all love her dearly.' She also made sure to notify the mothers with a description of the birth. One grateful mother wrote back, 'I was surprised to hear that she bore it so well. I was afraid that she would have an awful time. I am really proud to think she done so well.'[53]

Atwood also described every birth to the members of the Board. The new matron's attitude toward a young girl in labour was 'lovely in the extreme', Atwood reported.

> She had explained to her in words she could understand what to expect and that she was not to be frightened and when I saw her she was following Miss Prescott from room to room for assurance and solace and when Miss Prescott called me at 8:30 that night to tell me that all was over her own voice was husky with tears.[54]

Some residents gained the respect of the staff and board members for the way that they faced childbirth. Fern, for example, at fifteen was 'stormy petrel' and 'a thorn in the side of everyone'. Nevertheless in childbirth she proved herself to be a 'very brave and fine patient and possibly an example to some of our girls'. Annie who was fourteen and 'as underprivileged as any girl we have admitted in years', gave birth to a stillborn. 'The courage and self control of this child of fourteen was something to be wondered at: I saw her an hour and a half before the child was born and she made no complaint or murmur, only to reply to a question that she felt no better'. Nellie had an exceedingly tedious labour. Apparently she had been learning English for throughout her labour she 'constantly repeated over and over, Oh Boy!, Oh! Boy'.[55]

Atwood reported stories of the courageous deliveries to others who might be influenced by them. She wrote to the agent from the New England Home for Little Wanderers, of one resident that her

> baby was born after labor of two nights, which she bore with much courage after she got settled down to it: The doctor ordered a hypo to rest her and she did very nicely after that ... she was a very nice patient, Mrs. Pearson tells me, and the workers in the Home are quite impressed with her.[56]

In addition to assisting in labour, the women of the Board participated in the supervision of the residents by hearing regular accounts of the young women's actions within the Home, by visiting the Home to observe them when they could, by granting them permission to 'work out their fees' when necessary, and by 'voting them out' once they had heard their plans for the future. In their deliberations board members drew upon the small town community values that held older women responsible for younger women and that judged an individual by her age as well as her willingness to work. Atwood's monthly reports to the board provided detailed information that allowed members to judge the young women in a comprehensive way that paid attention to their circumstances.

Underlying all Atwood's judgements of the residents (whom she described as either 'satisfactory' or 'unsatisfactory' – or 'very' either one) was how well they fit into the community of the Home. Those who were satisfactory did their work and got on with the other residents. Atwood supplied enough information, however, for the Board to make allowances for unusual circumstances. Behaviour, she made clear, depended on circumstances and could change over time. When Odelie, for example, received a marriage proposal she 'lay down certain rules and regulations for the conduct of their affairs' and the man left. In consequence Odelie was 'consumed with remorse and fairly bursting with ugliness which makes her a thorn in the side of other girls and a decided problem to the staff'. Spring cleaning could also wear tempers thin.[57]

Louise's father had insisted she give up her child if she wished to return home. The Board voted to allow Louise to remain in the Home while they looked for a way to enable her to keep her child. She had been, Atwood noted, a 'pampered darling during her stay' as the workers feared she would pass out from her heart condition. Atwood and two doctors were convinced that her condition was nothing but nerves. It was not until the Home had a farewell party for one of the staff, however, that this was confirmed. Atwood reported:

> She danced merrily the evening through with no bad results. So in the light of past events during which she has shown a disposition to shirk all duty and responsibility it seems wise to me to permit her to remain the problem of her family and to wear down her father's resistance to the point where he will either assume the support of the child or encourage her to go to work to do so.[58]

Eda, on the other hand, 'made a very good adjustment since being told that the Board felt she should be dismissed. As she had no place open to her where she could be cared for through her confinement she decided to take a different attitude, which she has done'.[59]

The reports paid particular attention to the difference that age could or should make in a person's behaviour. When Buddy, having left the Home for a domestic job where the wage was not large but where she would be treated well, began to go around with a twenty-eight-year-old divorced man with three children, Atwood brought Buddy back into the Home. There, Atwood reported, Buddy was 'sulky over being held in the Home without the privilege of being allowed to go out'. Nevertheless, Atwood was determined to keep her there until she could persuade a family member to assume responsibility for the girl. 'At least she will be growing older every day she remains here', Atwood commented.[60]

On the other hand Nancy – who was 'penniless and without even the money to buy milk for the baby' – was a twenty-nine-year-old teacher 'who should have known better'. Nancy had engaged a lawyer to obtain a cash settlement from her lover, but the lawyer had taken the settlement, paid for the hospital and the doctor and pocketed the rest. 'She was advised that we could not admit her and that she had better wire her people for money', Atwood reported.[61]

The difference that age made led Atwood to deplore the marriage of young women with older men. When Marion's grandfather took her out of the Home and married her to the man responsible in order to 'save the family name', Atwood reminded the Board, 'we can readily envision the future of this fifteen year old married to a man over twice her age and against the wishes of both'.[62]

While young women could be expected to act irresponsibly, older women were responsible for providing them with supervision. Grace had been a ward maid in a local hospital and had been brought to the Home in labour by a doctor. When Grace's mother learned that her daughter was in the Good Samaritan Home, she hired a lawyer to obtain Grace's release. Atwood told the Board that she had written to the lawyer that his client had been, 'in our judgement', 'somewhat derelict in her duty and that it would seem that a girl that age should be under closer supervision and home influences and enjoying something of the privilege of obtaining an education, instead of being in an unsupervised position, earning her own living'.[63]

Friends of a woman as well as members of the board could be called upon to supervise her. Asked to help place a woman who wanted to come to Bangor after having her child in Guilford, Atwood replied that the girl would be 'better off if she remains in the vicinity of her home and finds work if possible where she will have the supervision of friends interested in her and her child'. And when Nancy, a former resident, became pregnant out of wedlock a second time Atwood commented, 'Her case seems to us pathetic, as we felt Nancy's trouble was caused through lack of suitable companionship and contacts'.[64]

No matter what their age, however, women were responsible for, and belonged with, their children. Letha was one of the very few women to be admitted after delivery. The child's father had been paying the expenses and board of the child but had disappeared. Letha 'felt it necessary to dispose of the child since it was impossible to find sufficient wages to support it'. She appealed to the state and other social service agencies until finally a doctor referred her to the Home. 'In our judgment, she was mentally as well as physically sick', Atwood reported. Atwood advised Letha to enter the Home to regain her strength and courage. Letha cried constantly for a week, Atwood informed the Board, but 'yesterday we found her improved. We almost feared at first that she might commit suicide but we feel that danger of this is now passed and we believe she will decide to keep her child with such encouragement and help as we may be able to give her'.[65]

Mildred remained in the Home for more than two years as the Home struggled to find a place for her. She had no home and no responsible relatives to assist her and, furthermore, Atwood noted, was 'emotionally unstable, and, in fact, a high-grade moron type'. Atwood determined that she was 'mentally unfit to be turned out into our community' and applied to the State for Mildred's support. Eventually the State assumed responsibility for Mildred as a state pauper, but Atwood encouraged the Board not to dismiss Mildred until there was some definite plan for her future as, she commented, 'we believe it unwise to have the state deprive her of her child, as we fear for her future should this be done'.[66]

Atwood disseminated her annual reports to organizations and doctors throughout the state. In her appeals for the support of the Home, she skilfully portrayed the women in the Home in terms that would appeal to the rural communities: the residents accepted responsibility; they had fallen because they were young and had not been supervised as they should have been; they had gained maturity by giving birth; and they would redeem themselves by hard work.

In her 1915 annual report, Atwood gave passing tribute to the 'Christian influence of the home' and the matron's 'splendid work' in doing so much for the refinement and 'salvation' of each girl. She spent most of the paragraphs in her report, however, emphasizing the practical problems faced by single mothers. Commenting on the difficulties of any single woman 'trying to earn an honest living for herself, hampered with the care of a child', she noted that the residents, 'neither vicious nor deficient', faced even greater difficulty. 'We challenge anyone', she commented, 'to parallel the hard task of the girl mother who faces the world and its scorn to support her fatherless child.' 'We who come in close contact with them,' she commented, 'never cease to marvel at what they do, and what they have to endure.' The residents' willingness to work hard and assume responsibility, she suggested, demanded the communities' respect. Year after year she repeated the same theme. Those who came to the Home were invariably young. They formed 'more promising material than is generally understood'.[67]

Atwood stressed the young women's self-sufficiency and willingness to assume responsibility. The Home trained the girls to become expert housemaids and homemakers, Atwood assured the public. The truest help, she commented, 'is rendered by giving people an opportunity to help themselves'. The Home found them suitable employment in which they could be 'self-supporting and self-respecting'. Even those who were fourteen, fifteen and sixteen, loved their children and almost never abandoned them, Atwood stated. 'When these girls are desirous of being good mothers, with all that involves', she told the public, 'they have retrieved the past, and should be shown the respect and dignity due them from a Christian People'.[68]

While Atwood called for the community to accept the young women because they had redeemed themselves through hard work and responsibility, she called the community to task for not assuming its responsibility for the young women. The older generation had failed the younger, she suggested again and again. The girls were extremely young and often motherless; they were in the Home not so much because they had failed but because the society had failed them. Many were 'little more than ignorant, misguided children who have not received the instruction and advice that they should'. Older women had not provided them with supervision and support or 'the most ordinary word of counsel against bad influence which even the plainest and most untaught mother might give'.

Society was at fault also for not providing the social life that all young girls need. 'Girls need some place where they may meet boys of their own age in a wholesome and natural way', Atwood pointed out. Mothers and employers should see to this. In addition, someone should provide sex education. She noted:

> Indiscriminate teaching of sex hygiene would be deplorable but somewhere in home, church or school definite teaching should be given every girl on the mysteries of her own being and the importance to the society of individual cleanness of life.[69]

The Home, she suggested, only did what a responsible mother would have done. Reminiscent of the *Argus* which noted that Rose's mother was 'unenlightened' for not helping Rose to take care of her child, Atwood suggested it was only an 'unnatural mother' who rejected a daughter who had given birth in the Home. 'We do not seek to palliate their faults', Atwood concluded, 'nor to shield them from the consequences of their sin. We believe stoning will not save them, but that counsel, sympathy and an opportunity to redeem themselves, may'.

Atwood emphasized the distinctions of age rather than that of gender. The residents became pregnant, she suggested, because they were young. The men involved were often 'no more than youths' themselves and also deserved help; the girls were seduced not by the men but by their own affections. There were men, however, that used the authority of their age and position to betray the young girls – men who were at least twenty years older and were often employers or brothers-in-law. They had no right taking advantage of women young enough to be their children, even when they proposed marriage. Commenting on a girl's imminent marriage to a man twice her age Atwood regretted:

> that such marriages are not prohibited by statute, thus preventing the inclination of such ignorant parents to marry the girl off, regardless of the consequences, in their belief that such saves the family reputation.[70]

In short, Atwood appealed to small-town communities to accept first time pregnancies out of wedlock as a sign not of immorality but of immaturity. The births marked a transition into more responsible maturity and were something for which the entire community was responsible. In 1925 Glenna Stearns, assuming the position of superintendent, explained to the *Bangor Daily Commercial*, 'Unfortunate – or unlucky – doesn't mean bad'. She pointed out that the Good Samaritan Home did not accept criminals or the feeble-minded but offered assistance to ordinary young woman. Many of us have broken laws of one kind or another, she said, but since the violations weren't found out we feel none the worse about them. 'These girls are very much like ourselves and anyone who would rule against them, would rule against himself'.[71]

If the women of the Board were themselves from small-town communities and, therefore, drew on small-town community values to gain support for their work, they were also experiencing upward mobility in the third largest city in Maine. Atwood's reports make clear that the Board sought to improve the condition of many of the young women who came to the Home and actively encouraged them to leave their small town communities and find independence in the city. The board paid particular attention to women who had proven they were willing to work hard to improve their situations and trained these women specifically to prepare them for better paying jobs. They also taught them English and improved their health with surgery when such measures would increase their job opportunities.[72]

The women who hoped for the privilege of remaining in Bangor had to live up to an additional standard. They had to prove that they could be self-support- ing. Atwood kept an eye out for the women who would be a credit to the Home. These she identified as 'good' or 'fine' – or 'particularly' or 'unusually' either. As with the term 'satisfactory', Atwood never described what she meant by 'good' and 'fine', but an examination of the women identified as such, even those who failed to live up to the expectations, suggests that the terms marked the women who were receptive, or appeared to be receptive, to self-improvement. In some cases, the words may have indicated a woman's middle-class sensibilities. Atwood noted of Celia, for instance, 'she appears to be a particularly fine type of girl and feels her situation keenly', but this was not always or even usually the case. In 1937 and 1938, when the Home took only those women who were most desti- tute, Atwood repeatedly referred to the residents as of an 'unusually good' and 'unusually fine type, exceptionally worthy of our assistance and encouragement'. While this may have been part of her public relations appeal, it may also have reflected the young women's courage and determination to improve their lives against almost insuperable odds.[73]

Atwood took care to describe the efforts of the young women who had worked for their room and board so that they could go to school or who had walked great distances to do so. When Hazel left the Home to marry her boyfriend, Atwood was not pleased. 'We regret this', she reported, 'as in our judgment he is inferior to Hazel, whom we consider an unusually good type of girl'. Hazel, she reminded the Board, had worked hard for four years so she could to go Bangor High School and then took a course in a local business college, working her way there as well. In addition, her baby had died soon after its birth, so 'there would not appear the same object in marriage as there might be otherwise'.[74]

Atwood also told in vivid detail the circumstances that women overcame in order to reach the Home. Grace was an orphan at an early age, 'an unwelcome addition in the family of an aunt who married her at fifteen to a man thirty-five years her senior, much against her will ... She suffered every form of abuse from him until last summer he returned home from an extended debauch, and in a drunken fury tore her clothing from her and burned it'. Grace left even though she was pregnant. She worked for a neighbour in order to earn the money to come in search of work and then came to the outskirts of Bangor where she got a job in order to earn the money for her confinement. She worked where four men were employed cutting pulp wood and did, Atwood reported, all the work for a family of seven till the day before her child was born. Mrs. Pearson tells me she had never seen a person so exhausted as she. Her feet were blistered, calloused [*sic*] and bleeding over the entire bottom and she has slept the greater part of the time since her baby came.' Her baby was stillborn.[75]

For those women who were willing to work hard to become self-supporting, the Board did what they could to protect them from the demands of their boyfriends and families. Hazel's boyfriend, for example, had visited the Home and demanded Hazel's release before she had worked out her fees. He 'naively promised to pay her fees when he could'. When Atwood would not release Hazel, he left to consult with a lawyer, 'swearing vengeance on the Home'. When Betty's mother was insistent Betty give up her child and return home, Atwood informed the family that Betty had 'decided to keep her child and seek employment away from her home in order to earn a sufficient wage to support the child … we believe her capable of assuming this obligation and will be of such assistance to her in so doing as we are able'.[76]

The Home placed a high priority on a woman's independence. Not only did it make every effort to support those who would support themselves, it expressed keen disappointment in those who could have supported themselves but chose not to. On the one hand, when Celia returned home with her baby, Atwood noted, 'It would seem she should have known better as she was among our older group of girls and capable of supporting herself and her child'.[77] On the other hand, Atwood noted with pride when a woman had gotten a job, attended night school and improved her position.

The emphasis on self-improvement and self-sufficiency, enabled Atwood and the Board to look upon the women in the Home as women in transition. Close to the end of her life, Atwood wrote to one woman applying for admission:

> I realize that these are very unhappy days for you but I wish to say to you that many worse things than this could happen and that it is not so much what we have done as it is what we do in the future that really counts. Some of the finest women it has been my privilege to know have been through the situation such as is now facing you. Keep up your courage and be of good cheer and all will come out well for you I am sure.[78]

The Good Samaritan Home successfully garnered the resources of the state to serve young women who got pregnant out of wedlock for the first time in a way that they and their communities were comfortable with. As a result, young rural women sought its services in ever greater numbers in spite of the hefty admissions fee – for many, a year's wages – and the requirement that they remain in the Home at least six months after their delivery.

The most notable feature of the young women who came to the Good Samaritan Home in 1915, Gertrude Atwood suggested, was their extreme youth. One was thirteen; two were fourteen; several were fifteen; and only one had reached twenty. They were not vicious nor deficient, but misguided – in want of the 'most ordinary words of counsel against bad influence which even the most

	1902–6	1907–15	1916–22	1923–31
Institutional				
Number of residents	57	95	67	149
Average Length of Stay (months)	4.2	9	10	10.2
Average Stay Prior to Delivery (months)	1.5**	1.5	2.2	2
Early Departure	0	9	3	0
Infant Deaths	0	24	17	14
Maternal Deaths	2	2	4	1
Population				
Average Age	20.8	19.4	18.6	18.9
Number Younger than 17	2	16	15	24
Marriage Impossible	Unknown	1	10	17
Marriage Undesirable	Unknown	Unknown	2	8
Family of Poverty	Unknown	Unknown	10	38
Catholic	4	13	19	46
Out of State	13	10	2	0
Outcome				
Placement		14	14	36
Marriage	4	16	13	41
Settlement	1	4	6	6
Stranger Adoption	1	4	4	15
Relative Adoption	0	0	4	1
Baby Committed to State	0	0	0	2
Second o/w Pregnancy	1	1	1	5

These statistics are drawn from the record of all women admitted to the Good Samaritan Home between 1902 and 1931, provided by Debbie Giguerre of the Good Samaritan Agency, 100 Ridgewood Drive, Bangor, Maine.

It should be noted that information was not always available so the counts in any category may be underestimated

Until 1913 the date of delivery is not regularly included.

The occupations of those admitted are listed regularly only through 1912. They include housemaid, housework, factory work, waitress, and nurse.

Those who leave early are either dismissed when it is discovered that they have a venereal disease or that this is their second pregnancy or the women chose to leave within the first week or are noted as having run away.

When the amount of the settlements is included it ranges from $150 to $500.

Marriage is counted as impossible when it is a result of incest or the birth father is already married, in jail, dead or out of state.

Marriage is counted as undesirable when it is noted that the parents object to a marriage or the birth mother and birth father are of different religions.

untaught mother might give'. 'We challenge anyone', she persisted, 'to parallel the hard task of the girl mother who faces the world and its scorn to support her fatherless child'. Nevertheless, with care, sympathy and training, the girls were able to go out into the world and become self-supporting and self-respecting, 'fine Christian characters, a power for good in the community'.[79] Year after year, Atwood repeated the same themes. The girls were invariably young. They provided 'far more promising material than generally understood'. Rarely did they fall again. Almost never did they place their children for adoption. They had, she suggested, given birth and therefore had grown up and were ready to resume their place in the community.[80]

A close look at the records of every fifth woman who applied for admission provides a portrait of the women who came in such great numbers to the Home. It should be noted that they represented only a subset of the single women who got pregnant in the state. Until 1940 when the Catholic Church established a home in Biddeford, there was only one other home for unwed mothers in the state and that, the Temporary Home for Women in Portland, by 1910 had implemented the same policies and procedures as the Good Samaritans though a little less stringently. It attracted far fewer women. There were however other options for young women.

While, in contrast to Tennessee, there were no foundling homes and no tradition of stranger adoption, women and their families who did not have or want to have their condition known to their communities had other recourses. Abortion was one. Although the Maine legislature had criminalized abortion in 1840, there were doctors who would provide an abortion in or near Bangor throughout the first half of the twentieth-century.[81] One charged $25 in 1927. This was a price substantially less than the entrance fee the Good Samaritans required. Women did not necessarily, however, have to rely on a doctor. In 1925 Dr Edmunds was indicted for the death of a young woman. He claimed that she had attempted to abort herself. Anyone could obtain a catheter at the drugstore, he asserted. 'I have known many women that have told me of aborting themselves'. As Dr Edmunds's trial suggests, abortions could be dangerous.[82]

Some women sought informal arrangements outside of the community's purview. When Annette G. became pregnant her mother sent her to the older man who was responsible and insisted he pay for the delivery. William G's mother had four children by four different men. Each of the men lived with and supported her for a year. Though both Annette and William G's mothers assumed responsibility for their daughters, they faced another hazard. The state eventually took the infants away from them.[83]

Some Irish immigrant families succeeded in handling a pregnancy without interference, but also with a cost to the pregnant women. One woman from Maine tells the story of her husband's great-great-grandmother who worked in the mill at the turn-of-the century and got pregnant. Her parents raised her child but confined her to her room. She died at a young age.[84]

Poor families were not the only ones who sought alternatives. In 1921 Sadie Marcus, daughter of a wealthy retail merchant on the coast, gave birth to a daughter. Sadie was Jewish. Her lover was a Gentile who, Sadie's father noted, died suddenly before the couple had a chance to marry. Sadie's daughter later claimed that her family had placed her in a series of foster homes and paid the superintendent of an orphanage to find the homes and pay the board. When Sadie's father died, the family made the superintendent her official guardian. Upon Sadie's death, the daughter sued for her share of the Marcuses' substantial estate.[85]

As disparate and fragmented as these stories are, they suggest a pattern. All of the women who sought alternatives were from ethnic minorities. They did not turn to the state to help take care of their children but attempted to do so in their own way, according to their circumstances. For Sadie and the Irish families, it is clear that secrecy was important. Those who, like Annette's and William G.'s mothers, attempted to deal with their situations on their own and did not have the money to do so secretly, risked the interference of the state and the loss of their children.

In contrast, the women who turned to the Good Samaritans – Catholics and Protestants alike – accepted community norms and community oversight. The Good Samaritans routinely rejected only those who had a venereal disease or were 'second offenders'. The board, however, required that every woman provide three references from her home community. Although these references were ostensibly to ensure a woman's good character, in practice they served to ensure that every woman came from a community that knew about and could be held responsible for her and her child's support.

Most often the women applied on their own and almost invariably offered to work hard in exchange for support. That they appreciated what the Home had to offer is made clear by their acceptance of the rigorous requirements. Before women entered the Home they signed a consent form in which they promised to stay six months after their delivery, do the work required, obey authority and abide by the rules. Having signed the form, they could still leave without obligation before the birth of their babies. In spite of the long-term confinement to the Home, the required uniforms and hard work, and the close scrutiny of their mail and visitors, relatively few women left early. In contrast to the Homes in Tennessee where the early departure rate was close to one-third, of the 602 women who entered the Good Samaritan Home between 1907 and 1941 only thirty-nine left before their time was up. Well over half of these left before their babies were born, complaining, as Atwood routinely pointed out, that the work was too hard, the required stay too long or the dormitory living too public.[86] Two who ran away returned to complete their stays.

Once a woman agreed to the terms, she remained in the Home for a long time. The average stay per year – excluding those who left within a week – ranged from seven-and-a-half months to over a year. Almost one-quarter, 124, remained over a year; some, for as many as two.

As Atwood made clear in her regular appeals to the public, the women who entered the Home were young. Of the 602 women only twenty-two were over twenty-five and only two over thirty.[87] The average age of the residents for every year after 1905 was eighteen or nineteen except for three years when it was twenty.[88]

The majority came from small rural towns or the northern agricultural centres of Fort Fairfield, Van Buren and Presque Isle. Only eleven came from cities other than Bangor that were larger than 11,000. While forty-seven came from Bangor, the records suggest that most of these came from rural areas in search of work. The women also were overwhelmingly involved in domestic work either in their own or in others' houses. The log of entrances and departures only occasionally listed a woman's occupation. Of 124 listed occupations, only six were in a mill or factory. In comparison, fifty-seven women identified themselves as having a position as some kind of domestic and of the twenty-eight identified as students, at least six were working in homes for their room and board.[89]

Many were living at home, but this did not mean they did not work. Letters from their parents and the Good Samaritan minutes make clear that the women's families relied upon them to provide childcare, care for the sick and household labour. Mothers wrote asking for their daughters to return because they couldn't do the necessary work without them and welfare agencies hesitated to remove pregnant women from their homes because, as older daughters, they needed to take care of their younger brothers and sisters. Atwood's reports regularly made such comments as, 'Ruth has had a hard difficult time. Her mother has cancer and she has six younger siblings', or, 'Margaret had kept home for father and watched over her insane sister for three years'.[90]

The women's hard work and acceptance of responsibility would have appealed to their neighbours and friends. In Maine, the townships and plantations were marked, as were rural families, by communal self-sufficiency. New England poet Robert Frost wrote in 'Death of a Hired Hand' which was published in 1914, 'Home is the place where, when you have to go there, they have to take you in'. The same could be said of the Maine communities in the first half of the twentieth century where state settlement laws required towns to support all who had lived in the town for five years or more and where towns, in turn, required all families to support family members.[91]

In the small towns, age was an important marker, for it determined one's ability to work and thus to contribute to the community. An infant needed support, but it promised to provide labour in the future; young people did not need support but instead needed to be reminded of their responsibility to support others; and older people, having already contributed their labour, needed to rely on those who were younger.

Just as the community assigned responsibility according to age, it had a vested interest in how each of its members behaved. Community members had a responsibility to keep an eye on other members of the community, to make sure they were doing their share. And finally, communal responsibility dictated that people take note of who was and who was not a member. Recognizing someone as kin or as a community member immediately drew that person into a set of obligations. While he or she might provide help, he or she might also call upon others for help. A stranger was someone outside of this circle of mutual obligations; someone who was not owed anything.

In their letters to the Good Samaritans, community members reflected this confluence of attitudes – recognition of the importance of age, emphasis on self-sufficiency and hard work, and suspicion of strangers.[92] Those who wrote the references repeatedly noted that the girls were not bad, only unfortunate and young. This was true even in the case of a fifteen year-old who had been involved with more than one man. Though she had been, Attorney Joseph W. Sawyer stated, 'a little loose for a year or two back, she is not what I would call a bad girl but one who is more unfortunate than anything else'. A week later the Rev. Alfred G. Davis concurred and added that with the right training she could 'develop into a virtuous and respectable woman and I trust a useful member of the society'.[93]

In another case, that of a sixteen-year-old, Attorney William Waldron wrote that she had been in the habit of going out at nights more than a girl her age should. 'From all I can learn', he added, 'she is not a bad girl naturally, but she certainly was in danger of becoming a bad woman. She was young and thoughtless and liked a good time, and could not understand why she should be restrained'.[94]

While the community accepted sexual misbehaviour in a young woman, it did so only when the young woman took responsibility for the consequences and only for the first pregnancy. The community did not tolerate sexuality that seemed irrepressible or irresponsible and suspected that it was an inherited trait. Commented the woman who adopted Gladys when she was twelve, 'I wrote to the Home for a girl and told them I wanted a girl of good parentage and learned afterward that the girl had a bad mother. We have done our best ... She is very good in some ways but has that very bad quality'. Later she wrote the Home that she hoped it would keep her adopted daughter for a while for there she was 'away from temptation. Poor child, she has that tendency born in her. I have faith that she will make a good woman though'. The girl went home and for a while behaved, but then she ran off with her stepfather and became pregnant again. Her adoptive mother considered placing her in a home for the feeble-minded. 'I know', she concluded, 'she never will be any different as long as she can get with the other sex ... She would be quite a girl if it wasn't for that'.[95]

The fear of the inherited 'very bad quality' made couples vigilant over the children they adopted. As one early adoptive mother wrote, 'We can't do a thing with __ as she won't stop her bad habits. She is smart and I have taught her lots of verses and she can count to twenty ... and I have tried to break her of touching her bottom but I have given up'. The adoptive father, she added, 'says he won't put up with her dirtiness and I don't want people to know that she is that way'. The couple that had taken the baby when she was three returned her in three months.[96]

While the community feared uncontrolled sex, it would forgive a woman's sexual misbehaviour if she worked hard. A field agent for the New England Home for Little Wanderers wrote in her reference for one young woman that her mother had three illegitimate children, all by different fathers. Nevertheless, the agent commented, 'The mother is said to have been honest and very hard working and intelligent'. 'She has always been the greatest of workers', she added in another letter, 'intelligent and although immoral took excellent care of her children. She worked in the best families in town although they knew of her reputation, they employed her because of her capability'.[97]

The community not only valued young women who worked hard, it also demanded that they do so. Families expected daughters who went off to work to send back money for the family and to return if their mothers were incapacitated. They expected those at home to help in maintaining the household and caring for younger siblings. As one wrote, 'Yes I keep the house clean ... mama isn't able to work so my sister and I do it. I can wash, iron, or do any kind of work'.[98]

Some potential residents, the records suggest, were unable to leave home because their families relied on their labour. Others who left were expected to send money home to help support the family and to come home when necessary. For example, Marie applied for admission to the Home from Van Buren in August of 1927. She was born in St Leonard's, New Brunswick. Her father, a woods cook, worked chiefly in Maine, and Marie moved to Van Buren for several months in 1915. When she was twelve she entered the Convent at St Pasile, but several months later her mother died and she was called home to help her father. At fifteen she went out to work as a waitress in various towns in Maine and Massachusetts. She was, however, all the while, sending money home to help support her younger brother as her father had been 'crippled' in a railroad accident.[99]

The women also, when necessary, went to work in the fields. Atwood wrote to the Immigration Service regarding Mattie. After Mattie was called home to care for her invalid stepmother and insane stepsister, her life was 'indescribably hard and lonely'.

> She tells me ... that she has taken the place of a man in the fields for years; That in the spring of '27 she herself planted thirty acres of potatoes, with a potato planter, that she assisted her father and step mother to cut them for the planter, that she and her father did the haying, and that she was all the assistance he had in harvesting the crops ... [100]

Orphan girls were routinely placed out to earn their keep when they were twelve. Said a woman who adopted a twelve year-old, 'I took her because I had no girl and I needed help'. Atwood commented of one, 'She has been cruelly abused, beaten, and ill-treated. She has done heavy manual labour in the fields, has milked six cows night and morning, has never attended Divine worship in any form and has had the privilege of attending school but little'.[101]

Any young woman who did not labour was considered a burden, especially if she were pregnant. The Immigration Service prohibited single pregnant women from crossing the border and was prepared to deport any Canadian woman who was a charge to the state in any way.[102] Even husbands considered a woman a burden if she did not work. One, whose eighteen year-old wife had become pregnant by another man, admitted he might take her back but only if she led a 'good life supporting her self with honest labor without the help of outsiders'.[103]

If community members expected younger women to go wrong without supervision, they relied on older women to train and supervise the younger. Older women supervised younger women by taking them into their homes and by engaging in gossip.

In the small-town communities, everyone kept an eye on everyone else. The gossip that resulted brought community opinion to bear on an individual; it could be a powerful tool for the enforcement of community norms in both men and women. In the letters to the Good Samaritans, community members reported on women's sexual behaviour, but they took care to place that behaviour in context. The fact that a woman contributed to the community through hard work could offset the fact that she had gotten pregnant outside of marriage. Furthermore, a woman could gain a reputation that was separate from that of her family.

Gossip enabled everyone in the community to know what was going on in every other household. The woman who employed Laura after she left the Home told a field agent for the New England Home for Little Wanderers that as far as she knew, Laura had 'been going straight'. The employer's brother had a garage and he 'hears all the gossip, has heard some of the 'hangers on' of the town say they had tried to make advances to Laura and she had shown her French temper'. So, the agent reported to Atwood, 'I imagine that they have not got along well with her'.[104]

The community gossip and control was directed at men as well as women. Seventeen-year-old Abbie wrote to the matron after she returned to her home in Milford with her baby, 'I have the best carriage there is in Milford. And I tell you I shine some'. She was placing her baby's name on the cradle call at the Congregational Church in a week. While apparently the community accepted Abbie and her baby, it made clear what it thought of the baby's father, Milliard, who was a married man. The father's brother, a dentist, had given Abbie free care, she confided to the matron. 'He's some different than Milliard ... Everybody is death on Milliard now. Hardly anybody speaks to him in Milford'.[105]

The community used gossip not only to reinforce community values by encouraging acceptance or rejection of individuals, it also used gossip to pressure a father into accepting responsibility for his child. Eva Scates, the field representative to the New England Home for Little Wanderers who referred a large number of women to the Good Samaritan Home and who represented the towns' interests as well as the girls', made extensive use of gossip. In 1922 she wrote Atwood that she had found the father. 'I can keep track of his whereabouts through one of the sheriffs here who knows the engineer on the crew. As far as I can learn, the man is not married. Also is earning good wages'. Scates suggested to Atwood that Atwood push the girl to name the father of the child as she was giving birth. Scates wanted to ensure that the man was forced to support the child and so relieve the town of responsibility.[106]

If the community used gossip to pressure people to abide by the norms, it also used its in-depth knowledge of the circumstances to judge individuals independent of their families. Attorney Joseph W. Sawyer, for instance, wrote Atwood about a fifteen year-old girl whose parents were poor and had five children. One of her sisters was married to a man who was in Thomaston State Prison for forgery, but the other was married to 'quite a decent fellow. I have never known anything against the father, excepting that he is not much good at earning a living, the mother is smart enough to work but her reputation as to chastity is bad'. Both the lawyer and the girl's minister recommended the girl to the Good

Samaritans. She impressed them as 'one who certainly is up to the average in brightness' and with training, could develop into a 'virtuous and respectable woman'.[107]

That community members themselves recognized the power of gossip is suggested in the case of a fifteen-year-old who was pregnant with her brother-in-law's child. The girl's grandmother fretted that the girl would write to the brother-in-law for 'if she writes and his wife finds it out she will tell it all over town'. The sister of the brother-in-law adopted the child, and the girl went back to her hometown where she worked for various families that needed extra help. She wrote to Matron Scoboria of one, 'You said maybe because I was unhappy at O'Briens I wasn't good. I was good and she started some stories about me ... She hates me and all my family as bad as anybody can and she would do anything to harm any one of us. My feeling for her is anything but love'.[108]

While community members expected their neighbours to know all about them, they did not expect strangers to do so. The word 'stranger' was used often by those writing to the Good Samaritans. It denoted those who did not belong to their circle of mutual obligations and who, therefore, did not deserve to know the intimate details of their lives. As one mother of a resident wrote to the matron, 'I don't know how to express myself to you as we are strangers'.[109] In 1938, when the Bureau of Social Welfare pushed the Good Samaritans to find out more information about the families, Atwood commented, 'It should be borne in mind that many of these girls come to us voluntarily and that many of them come from homes of great ignorance and limitations and that we are greatly handicapped by suspicions which such conditions of ignorance breed of any stranger or unfamiliar institution'.[110]

The suspicion of strangers, coupled with the importance of self-sufficiency, encouraged families to take care of their own children rather than have strangers adopt them. What adoptions of infants occurred, occurred within the community, where the natural parents and the adoptive parents were certain to know one another. Among the Good Samaritan residents, one had her child adopted by the sister of the man who got her pregnant and another by her lover's father. Hazel's priest objected to her marriage because her lover was 'dissipated and shiftless'. Nevertheless, the lover wrote that, although he could not get any money for a settlement, Hazel and her child should 'come here to my people. We ain't got very much. But she will be welcome to what we got'.[111]

If the community attitude towards unwed mothers was not harshly punitive, it was severely constricting. The women who applied to the Good Samaritans led lives that were marked by isolation, gossip and hard work. Commented one when she returned home, 'The harbor is all frozen now and this place is some dead. There's nothing but snow'. Their isolation was perhaps also reflected in the fact that for several years after they left the Good Samaritans, they wrote often asking for news about the other residents and commenting regularly on how much they missed the Home.

While their lives were isolated, they were also highly visible. Neighbours made it their business to comment on what the women did before and after they went to the Home. One reported that the day she returned she was 'busy all day. Many of the neighbours were in to see me and everybody about on the line called me on the phone when they heard I was home'.[112]

The women who came to the Home were not only isolated in rural areas, they were also often poor. The Red Cross, City Missionary and Overseers of the Poor referred or provided references for many. Others commented on the poverty of residents' families. In a number of cases the women were orphans, or their fathers were dead or incapacitated. Of the eighty-one full case reports of those admitted before 1930, thirty-five are clearly identified as poor. The degree to which poverty touched most of the women is made clear by the description of their obligations. An overwhelming majority performed hard physical labour as soon as they were capable of doing so. Whatever their degree of independence from their families, they had to work hard in order to survive.

On the surface, the Good Samaritans offered nothing new to the women who sought its services. Once at the Home, they were isolated by rules that separated them from the rest of the world, required to work hard, and expected to take responsibility for themselves and their babies. A sample of ninety-nine case files of the Good Samaritan Home taken chronologically from January 1918, to December 1941, suggests the ways in which the Home operated in these women's lives. Coming as they did from restrictive communities, the women found in the Good Samaritans a widening of their options. While the Good Samaritans reinforced the values and practices of the communities from which the young women came, it did this outside of those very communities and thus offered them an opportunity to change their lives.

In their letters of application the women offered their labour in return for the Home's support. It was a bargain that offered them a certain independence. It allowed them, for example, to keep their child against the wishes of their families or choose not to marry its father. They spoke of themselves not as victims but as unfortunates, who were willing and able to work to pay for their way. The Good Samaritan Home accepted their independence by supporting their wishes even when they went against those of their family. The Home called for respect for the women by emphasizing two things for which women were valued: childbirth and individual responsibility. It offered them a familiar but alternative community. Women applied to the Good Samaritans in ever increasing numbers and they fashioned their own solutions to their pregnancies out of the services the Home provided.

Some made considerable efforts to get to the Home and apply in person. In the summer of 1933 Jeannette walked almost the entire way to Bangor from Fort Kent, a distance of 185 miles. 'She was two days and a night on the way during which time she was without food. She was given the privilege of sleeping in a small outbuilding, and in the morning resumed her weary march', Atwood reported. When Atwood investigated her situation and found that Jeannette had already given birth to a child out of wedlock, she was forced to refuse Jeannette admission. But 'it seemed inhuman to turn her adrift, penniless', Atwood told the board, and Jeannette gained three months of room and board by her persistence. She went back to Fort Kent to marry and give birth to twins.[113]

Those who requested admission in writing explicitly bartered their labour for support. As one wrote, 'I am strong and I could work at anything until the time of confinement', and another, 'As for the fees I surely wouldn't be able to pay them. But I had in mind to work and I don't care how long as far as it will pay my fees'.[114]

If the women repeatedly offered their labour in exchange for the Home's services, they also offered no explanation or excuse for their 'condition'. One wrote specifically that her boyfriend was not to blame. 'I should have known better', she asserted, 'but I loved him better than my honor'. Occasionally they commented that they had only gotten pregnant because they thought they were going to get married.

Of all ninety-nine cases, only two claimed that they had been assaulted or blamed the man in any way. Both of these were from more privileged homes than the majority of the women. One mother provided a vivid description of her daughter's rape. The application of the other suggests that she blamed the man and emphasized her vulnerability because she could not offer her labour. She wrote that she had been 'brutally assaulted' while out riding. 'This is a terrible thing to happen to me in life when they are so alone as I am, and when I have tried so hard to not have any happenings like that but fate was against me', she stated, 'and now I have to look for someone to help me in my trouble so dear Lady I appeal to you to let me in your home'. In her very next sentence she made clear that she could not offer her labour. 'La Grippe', she noted, 'has left me weak so I can't do hard work for a while'.[115]

Upon entering, every woman agreed to remain in the Home and work for at least six months. Of the ninety-nine for whom we have complete records, only three broke this contract. Two left four months after their delivery. In both cases, they followed their babies home for their children had been dismissed a week earlier. One, whose lover had died of the flu and who had entered a week before she delivered, wrote, 'I felt as though I could not stand being in all summer so decided to come home'. The third, a student nurse who had moved to New York, decided with Atwood's assent to leave before the baby came so that she could place the infant for adoption immediately.[116]

Women could assume another name in the Home if they so chose, but Atwood warned them that the Home could not guarantee that they would not be recognized by someone from their hometowns. Almost invariably, they kept in touch with the Home and each other after they left. There is not one letter sent by a former resident that does not ask for or give information about other residents. They watched for each other's marriage announcements, visited each other and worked together. They also referred their sisters, nieces and friends to the Home.

The Good Samaritans strove to make the women self-sufficient and to allow them to make independent choices. As Atwood wrote to the mother of a six-teen-year-old resident, 'I do not think I can advise you about the baby, at least not until I know what Theo has in mind for her future, and I have not yet talked with her to find out just what her plans after she leaves the Home are'.[117] Just how successful they were in this pursuit depended primarily on the circumstances from which the women came. The few who were admitted from other institutions were without families or communities and had no one to mediate on their behalf. On the other hand, those with families and communities could find support but only at a price. They could be called home to provide labour or financial support.

Of the ninety-nine women for whom we have full case records thirty-two took the placements offered by the Good Samaritans. Thirty-one returned to their homes and an additional nine went to the homes of relatives. Twelve placed their children for adoption, five with relatives or friends. Three died, three married the father of their children immediately and three left early.

For many, the Good Samaritans had enabled them not to marry the man who got them pregnant. In twenty-four cases, almost one-quarter, the fathers of their children were either much older, of a different religion or objectionable to their parents. In a number of cases the men offered marriage, but the women rejected them.

Eleven women married men who were not the fathers of their children, ten before their children were two. Their marriages may well have been ones of convenience, a way of ensuring that their children had fathers to support them. As one woman wrote in 1919 about her intent to marry, 'I don't really care for him but you see it is like this. I never intend to marry for love now ... but this fellow is a dandy nice man, just as good as there is'. Another wrote that she was planning on getting married. 'I know I will have a good husband and a good home. He is very fond of __ and I think that is the main thing'.[118]

Of the one-third who went directly home, their stories suggest how limited and confining their lives continued to be. While the community offered basic support and tolerance, it extracted a price. Returning home was not easy. Seven of the women who returned to their homes came to the Good Samaritans in labour, and eleven came less than a month before they delivered. Most of them returned to their communities as soon as their times were up. This suggests that they came specifically for the delivery and were not expecting to hide their condition from their neighbours.[119]

The families accepted the return of their daughters with varying degrees of acceptance or conflict. For some the conflict was minor. As one mother wrote, 'I am very sorry __ done what she did but next to my God I love my children & no matter what they do. I try to bring them up good but I guess the best will make a mistake'. In a number of cases, the women wrote back with glowing details of how well their families had accepted their children. One, who applied to the Home to save her family the expense, wrote, 'My parents think the world of my baby, and she is just as happy as she can be. Mother tries not to spoil her, and Daddy doesn't see why she doesn't pick her up more often'.[120] Others, however, spoke of the conflicts within their families as family members struggled to accept the additional economic burden and the mark on their reputations. One mother told Atwood that she waited until her granddaughter's birth before she told her husband. He said, she reported, 'Well it's done and if she is a mother & keeps her baby & when her time's up there helps take care of it & leads a good deasent [*sic*] life she is welcome home and I'll do all I can for her'. He was cross at first, she acknowledged, 'but I talked to him & he saw my way of looking at it'.[121]

In other families the conflict was not so easily resolved. Ellen went home at the end of November in 1932 and three days later she wrote asking if she could bring her daughter back to the Home. 'I never would have come home if I had known just how things would be', she wrote. She had asthma that was bothering her, but her chief complaint was with her father. She couldn't ask him for anything for her child, she claimed. 'He has spoken to me just once since I came and not at all to her. Mother says he has been terrible this last year. He doesn't even speak to her now'. Before a year was up Ellen would give her daughter to the daughter's father and take a job in a chiropractor's office in the city of Augusta.[122]

While the families provided support sometimes grudgingly, they placed heavy demands on the young women. What distinguished the women who went home from the women who took jobs in the city was not their age or their rural backgrounds but the condition of their families. Overwhelmingly, the women who went home did so because their families needed them. In most cases their mothers were invalids or absent and the family relied upon the woman to take the mother's place. Jerrie's mother, for instance, wrote in 1920, 'I don't know how to express myself to you as we are strangers and I don't know how I can ever pay you and thank you enough for taken my deares daughter in your home'. Jerrie had not told her mother why she left home and her mother added,

> I didn't now why she didn't come home she nows [*sic*] my health is very poor and has been this last twelve years. I have got a lame leg and hip and I have got a big family and hast to work very hard. Jerry [*sic*] has been a big help to me I don't now how I am to get along without her she is all the help I have I have had the hardest time since she went away.

Jerrie at twenty-six was one of the older women in the Home. She was one of the very few who left their children with the Good Samaritans and she did so perhaps because she suspected her parents could not afford to keep the child.[123]

Annie was seventeen and came from a large family. The lawyer who referred her noted, 'the older children, more particularly the older girls, I understand have supported largely their mother and two younger children'. When Annie's baby died, she returned to her family and her old job as a telephone operator though, as the Assistant to the Special Agent of the New England Home for Little Wanderers wrote, 'I should think it would be rather hard on the girl to go back to her work among the girls who were there before she went to Bangor. Of course, none of them know for a fact what has happened but I do think many of them have the correct suspicion'.[124]

The Town of Saint Francis wrote the Good Samaritans, 'We have a family of paupers who are giving us some trouble'. The town paid for Lena's stay in the Home but hesitated to take her back. 'We have many reasons for trying to prevent (Lena) from returning home', the selectmen of the town wrote. 'The conditions there are beyond description, ' Lena's father was in Thomaston; her mother was 'reported to be selling liquor and her deportment is such that we have been compelled to take action to have her committed to some institution, probably to the reformatory'.[125]

Lena married the father of her child. This enabled her to return to the community and provided her with another source of support. For others, however, there was no way out; poverty and family obligations tied them to their families. Ivel, for example, left school in fourth grade to stay home and take care of her four brothers and her three younger sisters. Eva Scates, of the New England Home for Little Wanderers told Atwood, that although Ivel was at least five months pregnant, she would 'probably have to remain with the family until it is broken up as there is no one to get the meals for the children in school and it would be impossible to get any one to go into the home to do this'.[126]

Ivel entered the Home just one month before she gave birth and left as soon as she was allowed to. Atwood commented that Ivel had 'no desire to improve herself nor to increase her ability or earning capacity'. Instead, she returned home and a month after she did so Scates informed Atwood that the baby had lost weight. Her father, Scates wrote,

> brot [*sic*] her to a house that was hardly warm enough for a dog. When I went to see her, with the thermometer about 20 below zero at noon, she had one stick of wood in the kitchen stove and did not dare to put any more in because she was afraid the house would catch on fire as the chimney is all to pieces. The crib was next to the front grate of the stove and ... the mattress was wet.

Scates found Ivel a job with a family, placed her baby with Ivel's sister, and asserted to Atwood, 'She can't return to her father's place until he finds a rent that is livable, which he probably will never do'.[127]

Atwood blamed Ivel for her lack of desire to improve herself, but other cases make clear how strong a hold families had on the young women. Boby's mother wrote to Atwood asking her to keep her fifteen-year-old daughter's child. 'Why don't you take him', she wrote Atwood. 'I'm sick and have been for quite a while with Rhumatism'. Atwood informed the mother that Boby 'had a great desire to keep the child until such time as she herself might be able to provide a home for him'. She offered to go with Boby to court and to make the father pay for the child's board. She also pointed out it might take a while to find an appropriate Catholic home for adoption and threatened to sue the family if they left the child in the Home without paying its board. Her efforts were not successful. Boby's mother arranged for a Catholic adoption through the Holy Innocents Home in Portland, and Boby went back to her mother and obtained a job as a domestic. 'We feel deep sympathy for this girl who has in the past we feel been greatly suppressed by a domineering mother', Atwood commented.[128]

Ethel was one of two cases of acknowledged incest. She lived in a two-room shack with her stepfather and had taken care of her younger brother ever since the state had taken her crippled mother from the home. Ethel's child died at birth and Ethel returned home. Atwood noted, 'as we have no signed application we cannot hold her which we would very much like to do to take her from her surroundings'.[129]

If women were trapped by their families into hard work, dependence and poverty, those who had no families were even worse off for they had no relatives or towns of settlement to negotiate for them. The Good Samaritans negotiated with institutions as they did with families but with much less success. Without families, without communities, the cases of the three women who were involved with institutions before they entered the Good Samaritan Home reveal just how vulnerable these women were.

All three got pregnant when they were placed out to work in strangers' homes by the Industrial Training School at Hallowell and the State School at Pownal. Once pregnant, they had no one to help them bring the father of their child to court or to help them support their child on their own. When the man who got Rosabelle pregnant in 1923 got married, Hallowell referred Rosabelle to the Good Samaritans. Rosabelle had been working in various placements where, according to several letters admonishing her to be otherwise, she was 'slack and dirty'. In March of that year Miss Edith Cram from the State School warned Rosabelle:

> In regard to Henry Oakes, Mrs. Bryant doesn't think that he is a very nice sort of fel-
> low. I have not yet heard from him with any references, which I have asked him for. I
> don't want you to entertain the young man at the house, or to meet him outside, or to
> be writing him any letters or notes. If he is all right we shall see first. Just at present it
> does not look as if he were a safe companion for you.

In spite of Cram's efforts to protect Rosabelle, the girl became pregnant. Once she became pregnant, she had nowhere to go. When Atwood asked for the usual references the school staff replied they couldn't provide them as, 'Nobody else knows the girl'. Rosabelle delivered in the Home but then returned to the State School with her child.[130]

In addition, when women were in the care of the state, they automatically lost custody of their children. Ella, an orphan who had been brought up in the Belfast Home for Girls, stayed at the Good Samaritans and then went to the State Hospital and from there to Pownal School for the Feebleminded. There are indications that Ella was mentally unbalanced, but whether that was her natural condition or she was pushed to unbalance by the knowledge that she had no control of her life is unclear. 'Please don't let them have her', she wrote the matron at the Good Samaritan Home of her child. 'She is mind [sic] and nobody's else's. It nearly breaks my heart to think any one would be so mean not to let me know ... I swear right to it now that she can not go ... Gar promise me you will not let her go for my sake'.[131]

Atwood made clear in her comments and negotiations that she did not rec-ommend that the women 'dispose of their babies'. Nevertheless, twelve of the ninety-nine chose to do so. Their stories reveal how strong the pressure was for the girls and their families to take care of their own. Four placed their children either because they were already married or their families could not afford the responsibility of an additional child. As one woman who applied on her own to the Good Samaritans explained to Atwood, she had 'aged parents, and her father an invalid, and they dependent on her help; she must go out to work and feels that her mother is not able to care for the baby with the care of the father'. In the cases in which adoption was the only option, all but one came to the home ten days or less before their delivery and all left exactly six months after. They seemed to have chosen the Home to assist them in placing their babies as well as with their delivery. Secrecy could not have been the issue.

In two cases, the mothers were only fifteen and their families insisted that they give up their children. Atwood tried to intervene in one case; in the other, she commented, 'It seemed best to comply ... in as much as Naomi is dependent for her support upon a stepfather and her parents, living in a hotel'. Another woman who gave up her child for adoption was a minister's daughter who gave up her child to protect her parents' reputation.[132]

In the remaining six cases where the women chose adoption, they made every effort to appear to be complying with the expectation that families should take care of their own. Five placed their children with family members or friends. Two abandoned them slowly, that is, paid board and wrote letters affirming their support of their children for three years or more. The elapsed time gave them an excuse for taking the unorthodox path. As Alma, who explored giving up her child, explained to the potential adoptive mother, 'I have been home for over a year, and have kind of broken away from her. So it would not be so hard to lose her'.[133]

Irene, who combined these strategies, provides a clear example of the tightrope these women walked between community expectations and individual desires. Irene was the daughter of a poor farmer. She left her son in the Home when she went to Normal school, taught for a year, and then trained as a nurse in the hospital in her home town. In one of the many letters she wrote explaining why she would not be able to visit her child, she wrote, 'I suppose some of the girls thought it perfectly horrid because I didn't go see him on my week's vacation'. The father of her baby's father eventually adopted the child but not before an admirer of Irene wrote the Home to thank them. He wrote that he hoped to marry Irene and commented that, 'She loves her baby devotedly and in later years I know she will never consent to part with it. She is glad that it is alive and plans for it a fair future'.[134]

The Good Samaritans served as intermediaries in adoption. Those women who did give up their children gave them first to the Good Samaritans, who were no longer strangers. The Good Samaritans also enabled the women to keep in touch with their children, if only indirectly. As Atwood wrote to one mother who gave up her child, 'I will have more to tell you when they visit bringing the child'. In another case, an adoptive mother offered to send pictures. 'I have been thinking', she wrote, 'over the desire of the unhappy mother to see my baby. I am so happy and proud of her that I should feel most selfish and cruel not to let her look at the pictures, if it will bring her any comfort and peace'. She sent word through Atwood that when she had to tell her daughter 'about her other mother ... please tell her that I shall tell her as tenderly as I can'.[135]

Even when the Good Samaritans turned to stranger adoption in increasing numbers as they did during the Depression, they continued to serve as a conduit of information between the adoptive parents and the natural mother. Fern, for example, was sixteen when she gave birth to a daughter in December 1936. The father of her child, who was also young, had disappeared. When Fern's parents decided it was necessary to place the child for adoption, Atwood proposed that they consider leaving the baby in the Home for a while until Fern 'would perhaps get over missing her to the extent that she would if she parted with her when leaving the Home'. When the daughter was nine months old the Good Samaritans placed her in the home of a Massachusetts couple with ties to Maine. In recognition of the desire of the adoptive parent, Atwood noted that she could not tell Fern where her daughter was placed. She wrote to Fern, however, that she realized how hard it was to part from her daughter but that if she knew 'just how well she is situated I feel sure it would be a great comfort to you'. 'I shall keep in close touch with her', Atwood assured Fern, 'and anything you wish to know about her that I can tell you I will be only too glad to do so'.

The Good Samaritan Home required adopting parents to write monthly for the first year to keep the Good Samaritans informed of how the adoption was progressing and most adopting mothers complied with vivid details of their new child's life. In addition, many adopting parents visited Maine in the summer and often brought their children to the Home or invited Atwood to visit them. Atwood thus had many details to share with the natural mother. Fern asked if her daughter had curly hair, if she was walking at fourteen months and for how long, did she still rock herself, and how many teeth she had. She commented to Atwood, 'I wasn't surprised to learn that she loves dogs as I always did and tried to make friends with everyone I met. I am glad her hair is curly'.[136]

The adoption of Fern's baby was finalized in October 1938 but in December of 1940 Fern wrote one more time. She had found Atwood's letters when she was cleaning out a drawer and she wondered if Atwood could tell her any more. Atwood responded with more information.[137]

Atwood's ambition for almost every resident was to make her self-supporting and responsible for her child. As she wrote to one, 'You speak in your letter of having to remain at Home; What is the reason for this? and why are you desirous to be relieved of __ ? ... Please write me just what the situation is that you cannot have her, or cannot work like the most of our other girls, and either have her with you, or make a home for her'.[138]

Thirty-four women took advantage of the Good Samaritans offer to find jobs for them and to board their babies. An additional four returned to their old jobs. The placements were almost exclusively as domestics or as nurses. While placement in a domestic position or in a hospital provided women with what might have been irksome supervision and only limited income, it was in some respects well suited to the experiences of these rural women. They were accustomed at an early age to doing hard physical labour at home and many were in domestic positions when they got pregnant. Furthermore, Atwood placed many in the homes of board members and, in this way, followed the rural tradition of women working in homes of neighbours where they were needed. Housework might also enable the women to bring their babies with them and allowed them the flexibility to return home when their families needed them.

The women who took a placement were different as a group from those who did not. Two-thirds married. Almost one-half were Catholics. As this is a higher percentage of Catholics than was admitted to the Home, this suggests that Catholic women more often than Protestant women sought alternatives to remaining in their hometowns after an out-of-wedlock birth.

While placement provided them with an opportunity to move out of their hometown communities and to marry someone in the city, it also increased women's vulnerability by separating them from their families and their communities – the two institutions traditionally responsible for helping them negotiate with men. A full five of the thirty-four placed became pregnant out of wedlock for a second time. While communities generally accepted one pregnancy out of wedlock they did not easily accept two. Welfare agencies regularly gave the women in this situation the choice of giving up the second child or of being sterilized.[139]

A few cases suggest the ways that some women were able, with the Good Samaritans' support, to move themselves away from their restricted earlier lives. Mattie was working in the fields with her father and taking care of her invalid stepmother and insane stepsister when she got pregnant. Atwood told family members and the Immigration Service that Mattie was 'heart broken' at the prospect of going home and 'feels there will be no opportunity for her to earn her living there, nor that of her child; she also feels that the conditions of her home will be hard for her'. Mattie had come into the United States illegally and so was deported, but through a continual stream of letters to anyone remotely related to Mattie, Atwood found a distant relative in a Canadian city who agreed to supervise Mattie while she worked. A year after she left, Mattie married and her husband adopted the child. 'We are both so happy', Mattie wrote. 'He is so good to me that I couldn't possibly be anything else. I guess we are the only couple on our street that hasn't been caught drunk or heard quarreling'.[140]

Marie was also Canadian, but unlike Mattie she had entered the United States before she was pregnant. The Good Samaritans found Marie a situation in Bangor and assured the Immigration Service they would report Marie to the Immigration Service 'if in our judgment her conduct was such that we felt her presence in this country to be undesirable in any way'. Three years later Atwood reported to the Board that she had been told by the woman who employed Marie that Marie was 'the best maid she has ever had and the only one she had such a high regard and respect for, and one whom she felt she could make a companion of'. Later that year Marie married a streetcar conductor and remained in the city.[141]

Dana was one of the very few women who sought the services for the Home more for the protection of her reputation than for the economic support. She was a graduate of the New England Conservatory and living at home when, she claimed, a stranger entered her downstairs bedroom and raped her. Her step-father was the foreman of a papermill and her mother a music teacher. Dana left her child in the Home while she went to business college. Three years later Atwood was able to report that she 'has occupied a position of honor and trust in one of our local business offices and is now prominent in the life of one of our best known organizations for young women'. Dana married and her husband adopted her child.[142]

For Catholic Lilly, whose lover was Protestant, the Home enabled her to reject a marriage of which her family disapproved. Lilly stayed on in the Home as a night nurse after her six months were up, and nine years later she married a Catholic who worked with her father and moved into a home a three-minute walk from her parents. Her husband also adopted her baby.[143]

The Good Samaritans' primary aim was to make its residents self-sufficient and responsible for their children. The obstacles to doing so were extreme. Women relied on their families to help them negotiate in social relations; women were regularly paid less than men and families relied on their daughters to pro-vide whatever domestic work was required. The women, however, recognized their own value – their labour – and bargained with it. They did not come to the Good Samaritans empty-handed and they were not looking for charity. That the Good Samaritans achieved their aim with one-third of the women they served is remarkable. They were able to because they offered their services at just the right time in just the right way. Already by 1941, however, economic and social forces were making changes that would undermine the Good Samaritans' ability to offer women even limited independence.

4 PROFESSIONAL STANDARDS IN TENNESSEE: ONLY PERFECT CHILDREN WILL DO

On 15 September 1950, Tennessee Welfare Commissioner Shoat closed the offices of Georgia Tann, director of the Tennessee Children's Home Society, Memphis Branch. In thirty years Tann had placed over 5,000 children in every state in the Union as well as Mexico, Panama, Canada and England. Numerous parents had complained that she had offered to get healthcare for their children and when they signed a form authorizing it (so they thought) took their children away. Unwed mothers reported that she had told them their babies had died at birth or had forced them to sign a surrender form when they were still under heavy sedation. At least two adoptive families realized that she gave the identical description of the birth parents to them both. A large number of those placed were identified as Jewish, when the Jewish population in the state was very small.[1] Charging wealthy couples in New York and Los Angeles as much as $10,000 for an infant and falsifying her travel expenses, Tann had accumulated close to one million dollars. Four years later, Senator Estes Kefauver of Tennessee chaired congressional hearings on black-market adoption. Georgia Tann provided the perfect example of adoption gone wrong.[2]

Tann had violated almost every tenet of ethical social work standards and was the impetus for a Congressional investigation of black-market adoption and yet, ironically, the national child-placing standards initiated by the new social work profession combined with traditional child care practices in Tennessee, made possible Tann's adoption practices. By relying on Tennessee's tradition of improving children's lives by placing them in homes higher on the economic scale at a time when the new professional standards were limiting the options available to rural unwed mothers, she created a virtual empire as one of the most highly regarded, nationally recognized adoption specialists in the country.

There is no doubt that Tann created and abused power in numerous ways. She offered babies to couples and then threatened them with blackmail if they didn't support legislation that would protect her from supervision or oversight. She arranged with the city boss of Memphis (who also wielded power in the state legislature) to abort the laws that might have impinged on her practice. She also misrepresented the truth blatantly and continuously to birth mothers and adoptive parents. Even so, even when the facts were made clear, there were those who continued to maintain that she helped poor young women.[3]

When the Governor Gordon Browning threatened Tennessee Children's Home Society with an investigation what records there may have been disappeared overnight. The TCHS housed children of different ages, but a number were infants. These were the children of unwed mothers. There is no telling how many of these were from rural areas but they were often referred to as such. Tann sent 'runners' into the countryside to identify single pregnant women and to offer them free room, board and medical care. In addition, there is a high likelihood that those who were in one of the cities when they delivered were from the rural areas. As one contemporary scholar of 'unlawful motherhood' noted, 'the preponderance of traffic is city-ward'. The records bear this out. Of the twelve children who were born to unwed mothers who were in the Home when it closed, only two were from Shelby County, the county of Memphis. The mothers of others came from Mississippi, Alabama and Arkansas. Five gave birth in rural eastern Hamilton County.[4]

The turn of the century marked the beginning of a dramatic, long-lasting migration of rural people into the cities especially in the south where 'hundreds of thousands of rural families moved from the rural countryside to urban areas'. The migrants were overwhelmingly young and included more women than men. In Tennessee, they led to a preponderance of women in the urban areas (and a corresponding preponderance of men in the rural areas). When women reached the city, they were paid less than men, had no families to provide them with support, and were less educated than their urban counterparts. As a result, they competed with one another for jobs that, one study revealed, in at least 50 per cent of the cases paid less than subsistence wage. 'Many are the stories of disillusionment, defeat and ill fate of the girls who have left home and community environment to enter the complicated life of the city' one researcher concluded.[5]

In any event, the large movement of rural people into the cities of the south meant, as one contemporary observer concluded, 'the continuity between country and city was maintained and rural life was "highly valued" by a large proportion of the urban population'.[6]

By the first decades of the twentieth century rural communities in Tennessee were no longer as isolated as they had once been. Railroads and automobiles, travelling salesmen and warehouse catalogues had all brought urban values and the consumer culture to the rural world. As one observer of the south reported from his travels throughout the region in 1936, 'The most profoundly disturbing foreign agitators in the region are the salesmen ... The cabins ... are wallpapered with the pages of newspapers and magazines, and so much advertising has a practically permanent appeal'. Even those who couldn't read, he suggested, 'can desire. If they lack the money, they can wish for it'.[7]

Awareness of urban culture brought awareness of the limitations of rural life, especially for women. As rural Tennessee women who had moved to the cities explained to interviewers during the Depression: 'I wanted to have freedom and make my own way in the world', 'my wishes were not all satisfied and I was denied many things', and 'I could never go back now'.[8]

In spite of the freedoms and goods promised by the urban life, many of the rural communities retained their more traditional values as the pardon case of Lonnie Ball suggests. As in Maine, rural communities considered age more important than gender when judging sexual indiscretion and accepted premarital sex as part of a movement into marriage. They also considered individuals in their context and measured an individual's worth by the work that he contributed to the community.

In 1919 the court committed Lonnie Ball of Sneedville to state prison for having sexual intercourse with a woman under sixteen. Although the state had raised its age of consent for girls from ten to sixteen in 1895, Ball was the first in his county to be sentenced under the new age limit. The letters from the community that poured in to the Governor urging Ball's pardon suggest that many in this rural eastern Tennessee county held views that reflected traditional ideas of courtship and marriage.[9]

Lonnie Ball and Fannie Collins were neighbours who had known each other almost all their lives.[10] In 1915, when Fannie was fifteen and Lonnie a year or two older and both were students in the Sneedville school, they 'became sweethearts'. 'They were engaged to be married, loved each other', the jury later wrote to the Governor. Fannie had testified in the trial that 'she frequently kissed the defendant, put her arms about him and sat upon his lap, and that on an occasion when they were thus signifying their love for each other, the first criminal act between them occurred, she hardly knew how'. The 'criminal acts' continued and Fannie became pregnant. Lonnie offered to marry Fanny, to care for her and 'be as good to her ... as if nothing of the kind had happened', but Fannie's father rejected Lonnie's suit. Instead, he sent his daughter to Washington, DC, to work for the Board of Census.

Lonnie served in the Navy, and then returned to his family farm and married another woman. Four or five years after the event, when Lonnie was old enough to be treated by the courts as an adult, Fannie's father charged Lonnie with violating the age of consent law. When Lonnie jumped bail, Mr Collins followed him into Virginia and brought him back.[11] Lonnie was convicted and sent to prison, and his hometown rallied immediately to his support.

Ministers, court officers, justices of the peace and 'the good ladies of the town' wrote letters and an estimated 90 per cent of the town's citizens signed petitions requesting Lonnie's release. Lonnie's neighbours placed the blame on Lonnie's youth, not his sex. They argued that the boy was no more to blame than the girl.

W. S. Tyler, for example, commented, 'If a man of mature age and of experience had taken advantage of your Daughter', he wrote to Fannie's father, 'and seduced her to do wrong ... I would have been the last man to have requested a pardon ... But in this case it was a Boy and as I believe in many cases the Boy is not any more to blame than the Girl and so often ... the parents are to blame as much as the Boy or Girl'.

Others who wrote on Lonnie's behalf placed him within the context of his community. As Justice of Peace A. L. Livesy commented, Lonnie was 'ever ready to lend a helping hand to those who need help'. Those referring to themselves as 'the good ladies of the town' said, 'We have known this boy since childhood. We know his daily life, the record he made in school. We know that he never gave his teachers any trouble in school or his mother at home'. Others pointed out he that had a widowed mother and a wife and child to support.

If the community accepted as 'natural' the couple's premarital pregnancy, members of Fannie's family made clear that at least some in the community placed a high value on the developing middle class's concern with the reputation of its daughters. Fannie's father was a bank teller who had previously been a circuit court clerk of Hancock County. He called on his commercial and legal professional colleagues for support. As Hon. J. A. Maness stated, 'I am writing, not that I have interest in the case ... but that I am interested in the chastity and virtue of our young girls of our country'. The prosecuting attorney wrote that he had never seen a 'more outrageous violation of this law'. The young lady, he commented, was 'so humiliated and disgraced that she does not live in Hancock County any more'. The young man, he pointed out, 'admitted his promises of marriage, and offered no excuse whatever for his conduct'. Furthermore, he did not in any way attempt in the trial 'to question the good character of the girl he seduced'.

What the out-of-wedlock pregnancy meant to Fannie's family was measured in very practical terms. Collins was a man, W. H. Buttram wrote, who 'has and is working very hard to educate his children'. Of all his seven daughters, 'the one in question is the only one against whom anything has ever been said'. By having sex before marriage, Fannie had threatened her family's precarious hold on middle-class status. As Martha, Fannie's sister, pointed out in several letters, a certain reputation could ruin a woman's and a family's life. It could especially, she hinted, limit her chances for upward mobility. The child, she pointed out, must suffer from embarrassment because of his illegal birth; Fannie was striving to get on her feet again and working to provide for herself and her child. She had such great potential, 'being attractive and exceedingly brilliant', and now her chances were ruined because she has been deprived of a respectable name. Even worse, the suffering moved outward, for her sisters were 'suffering by the reflections cast upon them' and the family circle was 'robbed of the privilege of being unable to remove a stain on a history of refinement they had strived so hard to form'. It is important to note that Fannie was married by November 1920. Her child out of wedlock did not ruin her chances at marriage, but it may have ruined her chances to an advantageous match.

The 'good ladies of the town' commented to the governor that the people who had talked to Mr Collins 'say he don't use any reason'. He acknowledged, they said, 'the girl to be in fault as well as the boy but he says he wants to make an example of the boy'. Making an example didn't make sense to a community where everyone knew everyone else and knew what they contributed to the community. It did, though, to a man with seven daughters who was trying to hold on to his position in the middle class. Fannie might have married Lonnie and settled into a community which knew full well why she got married. The choice she (or her father) made was to leave the community and strive for a different life.

Fannie's family could afford to send her out of state, but for many rural women their options were limited to a much narrower geographic range.[12] They had to make their lives out of the options offered them. At the end of the last century, as we have seen, their options were defined by the laws that were created by those in power in each state. As the twentieth century progressed their options were increasingly influenced by the national standards emanating from an increasingly coordinated social work bureacracy.

In the early decades of the century, social workers were just beginning to solidify their position in society by carving out for themselves recognition as professionals. As with professions which had achieved professional status earlier, social workers sought a national organization, regular conferences, specialized training, and standards that would define the field. The fact that many social workers were women who had to make special efforts to get their professional expertise recognized had profound implications for unwed mothers.

Regina Kunzel has traced the development of the social work profession as it became increasingly dominated by women and at the same time struggled to separate itself from the maternal benevolence which proceeded it. It did so by emphasizing that its work was guided by scientific expertise. Trained social workers would use scientific methods to gather the facts, analyze them and then help those who needed to be helped. Its work would be both efficient and successful.[13]

The first professional schools of social work were established early in the twentieth century at Harvard and the University of Chicago. Soon thereafter, local professionals established social work leagues in Boston and New York. In 1911 the National Federation of Settlements was formed and in 1915 the *American Yearbook* made note of the 'increasing coherence in social welfare'. That year 2,600 people, more than ever, attended the National Conference of Charities and Corrections. Their major topic was the professional character of social work.

Soon after, those who had argued that social work was as much of a profession as law, medicine, and engineering, took over the leadership of the Conference and renamed it the National Conference on Social Work. In 1921 the American Association of Social Workers, 'the largest and most inclusive of professional organizations' was established.[14]

Over the next decades, as Kunzel has shown, the professional social workers struggled to gain recognition for their work as something distinct from the work of benevolent women who had organized charity work in the previous century. The two groups worked together, however, to gain federal support for women and children and in 1912 the US Children's Bureau was established. Although the Bureau initially had no authority and only a limited budget, under the guidance of Julia Lathrop it quickly became the authoritative source of information on the welfare of children and their families. While a large network of volunteer reformers was responsible for obtaining this federal recognition, the Bureau was 'firmly connected to the social work establishment'. In return, the Bureau's professionalism made it the 'main enclave of the welfare reform community'.[15]

Almost immediately, the Children's Bureau entered into the public discourse on unwed mothers. Its first major publication was a study of infant mortality. Richard Meckel in his study of infant mortality in the United States found that the first two decades of the century 'witnessed a virtual explosion of public concern over infant mortality'. While infant mortality had always been high, it was not until city and federal officials began to systematically collect and publish statistics on death rates that Americans discovered that between 15 and 20 per cent of all children in the United States died before their first birthday.[16]

The Bureau's study revealed that one-third of children born to unwed mothers died in their first year, a mortality rate that was three times as high as that of children born to married women. This revelation provided an impetus for the Bureau to carve a special niche for itself: the study and creation of national standards for unwed mothers. In the next two decades the Bureau would fund eleven studies on the subject and help organize numerous conferences on a local, regional and national level.[17]

In 1921 the Children's Bureau published a follow-up study based in Boston, 'Illegitimacy as a Child-Welfare Problem'. Although participants of the early conferences had taken care to point out that 'an exceedingly large number of illegitimate children are born to those who by virtue of wealth and position are enabled to shield themselves from public knowledge' and that the rates for these privileged women were as high or higher than those in the poor or middle class,[18] the Boston study focused exclusively on mothers who came into contact with social service agencies. Considering the poverty that forced these particular mothers to contact social service agencies in the first place, it is perhaps not surprising that the study concluded that unwed mothers were on the whole below normal mentality and that over half showed 'repeated violations of the moral code, serious alcoholism, dishonesty or general worthlessness'. By conflating poor unwed mothers with all unwed mothers, this new scientific evidence suggested that unwed mothers were not simply women who had 'fallen' but were women predetermined to fall.[19]

The concern generated by the discovery of the high death rate among children born to unwed mothers also raised concern over the circumstances of the unwed mother herself. In another Bureau study, Chicago Law Professor Ernst Freund reviewed state laws governing illegitimacy. He concluded that the allotments in bastardy suits were too small and that it was far too easy for reputed fathers to escape financial responsibility for their natural children. Julia Lathrop reminded those who attended the Children's Bureau conferences that 'we must not forget the awful social burden the mother has to bear'.[20]

In spite of the fact that child welfare experts expressed concern for the mother, their studies and reports marked a shift in public attitude toward unwed mothers. An unwed mother was no longer any woman who was seduced by an aggressive male, she was one of a group of women, a class, who shared in the responsibility of the pregnancy and, therefore, couldn't be entirely trusted to protect the best interest of her child. As the Juvenile Protection Association of Chicago concluded 'after careful study of the bastardy cases brought into the court ... it was impossible to reach the old-fashioned conclusion that the man was always the aggressor and villain'.[21]

Armed with scientific evidence and the support of the federal government, the Children's Bureau and other social-work experts sought to change the practices of the volunteer women who had originally opened unwed mothers homes. Children's Bureau staff visited the homes, wrote articles recommending new treatment, published standards, and, ultimately, controlled the dispersal of funds through influence with the newly organized Community Chests.[22]

In spite of its growing influence, the social-work establishment in the early decades did not have a unified vision of unwed mothers and how they should be treated. The importance of keeping mother and child together, the nature of the unwed mother, and how private birth records should be kept were all matters of discussion. What was clear, however, was that the concern for the best interest of the child, the separation of interests of the mother from her child, and the desire to find the best solution for each individual based on scientific rather than sentimental reasoning, opened the way for social workers to consider adoption as an option for all unwed mothers. By the 1950s the social work profession would reach nearly universal agreement on the necessity for a white unwed mother to give up her child and the need for secrecy in adoption. The decades prior to this, however, were decades of gradual cultural shifts during which the nuclear family gained prominence in the national discourse, adoption became a publicly accepted option for infertile women, and counselling encouraged individuals to adapt to society and its strict gender roles.[23]

Historian Julie Berebitsky traces the cultural changes that occurred in the first decades of the twentieth century as adoption, once seen primarily in practical terms as a way of providing for orphaned children, became a way of providing childless couples with infants to love. She notes that social workers were slow to endorse the placement of children with strangers but as adoption became socially acceptable as a way for infertile couples to complete their families, the practice grew in spite of social workers hesitancy to support it. In 1924 at the National Conference of Social Work, a Children's Aid Society member called for professionals to 'promote placement policies with a scientific basis'. A year later, the Children's Bureau published its first pamphlet on adoption policies.[24]

Once it had accepted the responsibility for promoting sound placement policies, the Children's Bureau became a major force in both the public discussion and the development of state laws. Social workers called for adoption procedures to be scientific and objective. They insisted on applying new testing techniques and interviewing protocols to ensure that investigations of both the child and her birth parents were thorough and scientific. To make this possible, they suggested, a child should not be placed until it was six months old. They also called for matching the child with his adoptive parents. In order for the adoption to be successful, they argued, the adopted children should 'fit' their adoptive homes in physical characteristics, intellectual capacities, temperament, and religious and ethnic affiliation'.[25] As class was seen by many as an indication of intellectual capability, this required that the new parents and child be from the same social class.

Having considered the possibility that the unwed mother might not be the best one to take care of her child, social workers now offered her a choice. She could choose to keep her baby or place it for adoption. This, in turn, called for casework with all unwed mothers. Katharine F. Lenroot, author of several of the Children's Bureau's studies of unwed mothers, pointed out that it was inappropriate to rely on one solution for all unwed mothers' situations. Provision for the unmarried mothers, she said in 1924, depended 'upon the application of the fundamental principles of case work – scientific understanding and adaptation of treatment to individual needs'. Psychiatric study would be especially valuable, she pointed out, 'since it gives a basis for decisions as to whether or not she should keep her baby, what her mode of living should be, and what vocational opportunities should be opened to her'.[26]

The casework method which both emphasized individual choice and required that a stranger explore the most intimate aspects of one's self and one's family could be difficult for a rural woman to accept. In addition in Tennessee, the suggestion that children should be placed only in families of equal status countered the state's long standing practice of enabling children to move up in society by placing them in more deserving (that is, more wealthy) families.

Tennessee courts had long distinguished between women who deserved to be mothers and those who did not. In 1825 the Tennessee Supreme Court stated, 'Perhaps the strongest law in animated nature is the disposition of the female to protect and support her offspring', and concluded, 'it was never intended, even by the marital relation of husband and wife, that the great law of nature be violated by a separation of the mother from her infant'. Nevertheless, Tennessee law made it clear that the 'great law of nature' did not apply equally to all women. The Tennessee court denied slave women the right to keep their children and denied other mothers their custodial rights when it determined they were economically unable to support their children or were 'immoral'.[27]

In contrast to Maine where the law and the communities pressured a woman to keep her child, Tennessee implemented laws that facilitated the transfer of children away from poor parents. Bastardy law authorized the court to 'dispose of' a child when it was three 'in such a manner as shall most conduce to the interest of the child' either by giving it to the father or by apprenticing it. The adoption law of 1852 authorized courts to sanction an adoption when it was satisfied with the reasons given by those who wished to adopt. The law did not require the consent of those releasing the child until 1917. The state's first child welfare law of 1885 authorized orphanages to receive or take charge of any 'destitute white orphan or indigent white child;' it authorized the boards of these institutions at their discretion to 'require the parents of such indigent children to surrender all right and claim to the control of them, and to consent for the said asylum to provide homes for them, by adoption by proper and suitable parties ...' A law establishing an industrial training school in 1887 authorized county judges to commit children three years old or older if the children were 'living with persons of bad character' or 'in danger of growing up in pauperism, lewdness, or crime' and authorized the school to place children for adoption.[28]

Tennessee social literature and news reports describe the formal and informal processes by which infants moved from undeserving to deserving mothers. Lide Meriwether, founder of the Woman's Christian Association's Mission, described how she and her Christian group came to adopt an abandoned child in 1872. A young man found it on the steps of St. Peter's Church. His mother gave it into the 'charge of a mulatto woman in the city who having lately lost her own child, would be able to give all her time and attention to it'. Meriwether, having lost a daughter several years ago, 'petitioned for the especial charge of the baby'. She named the baby after her dead child and soon it was 'taken to heart' by the women of her Christian group. 'Every Wednesday morning', she wrote, 'when I made my appearance at the weekly meeting, I was greeted from all sides with the question: "How is our baby?"' The group formally adopted the child.[29]

Judge John C. Ferris, founder of the Tennessee Children's Home Society where Tann eventually worked, wrote in 1895 of his role in assisting the transfer of children. Ferris took office in Nashville in 1872 and almost immediately, he reported, a clerk told him of an infant that had been left with 'an old colored woman on Front Street, just below the workhouse'. It was a judge's duty, he explained, to look after orphans and so he went to investigate. The woman told him that an old man had given her fifty dollars and a basket of fine baby clothes and had taken the infant's mother with him on the northbound train. The Judge left the fifty dollars with the old woman but gave the child to a 'lady friend'. The lady friend was single, but a 'gentleman loved the child so he actually married her adoptive mother'.[30]

In 1906 a 'band of charitable women' formed the Memphis Foundling Home Association to aid in this informal transfer. They established a free home where 'any white baby under two will be admitted and given the best care till a home can be found'. Although there were private foundling homes, Mrs John Oliver claimed that the women of Memphis had for many years felt the needs 'of a home such as this'. In the first report of the Foundling Home the *Commercial Appeal* described one of its early customers. The 'parties that had abandoned him' drugged the one-month-old boy and left him with a cab man at Union Station; the cab man took him to the police. He was 'sinned against, not sinning', the Board of the Home reported, 'and he has bright prospects for being adopted into a good family. He may some day be governor ... Who can say?'[31]

While these public stories stressed the fact that babies were abandoned, records of the orphanages suggest that in many cases mothers did not choose to give up their children but were forced to do so by poverty. As Clopper noted in his survey of social services in Tennessee in 1919, 'Institutions are compelled to accept children who should not be separated from their families because of the lack of any provision for social case work in their home communities'. Clopper cited the inadequacy of mothers' pensions, outdoor relief and the poorhouses.[32]

The history of the Protestant Orphan Asylum, founded in Nashville in 1845 and one of the oldest orphanages in the state, confirms Clopper's assessment. The Asylum's historian noted in 1945 that while there were many reasons for admission to the Home, 'probably the one recurring most frequently was the failure of one or both of the parents to provide food and shelter'.[33] 'I am a widow lady and have two daughters I wish to send to some orphan school', one applicant wrote in 1884. 'I have no way of making support for them. I have five children and wish very much to get the two oldest to school for one session if no longer ... please try and do all you can for me as I am a widow and have no relative to help me nearer than Missouri'.[34] The minutes are filled with such requests from applicants, many of them single mothers who needed to work and could find no childcare. They are also filled with requests from couples looking for children to adopt.

Once the Board accepted a child, board members exerted control over its future. In 1900 the Board asked the executive committee to consider 'the advisability of securing homes for some of the children whose parents have not relinquished their claim'.[35] Mr Hancock was one of those parents who, when pressed about giving his children up for adoption, 'expressed himself indefinitely, but agreed to consider the matter'. Three years later his daughter was placed with the wife of a minister 'with adoption in view'. Six months later, the Board agreed to send another of the Hancock children to a Catholic institution, 'principally that she might be permanently separated from a very unworthy mother'.[36]

Parents could initiate a *habeas corpus* suit to regain the custody of their children. When they did, the courts often supported the board's right to determine the best interest of the child and to define fit parenthood. When Hazel Taylor married and instituted a *habeas corpus* to recover the custody of her children, 'the testimony showed conclusively and overwhelmingly that neither the mother nor her husband was in any way qualified to rear the children, nor were they fit persons for them to be associated with'. The Judge sent the children back to the Asylum.[37]

Although those placing the children reiterated the belief that the placement was in the best interest of the child, children and parents contested the right of the elite to transfer children from one family to another. The Protestant Orphan Asylum, according to its history, had 'much trouble with the children' in its early years. 'The policy of putting them out in homes, or of binding them to learn a trade, was adhered to, with the result that many of them ran away', the historian recorded. In one month, six were placed and all ran.[38]

In Judge Ferris's account of his child-placing experiences, almost every case involved a parent who sought for his or her child's return. One mother worked at a gun factory and her husband, according to Ferris, wouldn't work and wouldn't mind the baby. 'I took the child', Ferris reported, 'and sent it to a lady friend of mine who had no children and was anxious to raise one. She and her husband came to the office the next day and adopted the child'. The father filed a *habeas corpus* for the return of the child. In the trial the Judge asked the adoptive mother if she really loved the child. 'She said, in a clear, trembling, motherly voice', Ferris reported, "Judge, before God and this audience I would rather have my right arm severed from my body than to part with this sweet precious babe." The Judge decided in favour of the adoptive mother.[39]

The Judge relied on the law to support his placement practices, but he also relied on community support. In one case he placed 'little Maggie' with a 'good family' in Williamson City where she was much loved. When her natural parents came to get her 'the whole community rose in arms and went in pursuit'.

With the help of these neighbours who saw that Maggie's life 'had been much improved', Maggie was returned to her adoptive parents.[40]

If poor parents had little support for keeping their children, poor unwed mothers had even less. The state provided mothers' aid to single women but unwed mothers were not generally eligible in Tennessee. Once they had placed a child in an institution for economic reasons, their moral standing made it less likely that the institution or court would return the child to them.[41] Unwed mothers did not often file *habeas corpus* suits, perhaps because they were so unlikely to win them. The fate of Mary Blalock, however, suggests what they might have found had they done so. Mary left an abusive marriage and attempted to support her child. She had held 'first one menial job after another in the effort to obtain clothing and food for herself and her little child and it was a great deal of pain or worry to her to live in such deplorable conditions'. When she reconciled briefly with her husband and got pregnant 'being in such a worried, downcast, broken-hearted and even hungry condition', she brought her infant to the Tennessee Children's Home Society for what she expected was temporary care. The Home placed the infant with an adoptive family and Mary sued for its return. By this time, she had inherited enough money to set herself up as a piano teacher.[42] Mary had a respectable profession and, she argued, came from respectable parents, but the lawyer for the Home took care to point out that 'at the time of (her) marriage she was already pregnant'. On this basis – and the fact she left her children with friends to go out to work – he argued that she was 'guilty of lewd and lascivious conduct and of immoral relations ... and is not a fit and proper person to have the custody of the child'. Mary did not regain her child.[43]

The new social work standards condemned this widespread informal practice of transferring children from undeserving to deserving parents and called for more support for the unwed mother. The state, however, was limited in its ability to interrupt the practice as it lacked adequate funding for social welfare programmes. The Tennessee legislature passed its first comprehensive adoption and child-placing statute in 1917. The act authorized the State Board of Charities to inspect and supervise all public and private child-caring agencies in the state and prohibited individuals, specifically doctors, nurses, midwives and hospital officials, from placing children.[44] The Board of Charities' role was supervisory only. For the next three-and-a-half decades, the state struggled to 'professionalize' the placement practices of autonomous private institutions and untrained county judges.

When the state attempted to define new practices by protecting the rights of and providing economic support for natural parents, a severe shortage of staff hindered its efforts. In 1923 the legislature established the Department of Institutions in order to centralize authority over the state's charitable and correctional institutions. Two years later it created the Welfare Division within the

Department. The Welfare Division's job was to visit, inspect and license private child-caring institutions and maternity homes as well as jails, workhouses and almshouses. The staff of the Division consisted of a director, a field agent and a stenographer. In its first report, the Division called child welfare 'the very heart of social work'. 'Such rapid strides are being made in Child Welfare that standards of two years ago are almost obsolete today, and many of today's standards will be behind the times tomorrow', the report stated. It called for workers in children's agencies not only to do their daily duties but to 'constantly study the new information and help that is available, else they will fall short of serving in a really complete way'. The Division's one field worker, however, had to visit every jail, workhouse, almshouse, maternity home and private child caring institution in ninety-five counties. It is not surprising that the Director requested additional workers 'should appropriations permit'.[45]

In 1932 a new Director of Welfare again called for more personnel, pointing out that state control over institutions for children and unmarried mothers was necessary, for without such control, 'abuses would be frequent and flagrant'.[46]

In 1937 the Welfare Organization Act created the Department of Institutions and Public Welfare and enlarged the division of public welfare. The new Department tried to organize child welfare committees in each county but succeeded only in organizing three county committees and one statewide subcommittee. All of these committees stopped operating within the next four years. Furthermore, from 1940 to 1943 the Department had no director of the child welfare division.[47]

Study after study confirmed that a lack of adequate professional staff in addition to a lack of funding limited the state's ability to implement its new professional policies. In 1919 a study of child placements found that in spite of the prohibition against private individuals placing children, 'some of the best people in the state' were doing so, and the state had no way of knowing how many or who all the people were. The investigator listed, as examples, the chairman of an orphanage who personally made a large number of placements and a doctor who did the same with no investigation.[48]

The state professional social workers were equally unsuccessful in their call for 'strengthening and preserving natural kinships ties whenever possible' and for providing services for unwed mothers whether the mothers gave up their children or not.[49] In 1937 the Children's Bureau published a study of infant mortality in Memphis in which it concluded that while the state had laws to provide for the licensing and supervision of maternity homes, the state had not provided the staff for these purposes. It pointed specifically to the fact that, though the state recommended that maternity homes keep mother and infant together for six months, in practice none of the homes investigated did.[50]

Ten years later a study of the Department's child welfare placements, noting a 'shortage of personnel as well as rapid turnover' found that a full three-quarters of the placements that it was able to identify had been independent adoptions, prohibited by law. There was, it concluded, 'no indication that judges were aware of the law prohibiting child placing by individuals and unauthorized agencies, or that they accepted responsibility for the enforcement of this provision'.[51] Another study that same year noted that, as late as 1944, Tennessee was one of the few remaining states which had not reached the level of standards outlined by the Child Welfare League and the US Children's Bureau.[52]

While the Division of Welfare lacked funds and influence, the Tennessee Children's Home Society (TCHS) lacked neither. Although not a home for unwed mothers, it touched the lives of more unwed mothers in Tennessee than all the other institutions in the state combined from 1907 to 1950. It did so by skilfully following the state's longstanding practice of supporting the best interest of the child by placing it in families higher up on the social scale and at the same time apparently complying with the best social-work practices.

The TCHS grew out of the work of John C. Ferris, Judge of Davidson County, who gave public addresses about and enlisted the interest of the press in the problem of children without responsible parents. From 1872 to 1910 when he retired from the court, he often used his own home as a temporary receiving home for these children. Later he built a home and a child placement agency which he operated. Nashville incorporated the agency in 1897 and, in 1913, the Secretary of State granted it a charter to extend its child placing work through field agents in Memphis, Knoxville, Chattanooga and Jackson. In 1915 the state began what would be regular, increasing support to the TCHS. By 1946 it was paying the agency $40,000 annually.[53]

The TCHS was praised for its professional practices. In 1920, the National Child Labor Committee compared the arrangements of the TCHS with the practices of other organizations in the state that regularly placed children. The Committee's survey uncovered widespread violations of the adoption law. Without exception, the Committee reported, these institutions relied on child placement committees that had not one member with previous training or experience. The courts failed to make careful investigations at the time of an adoption and thus led to the state to be 'frequently embarrassed by *habeas corpus* proceedings'.[54]

In contrast, the TCHS alone employed a 'full-time visitor'. It followed a policy of investigating both the child and the adopting family before and of visiting the family every three months following the placement. The Committee concluded that the methods of the TCHS 'were developed along the lines of the best modern standards' and compared favourably with any of the younger societies in other states.[55]

For several decades the TCHS relied on two to five field workers who 'under adverse traveling conditions' brought children from all over the state to the receiving home in Nashville where they would await placement. In 1924, the agency opened a branch office in Memphis and hired Georgia Tann as its director. Under Tann's direction this separate office would eventually gain a separate charter, open its own receiving home and ultimately place for adoption more children than any other placement agency in the South.

As did the TCHS, Tann promoted herself in a way that emphasized both her professional credentials and her connections to Tennessee's traditions. She graduated from Martha Washington College in Virginia, attended social work courses at Columbia University, passed the state bar in Mississippi and worked at child-placing agencies in Texas and Mississippi. In her own description, however, she emphasized the influence of her father, George C. Tann, 'noted chancellor' and founder of probation work in Mississippi. He was, she claimed, 'always bringing children home with him'. More than once she heard him say, 'I wish I had a doctor, a school teacher and a good, far-seeing minister to sit as a committee and help me decide what should be done with these children'. He didn't have the committee, but he had his daughter who began helping him – and other male officials – with children at an early age.[56]

Tann also stressed her work as a woman, for women. Numerous reports about her personality suggested a toughness that could be considered masculine. Her obituary noted that she had an 'unusually strong personality'. Her 'ability to make those to whom she talked see her point was commanding', commented one acquaintance. Throughout her career, however, she emphasized her womanliness and the insight being a woman offered her. Interviewed by the press in 1935, she told a story of her beginnings in child placement work. When 'but just a slip of a girl' her 'jurist father and other visiting bar notables' met her outside the courthouse.

> Beside her was a big policeman, in her arms was a tiny baby, a 'doorstep' baby. The policeman didn't know much about babies so he had asked Miss Tann, then a volunteer social worker, to go along with him ... Her father, with an expression she would never forget, managed to gulp, 'Gentleman, this is my daughter.'

In this one brief vignette, Tann managed to suggest that men, though physically larger than women, needed to rely on women when it came to dealing with children; that she was from a line of jurists who were expected to find places for children and was a social worker herself; and that while young women might have a baby and ruin their reputation, other women might save a baby by knowing what to do for it. She made a practice of primarily hiring women. One employee described her receiving home as a 'kingdom run by women'.[57]

Tann also emphasized the way her placements improved infants' lives. By 1935 she had placed 3,000 children in every state in the Union. They came, she claimed, from '"ordinary" poor families in which mothers couldn't or didn't care for them', and she placed them with professionals. She stressed the improved opportunities her placements provided. 'Many have finished college with honors, some are junior leaguers', she told the press. Claiming the power of a professional, she noted that 'our children' turned out better than children picked from homes at random, because 'we select the child and the home'.[58]

Similar to the professional social workers in the Children's Bureau, Tann allied herself with other female professionals all of whom gained recognition for dealing with women's issues in a professional way. One of her close friends in Memphis was Camille Kelley, Judge of the Shelby County Juvenile Court. When Kelley was first appointed as a judge in 1920, she was the second woman in the nation to serve on a juvenile court and the first female judge in the South. Kelley had studied law for two years in her husband's law office, but, as she suggested in her autobiography, she considered her perspective as a woman to be far more important. She started her public career as a member of the parent-teacher organization who 'naturally' felt women should serve on the school board. When she was asked to give a speech and hesitated, her husband encouraged her. 'Wrap the garment of womanhood about you and speak', he told her, 'not as a man or as a politician, but as one with a mission to perform. Do this and you will command the respect of all who hear you'.[59]

But she also made it clear that her professionalism taught her things that women did not know. 'My ideas of motherhood and home underwent quick changes after I became a judge', she wrote. She found that bad children were the result of bad environments and also 'that mother love was not sufficient to give the wisdom for guiding children'.[60]

Kelley continued the judicial practice of taking children from unsuitable homes and placing them in suitable ones and gained national recognition for her work. Her book, *Delinquent Angels*, became a national bestseller and in 1948 a national poll found her one of the 'Six Most Wholesome Women in the World'.[61] The juvenile court judge did not normally handle adoptions, but Kelley identified for Tann children who might be taken from their homes for care and protection and who could then be placed for adoption. With her position as a judge, her nationwide recognition, and her support, she added to Tann's formidable influence.

Another of Tann's friends was Ada Gilkey, a reporter for the *Memphis Press Scimitar*. In December of 1929 Gilkey told Tann she was looking for a story. 'Don't know a thing about news', Gilkey reported Tann as saying, 'All I know is the Tennessee Children's Home Society has twenty-five children ready for placement and nowhere to place them – twenty-five children who will have to make the most of a boarding house Christmas'. Gilkey realized that this was news, though not in the traditional male sense, and she began an annual Christmas campaign to find adoptive homes for children at the TCHS. The first story was wildly successful. 'Ten minutes after the first picture appeared ... the deluge began', Gilkey reported. Twelve years later the Christmas baby campaign had led to the immediate placement of 1,400 babies and the *Chicago Sun* had 'adopted' the practice. The ploy not only found homes for babies, but it also sold papers and ensured Gilkey a special place on the paper. The *Scimitar* continued to publish articles by her about the TCHS through 1951.[62]

If Tann quieted local opposition by presenting herself as a woman operating in a woman's sphere, she gained power and prestige by making clear her professional resumé. She pointed out repeatedly in the press and her annual reports that TCHS was following the best, the most progressive, adoption practices. Along with smiling pictures of babies and stories of her father the judge, Tann assured the public that she was following the best social work practices: studying every child, investigating every home, and providing a year's probationary period. Occasionally she wrote a letter to the local paper offering her professional evaluation of certain adoption policies. The national media also consulted her on adoption issues.[63]

Tann made it clear in her annual reports that she was also not the only professional running the Memphis Branch. In 1946, for example, she paid tribute to the chairman of the Board, Mrs M. J. McCormack who had died that year. Mrs McCormack, she pointed out, had a law degree and was admitted to the bar.

> She was one of the organizers of the Memphis Children's Bureau; first head of the Women's Division of the Memphis Community Fund, and one of the originators of the Community Fund and Council of Social Agencies. She was on the Executive Committee of State Conference of Social Work. She was active in all social welfare work of the City and State.[64]

While Tann publicly endorsed social work standards she also spoke directly to those who wished to adopt. She understood the cultural shift which was making it possible for infertile women to express their desire for and fulfil their idea of a family with a child. Tann made clear the power that her job gave her: the power to give or take away a baby at a time when the demand for adoptable babies far outweighed supply. The TCHS Memphis Branch's annual reports were filled with photographs of adorable babies. 'The laugh of a child will make the holiest day more sacred still ...' the 1946 report announced and, the 1947 report, 'A child is the plan of God, a distinct, wonderful work begun by Him to be completed by you'. Filled with pictures and sent throughout the nation, the reports equated children with religion and suggested that only with children was a home a 'real home'.[65] Many of the members of Memphis Branch board had adopted children with the help of Tann. As one director commented, 'She did for me what God himself couldn't do'.[66]

Although she claimed the status of a nationally recognized child placement specialist, Tann violated basic social work standards. She made no effort to place children within families with similar religious backgrounds. Abe Waldauer, one of the city's most prominent attorneys, was a board member. From 1940 on, he served as its legal counsel. Waldauer had two adopted children. Although he did not adopt through Tann, he understood the difficulties that national social work standards could create for those who wanted to adopt. Waldauer was Jewish, and professional placement standards called for a child's religion be matched with that of its adoptive parents. Waldauer was a Zionist who travelled across the country urging the creation of a Jewish homeland. He also, the evidence suggests, found adoptive homes for the children at the TCHS. Those investigating the illegal practices of the TCHS in 1951 found that forty-one children whose adoptions were pending in New York were placed in Jewish families. The investigators concluded, 'it appears that it will be impossible to establish for more than three or four ... any Jewishness in their natural family heritage'.[67]

Tann also provided no time for young women to think about the choice that they were making. 'We found many occasions of babies taken from their mothers at the hospitals when they were only a few hours old and placed in nursing homes in and about Memphis', an investigator found. Mary Reed, one of the few unwed mothers who challenged the TCHS with a *habeas corpus* surrendered her son the day after he was born in 1943. She testified in the suit that she had signed a release while still hazy with anesthesia. She thought she was only agreeing to have her child boarded temporarily. Her physician claimed that Reed and her mother had arranged to give up the child two months before it was born. No matter who was telling the truth, Reed surrendered her child at a time when she was most vulnerable.[68] Furthermore, the TCHS emphasized single women's inadequacy. Attorney Waldauer wrote of his cross examination of one young woman, even 'her own counsel has indicated that I have convinced her of her unworthiness'.[69]

Beginning in 1941, in spite of the authority given her by tradition, professionalism and her job, Tann faced increasing questions about her practices. In 1941 the Child Welfare League expelled the TCHS from its ranks. The TCHS, it explained, had made hasty placements without careful study, falsified its records and placed too many children out of state.[70]

In 1944, Dr Clyde Croswell resigned his position as pediatrician for the TCHS Receiving Home, claiming that the staff had ignored his order not to accept any new children during a diarrhoea epidemic. As a result, he claimed, forty or fifty children died. Later, Croswell told the papers that when he had 'offered to show (the board members) the list of infants that had died at the time

– a staggering toll – they didn't want to see it'. Tann had told them already that the deaths were exaggerated.[71]

Two years later, Shelby County Probate Court Judge Sam Bates wrote to Public Welfare Commissioner William Shoaf asking that the Department make a 'thorough and unbiased' investigation of the Home. Citing dozens of complaints against the TCHS in Memphis, he concluded that 'unless these charges are untrue, I shall feel compelled to discontinue the sanctioning of adoptions sponsored by the Tennessee Children's Home Society'. When no investigation followed, Bates refused to accept any TCHS adoption requests. Undeterred, the TCHS referred its adoptive parents to the county courts outside of Memphis.[72]

It was not until 1950 that Governor Gordon Browning, recently re-elected, appointed Robert L. Taylor, member of the Memphis Bar Association, to conduct a full-scale legal investigation. 'For many years', Welfare Commissioner J. O. McMahan reported to the Governor in his request for the investigation, 'I had heard the weirdest forms of stories about Georgia Tann and the TCHS. Stories were being repeated that the local nursing homes were filled with unwed mothers who year after year returned and gave birth to children for the market'. Other stories suggested that children born to patients at the Western State Hospital for the Insane were being placed for adoption with false background information. 'By far the most often repeated rumor was that children were being exported to California and New York in large numbers for a price while childless couples of Memphis and West Tennessee begged for a child without success'.

In a short time, Taylor found evidence to confirm all the rumours. The full extent of the TCHS practices was never ascertained, however, for the TCHS destroyed a large number of records during the investigation. When Tann died of cancer almost immediately after the first press reports of the investigation, the Governor stopped the investigation and the state took over the TCHS operation.[73]

Taylor, however, described the workings of the operation. Between 1940 and 1950, the Memphis branch of the TCHS placed at least 1,016 children outside of Tennessee and claimed in its reports to the Nashville office that the children were placed in the state. The TCHS would send one employee to California and New York with four or five children and charge each adopting couple for the cost of the flight and the hotel stay. Couples paid an average of $750 for a child when the actual cost was around $100. In addition, many foster parents contributed large donations to the Memphis Home. They had been assured that their contributions would pay for improving the receiving home; the contributions went instead into Tann's personal bank account.

The investigation confirmed that the TCHS of Memphis made no investigation into the background of the children and in many cases provided false descriptions to the foster parents. Later, two adoptees searching for their families found that Tann had given them identical backgrounds. Their mothers, according to Tann, were eighteen, American Protestants, of English, Irish and Scotch extraction, and 5'6" and 120 pounds. They had blond hair, blue eyes, fair complexions, and a high school education. Their fathers were twenty-one, 5'8" and 175 pounds, in excellent health, and had served in the navy overseas. Both had been respected in the community and had no inheritable diseases.[74]

Taylor's investigation revealed that far from being the ideal American couple described by Tann, many of the natural parents had backgrounds that would make their children not suitable for adoption by any of the contemporary professional standards. Taylor confirmed that one young girl gave birth to a child by her own father; that an unmarried inmate of the State Hospital for the insane had three children and placed all three; that one mother had received recurring treatment for syphilis well along into her pregnancy; and that several couples were of mixed race. A large number of the couples were fictitiously identified as Jewish.[75]

In addition, Taylor made clear that he and others questioned the appropriateness of placing a child from an impoverished family into a wealthy home. One couple that had been promised a child 'were people of considerable means and maintained a high cultural and social standard of living'. The Home had promised them a child whose social history 'suggested many questions that required further exploration concerning the child's educability in terms of the achievements and cultural level of the natural parents'. Although 'there had been no psychological evaluation of the child's own development which physically appeared to be normal', Taylor suggested that in such a case the risk of future rejection of the child was too high 'because of the possible inability to measure up to the high intellectual standards of these adoptive parents'. When the Division of Welfare took over the case, they placed the child in a home 'where there is realistic understanding and acceptance of the infant's average intellectual endowments'.[76]

While national publicity of the Tennessee Children's Home Society scandal focused most attention on the married couples who lost their children without due process or on the adoptive parents who unwittingly adopted an 'unplaceable' child, Tann also violated standards with regards to unwed mothers.[77]

Both Taylor and court records confirm that the TCHS used coercive measures with unmarried mothers. Tann, he said, 'sent envoys to doctors and hospitals ... advising them that the THCS would gladly accept unmarred expectant mothers for prenatal care and advised them that the Society would pay all expenses until the child had been born'.

The mothers signed surrenders of their children when they were pregnant and the TCHS had complete control over the child as soon as it was born. 'We found on many occasions babies taken from their mothers at the hospitals when they were only a few hours old and placed in nursing homes in and about Memphis', Taylor reported. One mother wrote about the promises that were never kept, 'Please help me git my baby back. I am so heart broken about the way it has bin take from me until I am about to have a nervous break down ... Miss Tann said she would all ways let me hear about her but it is just like asking about the dead ...'[78]

No matter what home or agency an unwed mother appealed to in the 1920s, 30s and 40s in Tennessee she almost certainly came in contact with and in most cases took assistance from the TCHS.[79] It would be wrong to assume, however, that all roads led to Tann only because she was so powerful and unethical. A closer look at the maternity homes in Tennessee in these decades reveals the way in which efforts to implement new professional standards severely limited the options for rural unwed mothers. Either by withholding funds from those homes that didn't comply with the standards or by insisting that homes adopt standards that appealed to middle-class women, the pressure to standardize services to unwed mothers dramatically altered the social landscape. This pressure to standardize came at the same time as rural communities were facing a severe economic crisis.

For those in rural Tennessee the depression persisted for a long time. It started at the end of World War 1 when the down turn in the agricultural economy affected tenant and small farmers alike. Most had turned to cash crops after the Civil War and were thus dependent on tobacco and cotton production. In 1920 the price for each fell dramatically. Although the average farm size was decreasing, rural families continued to be much larger than their urban counterparts. Once part of a successful economic strategy, by the third decade of the century large families were more of an economic disadvantage. Children were limited in bringing in extra money when the 1938 Fair Labor Standards Act prohibited child labour, the New Deal Agricultural Adjustment Act paid farmers not to plant, and the jobs that had once supplied seasonal income dried up. As the Depression deepened and those who had left the farm returned to it as a last resort, the farm families struggled to support their own.[80]

Surveys of conditions in the rural areas confirmed the destitution of its residents. In 1937 W. C. Holley found that 'the dietary inadequacies of the agricultural families at the bottom of the economic ladder in the southern states are accompanied by poor housing' and high rates of illness. He cited a study of the dietary intake of six southern counties including Hawkins, Tennessee, that found, 'The results were little short of appalling'. An earlier study in Jackson, Tennessee found only two of 121 homes had running water and only four had electric lights. Many had no toilets. In spite of extreme poverty, the same studies found that welfare support was extremely limited. 'On a per capita basis', Holley noted, 'the south has not received as much federal aid as most other sectors'.[81]

Under these conditions, unwed mothers would have had an especially difficult time supporting themselves. In Maine a position as a domestic might offer a woman an opportunity to keep at least one child with her where she worked. In Tennessee, such jobs were not as often available to white women because black domestic workers were forced to work for less. In addition, the textile mills had so many applicants that they could, and did, restrict their jobs to those whites who carefully followed the middle class model of decorous behaviour.[82]

If unwed mothers had difficulty finding jobs, they also had difficulty finding financial support. Until Social Security funds became available in 1937, public aid in Tennessee was provided almost exclusively through the county poor farms. As the state had no standards for the farms and ran them by contract, investigators periodically submitted 'horror reports' on the conditions that prevailed in them to the legislature. The Tennessee Legislature passed a mother's pension law in 1915 but the law specifically stated that the benefits provided under the law were limited to 'proper persons morally, mentally and physically'. In 1921 the legislature amended the law to allow counties to extend the benefits to children of unmarried mothers but only two disbursed any aid for it. In 1937 Tennessee began to provide Aid to Dependent Children with funds from the federal government. Once again, however, the benefits were limited to children whose homes were deemed 'suitable'.[83]

We have no descriptions of the lives of the poor rural unwed mothers, but the lives of other poor rural single mothers suggest the desperate condition of their lives. In 1939, Bernice Gibson Pulver's parents and her sister-in-law fought over the custody of her son Edward. Bernice had been three months pregnant with Edward when her husband died of tuberculosis. Bernice returned to her family's farm where she lived for three years until she remarried. When Bernice found it 'impossible to keep employed regularly so as to enable her to support her children', her sister-in-law offered to adopt him. Bernice's parents contested the adoption. They had 'joined in the support of the child from its birth up and will continue all types of aid', they argued. But the court concluded that returning the child to his grandparents was not in the best interests of the child. The Wisemans had two bedrooms for nine to twelve people. The house lacked screening, the water was 'very bad' and tubercolosis was prevalent in the family.[84]

In spite of the dire poverty, perhaps because of it, rural women sought out the services of Georgia Tann even when other options were open to them. They especially did so when social work standards limited their options. In the first three decades of the twentieth century there were five unwed mothers homes in Tennessee and all of them provided free room, board and medical care for those who could not afford to pay. Nevertheless, in spite of their critical economic conditions, single pregnant women chose only to go to two. When the social service community systemized its fund raising and imposed uniform standards on all charitable organizations, one home that had been popular with rural women closed and the other changed so that it became attractive to middle class women from across the country. Whether the rural white women no longer found the home suited their needs or they couldn't compete with others who were applying for admission can not be known. What is certain is that the rural white women turned to Tann in great numbers. Denny Glad, who founded Tennessee's Right to Know to help members who had been separated by adoption find one another, pointed to 1937 as the time when Georgia Tann began her wholesale adoption practice. That was also the year when unwed mothers homes lost their diversity.

The homes in Nashville and Chattanooga were affiliated with the Florence Crittenton Mission. The Mission emphasized the importance of keeping mother and child together. Nevertheless, the evidence suggests that in 1920 a substantial portion of the women in the Nashville Home placed their infants for adoption. A later history of the Home stated that at this time the Home placed pictures of babies available for adoption regularly in the local papers and that there was a standing adoption committee. In 1920 the Home placed ten children.[85]

A US Children's Bureau survey recognized the Chattanooga Home as being one of two homes in the state to encourage mothers to keep their children.[86] It did so, however, by emphasizing the need to transform all the young women who came to the Home. The *Tennessean* pointed out in 1898 that it was a 'miracle of God's love' to see the 'often irresponsible young mothers urged to love and care for their children' and to note the result. In 1918 it noted that the babies in the Home 'were not occasions for rejoicing', but, nevertheless, had 'wormed their way into hardened hearts, and are now in their subtle, baby way, helping the Home to "bring back" those girl mothers'. A mother had to agree to stay six months with her child, it continued. 'Invariably she reluctantly promises and even at the birth of the child, it is frequently noticed that the mother is indifferent toward her baby'. But as the child grew older, motherly love was awakened. 'Even the most stubborn, hardened girl has never failed to respond to the caress of baby fingers, and not once in the history of the institution has a mother who stayed with her baby deserted it'.[87]

Both homes had trouble appealing to pregnant women. Chattanooga regularly reported a low number of residents and Nashville a high number of runaways. In 1898 and in 1900, the Chattanooga Home noted that it had only nine residents though it could accommodate twenty-five. Even in 1942, when World War 2 was 'increasing their work', the Nashville Home was not filled to capacity.[88]

There were three homes in Memphis. Each had responded in a different way to the dominant culture that placed men in authority over women's reputations and that emphasized the importance of a woman's chastity. Each was also pressured by the local Community Chest to adopt new social work standards..[89] The three homes as a result offer a window into how the developing national influence of professional social workers affected rural Tennessee unwed mothers

The Woman's Christian Association Home, now called the Ella Oliver Home, continued to emphasize the importance of reputation and to support men's role in protecting it. In its 1936 fundraising appeal board members pointed out that it was the 'only local home for the un-married mother where the patient is NOT sent to the hospital for delivery'. It provided a refuge, a place where women could find seclusion and privacy and have her secrecy 'faithfully guarded'.[90]

While the Home promised secrecy it did not offer women a choice but instead cooperated with men who wished to protect their daughters' reputations. Denny Glad, who founded Tennessee's Right to Know to help those separated by adoption search for one another, described the women who came to the Ella Oliver Home as 'young women from small rural areas around here who had become pregnant and whose families had sent them to a maternity home ... and would not allow them to return home with the children'.[91] Newspaper accounts, scattered adoption records and social service surveys corroborate her findings. Many women who entered the WCA Home released their babies even before they were born to the Tennessee Children's Home Society and most left the Ella Oliver Home a month after their delivery without their child.[92]

Glad chronicled the way that the Ella Oliver Home used coercive measures to support fathers' desires to protect the reputations of their daughters. She told the stories of two women who delivered their children in the Home in 1924. One was the daughter of a Baptist minister in a 'little town over in Arkansas'. She was not given any choice about what to do with her child, she later told Glad. She had run away with the baby when it was a month old, but, Glad reported, the 'Ella Oliver people got the police after her and they caught her at the bus station and brought her back'.

> When they were ready to place the child, they forced her to stand at the head of the stairs. The people who got the child came in and they handed the baby over to them and she really was restrained at the top of the stairs there while they, they went with the baby. When she left there she was very bitter, very angry, at her family, at society, at everybody.[93]

The other was from a family with 'deep fundamentalist beliefs'. 'Her father put her on the train in Louisville, Kentucky, and brought her over here, would not ride in the same car with her. He rode in one car, she rode in another. And he delivered her to the steps, he did not even go in the building, and left her'. Ruby Mink McElhaney told her story to the newspaper. She was eighteen when she came to the Home from Jonesboro, Arkansas. In 1930 she told the *Commercial Appeal* of the pressure. 'I wanted to keep my baby but my father wanted me to give her up', she said. 'And of course, the people at the Home gave me a lot of pressure.[94]

The Home struggled to retain its practices when they came in conflict with the new social-work standards. When the Community Fund pressured the Home to register its residents with the Social Service Exchange and hire a case-worker, the WCA board refused. The Fund then dropped the Ella Oliver Home from its list of participating agencies. At the same time, the Home was struggling to justify its existence as 'fewer girls were coming all the time'. Often, many of the Home's thirty beds remained empty. In 1937 the Home closed.[95]

A second home, run by a working-class, self-made minister offered women a certain element of control and attracted rural women in large numbers. Unwilling to adopt professional standards, however, it closed for lack of funds. In 1916 A. J. Vallery came to Memphis to provide for 'unfortunate girls'. He approached businessmen and firms of Memphis and drove through the country districts of Tennessee, Mississippi and Arkansas soliciting funds. In this way he raised enough money to purchase five acres, 'the old Hunt estate', in North Memphis. For the next twenty-one years this Nazarene minister, pastor of the First Church, battled city officials in his efforts to provide room, board and some means of making a livelihood to unwed mothers and their children. Vallery himself came from a poor rural background. He had a radical economic analysis and offered the women an opportunity to redeem themselves by accepting religious conversion. He also encouraged them to keep their children. His efforts were marked by constant economic struggles and conflicts with local authorities.

Vallery was born near Lake Charles, Louisiana, in 1868. He worked in a mill until he was thirty when he experienced a religious conversion and entered the ministry. He began as a Methodist but within five years had accepted the creed of the Nazarene Church. Vallery founded homes for unwed mothers in New Orleans and Monroe, Louisiana, and El Paso, Texas, before coming to Memphis. There he became pastor of the First Church. His obituary in the *Press Scimitar* claimed that he had a total of six months schooling but that he 'studied diligently all his life, reading all of his spare time'. 'White haired, erect', the *Scimitar* said, 'he hurled patient defiance at the Memphis authorities for years on behalf of the rescue home founded for unwed mothers'. His only son, chief physician of the I. C. Railroad, was one of the medical advisors of the Home.[96]

Vallery established a board that included three women and five men. He kept cows and chickens on the Home lot and maintained a 'mattress factory' in the upstairs room where the women stuffed mattresses with donated cotton. A 1922 promotional pamphlet showed six babies in cribs surrounded by other children. The age of the other children, some apparently close to three years, suggests that women stayed in the Home for long periods of time. A 1923 pamphlet announced that Bethany had cared for 215 girls and babies the previous year. 90

per cent of these, the pamphlet claimed, were 'blessedly converted. At least 85 percent are standing true to God. A number of them have married and are doing well'.[97]

Like the board of the Ella Oliver Home, Vallery resisted the new standards being imposed by the Community Fund. Like them also, he suffered the consequences. Bethany was supported entirely by donations and the women's work until 1922 when the Community Fund assumed the task of fundraising for the Home. When the Fund asked for an accounting of the budget, however, Vallery refused to comply. The Fund also questioned the unsanitary conditions and inadequate heating in the Home where there was an open fire in the nursery. When the Fund refused to solicit funds for the Home unless Vallery resigned, the Board forced his resignation. He immediately established another Home and called it Beulah, a word designating peace.[98]

From then on, his obituary stated, he was in 'almost constant conflict with city officials in his efforts to support his work'. In 1924 Chancellor F. H. Heiskell placed a restraining order on him after a jury had found he had no right to interfere with the Bethany board. In 1929 during the Christmas season, he was arrested for leading a 'parade of protest' planned to capture attention and gain funds for Beulah Home. The judge fined him one dollar; then paid the fine himself. In 1932 when the city's mendicancy board refused to permit him to solicit funds, Vallery staged another 'parade of protest'. In 1933 he staged a hunger strike. Drawing his will and making arrangements for his funeral he announced, in a public speech after his last meal, that the strike would end 'either in my death or in a victory for my cause'.[99]

Vallery died on January 25, 1937. Two days later the nineteen women in Beulah Home 'walked out'. Dr. Vallery's family had moved in to take over the operation of the Home, so 'we decided to move out', the young women said. 'We've been cold and hungry. We've had little heat and inadequate food'. Although the matron had been buying some green vegetables with her own money, the women noted, 'we've led pretty much of a hand-to-mouth existence and we can't go on'. The women went directly to Georgia Tann of the TCHS who called together representatives of the social service agencies to help work out a plan for them. Within an hour the agencies had placed every woman. 'The girls turned to Miss Tann', the paper reported, 'because her agency has kept a watchful eye on the home to see that infants had proper care, and in many instances placed them for permanent adoption'.[100]

Vallery left little record of his work beyond his conflicts with authorities but what record there is suggests that he offered women redemption and the opportunity to work and to keep their babies, and that he regularly attracted a large number of women.[101] As a pastor for a Pentecostal Church, he perhaps believed that conversion absolved unwed mothers of their past sins. That he kept track of conversions is clear from his 1922 promotional pamphlet that recorded the number of conversions.[102] His was one of only two homes in the state that encouraged women to keep their children according to a 1922 children's services survey. In 1935, when the Ella Oliver Home was reporting that it had 'fewer girls coming all the time' Valerie claimed to have served seventy-one women.

The third home – Bethany Home after Vallery resigned – accepted professional advice and thrived. Over time, however, the services it provided became more attractive to middle-class women than to the poor rural women Vallery had created his home to serve.

The Bethany board made its first choice to accept professional advice when it forced Vallery to resign in 1922.[103] In 1927, Judge Charles Burch acknowledged the change this had meant for Bethany when he recommended a change in the charter as the 'wording used by the Nazarene Church no longer applied'. From then on the Home accepted women from every denomination.[104]

In 1934 the Community Fund voted to support only one unwed mothers home. According to Lois Ware, long-time superintendent and executive director of Bethany, Bethany board members agreed to all the requests of the Fund including hiring a full-time caseworker. The Fund chose to support Bethany and by 1937 Bethany was the only unwed mothers' home in the city.[105]

From the beginning Bethany combined elements from each of the other homes. Similar to the Board of the Ella Oliver Home, the Bethany board women were prominent in Memphis. They stressed the need for protection and relied heavily on the adoption services of the Tennessee Children's Home Society (TCHS). Like the Vallery Home, Bethany stressed the fact that the women who came to the home did so on their own.

Bethany was unique, however, in that it accepted the Community Fund's demand that it comply with professional social-work standards. With acceptance of professional standards came a new definition of illegitimacy – one that made choice an essential issue (and marriage a hoped for outcome). Illegitimacy, Bethany staff and board members repeatedly asserted from this time on, was not a matter of sin or economics but of personal despair. Women got pregnant out of wedlock not because they had fallen or were poor but because they had not been loved. What they needed was to be supported with love. In return, their love for their children, if they chose to exercise it, would make them whole.

While this new definition of illegitimacy brought widespread support for the Home it also changed the nature of the services provided and ultimately changed the population that the Home served. From then on the population of residents in the home became increasingly better educated and less impoverished until they became more like the members of the board and the people it appealed to for funds.[106]

The gradual transformation of the Home was completed in the 1950s. In 1957 Lois Ware, who had managed the Home for thirty-one years told the public, 'It used to be that unwed mothers who came to Bethany ... were generally products of 'underprivileged backgrounds' but times have changed. Now the majority ... are from brackets that you certainly could not consider underprivileged'. She pointed to the educational backgrounds of the sixty-five women served in 1956 as proof. Only thirteen had failed to complete tenth grade; more than half had graduated from high school; seven had attended college'. As the women in the Home became more like those who supported the Home, the financial support of the Home increased. As the Exchange Club noted in 1951, because of Bethany, many girls 'who might have been the daughters of any of us, have been lifted from an abyss of hopeless despair and restored to useful places in society'. The Home no longer needed to transform the women, it only needed provide them with affection to restore them to their former place.[107]

From the time that Bethany accepted the Community Fund's call for implementing professional social work standards, the Home gained widespread support from the community. In 1935 when the Beulah Home was asking for $7,000 to survive and the Ella Oliver Home was making an urgent 'Mother's Day' appeal, Mrs Dan Hamilton gave Bethany $7,500 to build a new wing and $1,000 to create an occupational therapy department. 'Representatives of all city departments, of all local social agencies, leaders in Memphis philanthropic enterprises' attended the opening of the new wing and were unanimous in applauding 'the favor Mrs. Hamilton has done us', the newspaper reported.[108]

Mrs Hamilton was not a lone supporter. Throughout the 1930s, 40s and 50s, lawyers, doctors, teachers and ministers donated their services to the home. Bethany acknowledged this widespread support with an annual tea and open house. In 1941, two hundred people attended the tea 'overlaid with lace' and afterwards had an 'inspection tour' of the home. In 1944, the Exchange Club began its annual $500 contribution to the Home. In 1949 it provided the Home with an additional $4,500 to build another wing; in 1951 it began to provide a 'rehabilitation loan fund' to enable a woman to 're-establish herself on a firm footing'. The loan fund enabled a woman to repair a broken tooth, go to beauty school or do whatever was necessary to obtain a job that paid well enough to support her and her child.[109]

The services that Bethany provided changed over time and changed with the changing status of its residents. In 1930, for example, Mrs Hamilton opened an occupational therapy room in the Home where women were taught sewing. At the same time, she began the practice of providing every woman who left with a going away suit and a layette for her baby. The Home encouraged the women to come six months prior to delivery to receive prenatal care. It provided a well baby clinic in the Home and took the mothers to the John Gaston Hospital, the charity hospital, for their delivery.[110]

In 1944 the Exchange Club noted that the patients were 'principally those of limited resources'. A year earlier the Club initiated a bridge fund, to provide residents with training and incidentals such as a haircut or dental work to enable them to get a job. The *Press Scimitar* described the image of the 'girl' that the Exchange Club had in mind when it announced the opening of its Bridge Fund. Describing the fund as 'the dream of social workers', it described what it offered to Jane.[111]

Jane was a naive girl from the country who was attracted to the bright lights of the city. She lived in a small Mississippi town and dropped out of school in eighth grade to help her mother take care of the younger children. When World War 2 opened up new job opportunities for women, Jane heard from other girls that Memphis was 'where everyone had a good job and lots of fun'. She came and got a job as a waitress, and then, to her surprise, discovered she had 'as nice a personality as any of the other girls'. 'Jane had never been around a lot of people before but she liked them and wanted to be like them', the paper reported. She went out on blind dates, found a steady, and soon was pregnant. 'You could look down your nose at her', the story admitted; the Bridge Fund of Bethany chose to provide her with a loan so that she could get training and not be forced to go back to the 'same environment that was partly responsible for her error'. Jane could go to beauty school or enter one of the defence schools. At any rate, she would improve her situation, gain self-respect, pay back her loan and achieve 'self-sufficiency. She would then no longer need agency help'.[112]

The story rooted Jane's problem in her personality. Being from such a large family, she hadn't known that she could be loved for herself. The story also suggested that Jane was different from many of the *Scimitar* readers, commenting that her environment had been 'partly responsible for her error'. The Bridge Fund, it suggested, promised to make her self-sufficient.[113]

Within the next five years the public presentation of the women who came to Bethany changed. As the public description of the women changed, so did the services. While in 1944 the Exchange Club referred to the residents as 'principally those of limited resources', in 1948 it reported that they came 'from no social group'. In 1951 it claimed that they 'might have been the daughters of any of us'.[114]

Which came first, the changed description (and public image) of the women in the Home or the changed population is hard to say, but clearly by the late 1940s the city's newspapers were presenting a new image of unwed mothers – one that called for sympathy and understanding. Illegitimacy, the stories suggested again and again, was part of a deep underlying personal problem – one that caused an individual more pain than the individual caused society. The new definition allowed the community to continue to define pregnancy outside of marriage as wrong and at the same time to call for love and understanding instead of punishment for the pregnant woman. It did so by stressing the anguish the women experienced for what they had done and in this way justified their return to the community.[115]

'A girl who is going to become a mother without a marriage license has violated a moral code. It cannot be condoned', the *Commercial Appeal* announced in an article on social services for unwed mothers in 1951. Nevertheless, the article continued, while not minimizing a girl's mistakes or her moral obligations, the society should help her and 'mold her gently into a useful happy member of society'.[116]

The case histories of unwed mothers were filled with suffering, the Home and newspaper accounts confirmed. 'They are stories of the bewildered, the shamed, the desperate, the tortured', a newspaper suggested in 1949.[117] Unlike the earlier Jane who was identified by a plain and common name, the later residents were all referred to as Mary – most likely to remind readers of the Mary Magdalene and Christian compassion. They were also, according to newspaper reports, invariably driven by their plight to consider suicide.

A *Memphis Press Scimitar* article of 1946, for example, described how a businessman and his wife saved a young woman who was wading out into the river to drown herself. 'She was desperate', her rescuers claimed she told them. 'She had tried every way in the world to get a message through to the father of her unborn child to tell him of her condition. She was certain he would want to marry her if only he knew'. Her boyfriend, however, was working as a technician on a secret government project. Her family, horrified at the disgrace, told her she must give her baby up for adoption. This she could not do and yet she could not bear the idea of her child being branded for life with the stigma of illegitimacy. 'There was nothing to do but kill herself, she sobbed'.[118]

A 1953 clipping commented, 'There's magic in having a baby ... And there's grief and anguish and black despair as well'. Mary was a waitress with no money whose new employer had fired her when he discovered she was pregnant. She took a cab to the bridge. The cab driver talked her into not jumping and took her to Bethany. There she received medical attention and the best of food and 'her mental condition improved steadily'. Two weeks after her baby was born, she left for a new job. At her request, her child was placed for adoption. She took up her interrupted life, the paper concluded, a 'wiser woman matured in the crucible of travail'.[119]

If the women were desperate to kill themselves, they were also filled with love for their children. This love, Bethany suggested, could help to save the child. In 1948 a newspaper article highlighted a picture of babies. 'These babies did not ask for life', the caption stated. 'Though deprived of the loving protection of a legal father, they are given a chance in this world'.[120].

The statistics that Bethany offered to the public confirmed that the population of Bethany Home was changing. By 1947 the Home could report that the seventy-three women admitted that year 'were not illiterate, nor were they from the poorest families'. Twenty-five had completed high school; the largest group consisted of students in high school and colleges. In 1951 the Home reported that the residents were 'older, better educated and better trained to earn good salaries' than previously. In 1957 Lois Ware wrote that 'the majority ... are from brackets that you certainly could not consider underprivileged'.[121]

As the population became increasingly more middle class, the board implemented changes that got rid of, or hid, the institutional aspects of the home. In 1947 the board changed the title of the superintendent to housemother and the title of the secretary to executive director. Sometime shortly thereafter, they dropped the word 'training' from Bethany Training School. In the 1950s, the director of Baptist Memorial Hospital offered his hospital for the delivery of Bethany women. 'What this has meant to Bethany girls', Ware reported, 'is difficult to put into words'.[122] As the hospital where the residents had formally delivered was the one hospital in Memphis that took the poor, one can assume that one thing that this meant was an escape from the stigma of charity.

While the Board continued to offer employment training, it emphasized that it taught residents how to run a home. 'They work in the nursery, serve food, learn cooking, take sewing lessons – do all the chores that arise around the house', the newspaper reported in 1949. It also continued to require women to pay board if they were able to do so and it noted in 1957 that many of the residents were unable to do so. This was not, however, because they were poor, Ware pointed out, but because they didn't 'want their families to know of their predicament'.[123]

Meanwhile, protecting the woman's secrecy became ever more important. 'One of the main reasons for Bethany Home's existence is to shield these girls from stigma and ostracism', Miss Ware said in 1953. Even when the girls did keep their children it required 'complete disassociation with former ties'. In 1954, Ware and the president of the board, Mrs Scott Stewart, opposed the development of a filling station across the street. Not only would the filling station create noise, they stated, it 'would infringe on the privacy and seclusion of the Bethany Home, possibly revealing to the public the identify of the home's unmarried mothers'.[124]

But if the Home was a place of concealment, it was also a place of choice. Bethany emphasized that most of the women who came to the Home applied on their own, 'many by going to the Home and knocking on the door'. Once in the Home, the executive director emphasized to the paper in 1957, they made their own decisions about plans for the babies, 'without any influence from the home'. They could keep them, she noted, or place them for adoption'.[125]

There are no available records, so it is impossible to know what happened to the women who came or what choices they made for their babies. The evidence suggests that this too changed over time. In 1935 a nurse in the Home reported that, 'Most of these girls make every effort to keep their babies. When they are strong and able to return to their positions or find new ones, they find some way to provide for the baby and keep it'. A decade later, a newspaper report claimed that one-quarter kept their children.[126] Whether the residents chose to keep their babies or not, the Home for the first time was calling on the sympathies of the public to support a young woman making her own choice. It could do so in part because the women were no longer poor and, therefore, did not threaten to produce one more baby that needed support.

The role of the Home was to provide love and understanding. 'I try to take their mother's place and encourage them to come talk to me', said Mrs Eva Neill who had been the house mother from 1947 to 1960.[127] The combination of love and choice was described by one woman who wrote that her heart 'would not let me rest until I had written it'. She thanked the executive director for making Bethany a haven, 'a place I needed desperately' and the matron, for the 'helping hand, those well-spoken words, and the shoulder that was there, ready'. Even a mother 'could never have had a more understanding heart'.

> When I entered...I felt my world had ended. I had expected to be behind lock and key and to have all privilege denied me. I had heard it was compulsory that all babies be adopted, that outside contacts were forbidden and many other things too dreadful to mention. Thank God! They were ALL UNTRUE.[128]

The Home provided, in short, what the men of Exchange would want for their daughters.

With this combination of 'tender love, kindness, understanding and instruction', the Exchange commented in 1956, rehabilitation was 'easy and successful'. For Vallery who founded Bethany in 1916, the name may have implied that Jesus was able to work the most spectacular miracle, raising Lazarus from the dead. Forty years later the Exchange stated specifically that Bethany in Memphis, like Bethany in Judea, was 'a place of Christian love, friendship and understanding'. Earlier Homes in Maine and Tenessee had demanded transformation through religious conversion or through hard work and commitment to support oneself and one's child. By the 1950s Bethany provided a place of concealment, where a pregnant woman could go and have an easy time and come out pretending that the pregnancy hadn't happened.[129]

The Nashville and Chattanooga Homes were also changing their practices and attracting more women. When World War 2 arrived, and, with it, a dramatic increase in the illegitimacy rate, there were three remaining homes for unwed mothers in Tennessee – all of which were filled to capacity.[130] All of them also now had to turn women away. In 1946, for example, the Nashville Home referred as many women as it served in its first three months. 1949 Bethany noted that it had been crowded almost to capacity for some time, but in 1949 the situation became acute.[131]

Not coincidentally, they all also offered the utmost secrecy and choice. As the director for the Chattanooga Home noted in 1945 for the first time, the women entered in 'strictest confidence' and each woman who entered received a code name. If people called asking for the girl by her real name, the staff told them there was 'no such girl at the home'.[132] He placed their children when they were in desperate need and did so with no questions asked.

Poor rural women made choices. They chose not to go to homes where the staff looked down on them or where they had no choice. By the 1950s the Homes in Memphis had changed. They all offered support and choice. They also, however, could choose whom they wanted to serve. Whether rural white unwed mothers did not choose to go to these homes, or could not compete with others who chose to go to them, is not known. One can understand, however, that they might have chosen to place their children through Georgia Tann in any event. Tann was from Hickory, a small rural town in Mississippi, and she may have let young pregnant women know that she understood where they were coming from. In a time of extreme economic crisis she offered to place their children with no questions asked and no matter what the conditions of their births. In addition, she provided them with room, board and medical care though their delivery. With no casework investigations, they could feel secure that their communities would have no reason to suspect their pregnancy if they gave up their child or be subject to scrutiny by strangers. If Tann didn't investigate their families, she did offer – in the Tennessee tradition – to place their children in homes superior to their own, in homes 'capable of lavishing every affection and advantage which wealth can give'.[133] She might even place them with movie stars.

At a time when three-quarters of the placements were made informally, Tann also offered the women an element of control. The TCHS adoption agreement required adopting parents to 'rear, nurture, and support said child tenderly and affectionately and give it a Christian education'. Furthermore, they had to agree not to give the child away to a third party without consent of the TCHS. If they failed to follow this agreement, the TCHS could retake the child 'with all her clothing, wherever she may be, whether in this or any other state or nation'. Later investigation would show that Tann did not enforce these requirements, but she publicly supported this idea when asked her opinion as an adoption expert. As she noted of a couple that wanted to return a child with cerebral palsy.

If the White Plains couple had borne this child they would have had to cope with his handicap. Whatever their solution would have been, it is the answer to their adopted child's problem. They finality of adoption must be upheld or the whole structure of the institution, based upon the concept that 'the adoptive parents stand in the place of the birth parents' is destroyed.[134]

And finally, as the investigation showed, the TCHS placed children who would have been determined 'un-adoptable' by the professional standards of the day – children who were bi-racial, the result of incest or of questionable family background. The TCHS not only placed these children, but placed them in homes that were privileged. Rural white women did not have a wide range of options, but even so they made choices which in turn affected the homes that were opened to them. There was in fact a dialogue between the country and the city, one that lasted well into the twentieth century.

5 PROFESSIONAL STANDARDS IN MAINE: RELYING ON STRANGERS

On 20 October 1939, Maud Morlock, specialist on illegitimacy for the US Children's Bureau, addressed the trends in work with unmarried mothers at the Maine State Conference of Social Welfare in Bangor, Maine. Gertrude Atwood, Superintendent of the Good Samaritan Home, expressed her excitement at the opportunity to hear the latest in the care for unwed mothers and urged all the Good Samaritan Board members to attend. To her surprise and disappointment, Morlock spoke disparagingly of Maine's efforts. In her public address, Morlock pointed out that Maine had one of the highest illegitimacy rates in the country and suggested that the Good Samaritan Home had outlived its need.[1]

For two decades Atwood had enthusiastically promoted cooperation with national social-work organizations. From 1918 on, she regularly announced in her annual reports that the Good Samaritan's cooperation with such agencies was a cause for pride. In the *Annual Report* for 1939, however, following on the heels of Morlock's criticism, she raised a note of caution. There was a tension, Atwood suggested in her report, between keeping what was good of the old and accepting the new. Drawing explicit comparison with Morlock's assertion that it was time to get on with the new, Atwood pointed out that techniques and methods had been changing so rapidly it was hard to keep up with them. She herself preferred the opinion of another Children's Bureau staff member, Field Consultant Mary S. Labaree, who had suggested that workers with unwed mothers would benefit from 'the experience and guidance of those who had been in the field a long time'.[2]

For Atwood, however, the question was not simply one of old versus new. The new standards, she insisted, came out of work in the larger cities.

> Nothing we have seen or heard applied particularly well to work in rural states ... It would be interesting and helpful if the subject could be considered from the standpoint of such rural states as ours where conditions and the character of those we work with are very different from such work with the city girl.[3]

Though professional social-work standards came to Maine through different channels than they came to Tennessee, and though those who brought them emphasized different aspects of the new standards, the end result was the same: limited resources for poor rural unwed mothers. In Tennessee, professionals emphasized the 'deep underlying' psychological causes of illegitimacy and the need to recognize the rights of the unwed mother. This led to making the services they offered more acceptable to middle-class women who increasingly dominated the limited services available. In Maine, professionals stressed the importance of providing increased options to unwed mothers and of limiting institutional control over them. They urged the Good Samaritans to consider adoption, reduce the required length of stay in the home, and offer their services to second offenders. When the Good Samaritans adopted these suggestions, they moved increasingly further away from the practices of the rural communities from which their residents came. As a result, the rural unwed mothers in growing numbers rejected the services the Good Samaritans had to offer.

The Good Samaritan Home had for a long time welcomed interaction with national professional social-work organizations. It began to pay dues to the National Conference of Social Work in 1918, and Atwood regularly attended the annual Maine State Conference of Social Welfare. In 1924, the Good Samaritan's Annual Report noted the 'endorsement of our policies by foremost social service organizations in New England, two of which changed policies along certain lines to conform with ours'. In 1926 it commented on the 'aroused and quickened spirit of progress' among members of the Board through affiliation with the Girl's Social Service League of America and the National Conference of Social Work. This contact with worldwide welfare, it asserted, brought an 'added breadth of vision and increased efficiency for the administration of our policies'. In 1928 it announced that not only had colleges and universities requested information on its methods and policies, but also the Children's Bureau had paid the Home the high compliment of asking for its training policy and 'highly' praised the 'outstanding excellence' of its system of case records.[4]

In 1933, however, Atwood recorded the first note of caution. 'We are keenly awake to the fact that the technique of living and serving is changing swiftly, but despite the bewildering conditions prevailing, we have an abiding faith that a wisdom as permanent as the oldest yesterday of man still endures...'. She was referring not only to the severe economic pressures of the Depression but also to the 'changing trends in the field of work with the unmarried mother'. She called on her fellow Good Samaritans to:

> consecrate ourselves to the task before us, with courage and determination to face the new age, but to conserve the best of the old; to follow truth wherever it leads, and to apply it; to be open mindedly critical of our methods, but alert to our dangers, and to be courageously loyal to our fundamental purposes in our chosen field ...[5]

In contrast to Tennessee, state government in Maine was quick to extend its control over the practices of private welfare organizations through licensing requirements. In 1931 the Legislature created the Department of Health and Welfare with broad licensing and advisory powers. The new department assumed the responsibilities of earlier state boards of Health, Charities and Corrections, and Mother's Aid.[6]

Each division of the new department had its own licensing requirements. By 1935 when the Legislature passed a law requiring child-placing organizations to obtain a license, the Department of Public Welfare required a total of four licenses from the Good Samaritan Home: as an unwed mothers home, a boarding home, a hospital, and a child placing agency.[7]

Maine's licensing requirements became increasingly onerous. At first licences required lengthy reports that involved describing the facility, the numbers served, and the money spent. These may have been time-consuming but they did not interfere with in the operation of the Home. The Bureau of Health, for example, required that the Good Samaritans measure each room in the house and count the number of toilets, faucets, windows, sinks, etc. By 1937, however, representatives from the Bureau of Social Welfare were visiting the Home to inspect its record management systems.[8] In 1938 Miss Fuger from the Bureau spent five-and-a-half hours reading records 'with a critical eye'. From then on, the visits multiplied in number and scope. Mary H. Merrill, who followed Atwood as superintendent, mentioned numerous visits from the Fire Department, the Department of Health and Welfare, the District Sanitary Engineer, and the District Health Officer. In October 1947, Merrill reported that the Director of the Division of Hospital Services 'went through the Home examining every corner from cellar to dormitory' as well as examined the books; and Mr Downy visited 'to get acquainted with our routine'. Mr Downy also suggested that the Board send him its minutes.[9]

In addition, public officials demanded that the Good Samaritan Home change its practices in order to comply with state standards. At first these changes were practical. While they consumed the staff's time and the Home's money, they left the basic structure of the Home intact. In 1936, for example, the Bureau of Social Welfare requested that the Home revise its application blanks; in 1945 the Bureau of Health required it to purchase an oxygen tank and a heated bed for infants and the District Sanitary Engineer required it to make changes in the plumbing and raise all the taps a fraction of an inch.[10]

By the 1940s, however, the state department agencies were placing increasing pressure on the Good Samaritan Home to implement more fundamental change. This pressure extended from requiring board members and staff to participate in educational meetings to threatening to withdraw funds if the Home did not change certain practices.[11]

The changes that the state urged on the Good Samaritans included hiring a social worker to implement an adoption programme, decreasing the length of stay required, and admitting the second offender. In every case the changes moved the Good Samaritan Home further from the local communities that it sought to serve. In every case, as well, the Good Samaritan board resisted the changes. It was only when the Depression and then World War 2 changed the conditions both within and without the Home that the Board complied with the professional social workers' demands.

It was the Depression that persuaded the Good Samaritan Board to accept stranger adoption as an option for its residents. Adoption in Maine was traditionally a community, if not a family, affair. Unlike Tennessee where adoption was considered a means to improve a child's social standing and to ensure the adopting family a line of inheritance, Maine expected adoption to support the status quo. The original Maine adoption statute of 1855 expressly excluded the rights of inheritance and applied only to the rights of custody, obedience, and maintenance. In 1880, the Legislature modified the law to enable those who adopted to include the right of inheritance, but many adopters opted not to do so. The formal adoption decree explicitly called upon the adopting parents to bring up and educate the child 'with reference to the degree and condition of' his or her parents; the most commonly cited reason for the adoption was that the child had been living with the petitioners for an extended period of time.[12]

The preponderance of the adoptions in Maine prior to the mid-1920s occurred between members of the same community or within the same family. Even when the adoption occurred across communities for the purpose of providing support for a child, the parent retained the right to keep in contact with the child. In 1881, for example, Melissa Douglass of Bath surrendered the care and custody of her infant child to a couple. The decree suggests that Melissa may have been seeking to improve her child's social standing as well as provide for its support. She, however, remained nearby. Although she renounced all her rights as a mother she reserved the right to visit the child 'at reasonable times'. The couple was called upon to support and rear the child in a comfortable and proper manner and to provide the advantages afforded by the neighbourhood 'where they do and I shall hereafter reside'.[13]

Appellate court cases, Penobscot County court records, and the Good Samaritan case files all confirm that adoption occurred within communities for the purpose of providing children with practical support when one or both of their parents had died or were unable to care for them. Adopting parents expected the children to help support them in return. As one woman who adopted a girl from the Girls Home in Belfast wrote to Gertrude Atwood in 1921, 'I took her because I had no girl and I needed help'.[14]

The early case records of the Good Samaritan Home support such findings. Out of forty-six cases from 1918 to 1930, only sixteen children were adopted – six by the husbands of the child's mother when she got married, four by relatives or friends, and only five by 'strangers'.[15] In the five cases of 'stranger' adoptions, the mother had either died or abandoned her child for a long period of time. The relatives who adopted included members of the father's family as well as those of the mother. Throughout the 1930s and later, family members of both the child's mother and father continued to take the child informally or through formal adoption proceedings. As one mother of a resident wrote in 1939 when Atwood suggested a possible adoption placement, 'It was never my intention or __'s[16] wish to have the baby go to anyone outside our own family. I intended to tell you ... that my eldest daughter wished to adopt it'.[17]

Community or extended family adoption meant that the mother often had the opportunity to keep in touch with her child after it was placed. The father of Irene's lover adopted her child. He invited her to dinner, found a job for her where he worked so that she could return to the area, and encouraged her to come see her child whenever she wanted to.[18] Even in a case of stranger adoption, the Home did not require – as did the Tennessee Children's Home Society – that the mother agree not to gain information about or make contact with her child.[19]

Adoption by related kin had one further advantage. As family ties were the reason for the adoption, the child's 'adoptability' was not an issue. Her or his mental and physical condition was rarely called into question. When the sister of the man who got Stella pregnant adopted Stella's child, she carried on a long correspondence with Superintendent Atwood. The child's father brought the child presents and insisted that the adopting parents change the child's name back to the name the natural mother had given it. Later the adopting mother wrote to Atwood: 'You spoke about the baby being backward. Of course you know we have no others to compare with so perhaps can not judge but we think she is darling. Of course, we took her on account of her parentage mostly and would probably have loved her anyway'.[20]

The people from Maine chose to adopt within the community not only because they wished to care for their own but also because they distrusted strangers. Mothers, lovers, and the women themselves repeatedly referred to 'strangers' and expressed their distrust of them. 'It is going to be a hard battle for us both. Just think you have got to go among strangers', wrote one man from training camp to his lover who was in the Home. A mother of another resident wrote, 'I don't know how to express myself to you as we are strangers'. Atwood worked to reassure the women and their families that the Home would treat the women and their children, 'in the place of her own kin', as if to reassure them that the Good Samaritans were not strangers.[21]

Social workers began making recommendations related to adoption in the mid 1920s and began at the same time suggesting adoption as an option for unwed mothers.[22] Although many promoted adoption in the state and national social welfare conferences that Atwood and others attended regularly, the Good Samaritans were slow to accept the practice.

It was the conditions of the Depression that led to Atwood's acceptance of adoption as an option. The Depression in Maine came early, stayed late, and hit the rural areas as well as the manufacturing centres. Potato farmers, part-time farmers who supplemented their incomes with work in the woods, and those who earned their living fishing or processing seafood all faced steep declines in their incomes.[23] At first, the severe economic hardship experienced by so many led Atwood to call upon Maine's traditional structures for supporting unwed mothers. Even as well endowed as the Good Samaritan Home was, it could not survive the times without exploring every option for financial support for the women it served. Unable to find jobs for the women in the city, the Good Samaritans sent more back to their homes than ever before. As a result, Atwood noted, more were getting married to the fathers of their children.

With families and the Good Samaritans short on funds, Atwood turned to the courts to obtain child support from the fathers with a vehemence noted even by herself. Her efforts in 1931 were mainly devoted to collecting for board and fees and she felt 'in spirit similar to an ogre or dragon, or some horrible thing. Threats of suits have brought some results, promises galore, some notes and considerable money'. In pursuit of fees and money for the residents, Atwood brought into court unemployed husbands as well as chauffeurs of wealthy summer residents. Of one she commented, 'We had him arrested and, as he could not get bonds, had him committed to jail, but released him upon his personal recognizance as he was worth nothing to us lying in jail'. Of a lawyer who came looking for legal technicalities favourable to his client, a chauffeur, she commented, 'Being a verbose gentleman, he accused us of being narrow-minded, unscientific, and non cooperative, but in spite of all arguments to the contrary we stuck to our guns and after a lengthy session he took his departure'. Atwood noted with pride that she rarely lost a child support suit. In one case where she thought she might lose, she made arrangements with the county attorney to bring the more serious charge of violating the state's age-of-consent law.[24] Atwood did not limit her efforts to the man responsible. She also pushed the towns to provide for the women who had settlements within them and, occasionally, took towns to court to ensure that they did so.

At the same time that the Good Samaritans were working to enforce Maine's traditional support laws, economic conditions were widening the social gap between the women of the Board and the women which the Board served. From 1929 to 1940 the Good Samaritans regularly received twice as many applicants as they could provide for. In 1930 they renovated the Home to accommodate more women; still they were forced to turn away as many as they served.

Not only did more and more women apply, but those who applied were in increasingly desperate straits, unable to pay anything toward their delivery or support. As a result, the Board determined that while no destitute or homeless woman should be turned away, 'such girls as had homes or responsible relatives to care for them were referred elsewhere unless relatives were willing to pay for at least the required clothing and medical fees'. In 1933, the Board voted to admit only those unable to pay anything.[25]

Five years later Atwood reported that there was an even a greater degree of destitution among the women seeking admission than ever before. 'Many of them', she reported at the annual meeting, 'were without adequate underwear, shoes, stockings and outer clothing sufficient to protect them from the rigors of a climate such as ours. Among the present family there are several without sufficient money to pay postage on letters home or to friends'.[26]

The result of this screening – necessitated by the harsh economic conditions – was a widening gap between the women of the Board and the women they served. Many of the original women of the Board had themselves come from rural Maine communities. They had not, however, been destitute. Their families or their husbands had the resources to move into the city to take advantage of opportunities that enabled them to lead middle-and even upper-middle class lives. The women who entered the Home now had little opportunity to change their lives; their primary concern was survival.

Fern, for example, entered the Home in 1934 when her landlady evicted her. She had eaten only a candy bar in twenty-four hours. The fact that she was almost totally deaf meant that she was unable to obtain any work but heavy cleaning which she had been doing up until a short time before coming to the Home. She gave birth shortly thereafter. She was, Atwood asserted, 'absolutely destitute'. Her boarding mistress, Atwood noted, had kept her personal belongings.[27]

A doctor brought Ethel to the Home at 3 a.m. He had gone to Ethel's two-room shack but found conditions there such that it was 'impossible for him to deliver her there'. The Home admitted the girl of sixteen, but then the staff called the ambulance to take her to the hospital where her appendix burst and she delivered prematurely. Ethel's mother was disabled and a state pauper. She had been cared for away from the home for three years 'presumably to avoid more children'. Ethel had cared for her mother through the last confinement and 'carried on the home since her mother was removed'. The doctor claimed that the stepfather was responsible for Ethel's condition.[28]

Women from these backgrounds were, Atwood declared, 'utterly untaught in the very rudiments of household duties and generally speaking lacking discipline of any kind'. They were also young. Atwood conceded that she did not expect them to be proficient on account of their age but, she concluded, 'that they are so untaught in every line is an indication of what their home condition must be'. Atwood referred to those who returned to their homes after the required stay as 'missionaries' who 'spread the gospel of better housekeeping'. One of the residents herself acknowledged the huge difference in conditions between the Home and her home. Velma's parents refused to let her return home unless she consented to give up her child which Velma refused to do. The Board found her a domestic position in Bangor but she had been away for a year and was homesick and 'unable to adjust herself'. She took her child with her to her home in Calais; a month later she returned once more to Bangor, this time asking the Good Samaritans to place her child for adoption. 'She said she had not realized the conditions existing in her home until she had an opportunity to see how other people lived', Atwood explained.[29]

At the same time that there was a growing recognition of the poverty from which the residents came, couples were applying to the Home in ever-increasing numbers for infants to adopt. Many of these were professional couples who had regular salaries and owned their own homes. A large number were summer visitors from other states. They included college professors, architects, and social service administrators, as well as the head of the pediatrics ward of one of the largest hospitals in the Midwest. The contrast in social class between the residents and the couples seeking their children was striking. Atwood described one adoption in which the husband was an engineer working for the federal government and both husband and wife were college graduates. They adopted the child of a destitute fifteen-year-old.[30]

It was at this time that Atwood began to note the advantages of adoption. While she had regularly referred to the residents as 'satisfactory' or perhaps 'very satisfactory', she began to refer to the adopting couples as 'extremely satisfactory', 'unusually good' and even 'superior in every respect'. She noted the educational and cultural advantages of adoption and emphasized the care given to investigating the parents. 'Every child', she asserted, 'has a right to the very best type of American parents and home'. As the adoption programme began to grow, so did Atwood's sense that there was no perfect solution. She felt the tension between her commitment to the residents and to their children. 'As the years pass', she acknowledged at the end of 1935, 'we become more and more cognizant of the fact that the best we can do for these little ones and those unfortunate other children – their mothers – seems very little in comparison to what we desire for them'.[31]

While the Depression made starkly clear the discrepancy between the social standing and financial security of the would-be adoptive parents and that of the unwed mothers, it was forcing other poor families to turn to adoption in order to provide for their children. Atwood noted in 1935 that the Bureau of

Social Welfare and 'many outside sources' were requesting assistance in placing children for adoption. This suggested, she posited, 'an unusually large number being offered for adoption through the inability of the families to provide for such unfortunate children'. Doctors, the city, families and 'various organizations and social agencies' all sought the Good Samaritan's assistance in finding homes. Atwood noted that these referrals were 'a distinct compliment to our success in this important field' and proudly reported that the court also had 'highly complimented ... our conscientious efforts and methods in cases of adoption'.[32]

At the same time that the Good Samaritans were developing their adoption policies that eventually included psychiatric tests of the children, thorough investigation of the prospective parents, and a one-year waiting period, they observed that desperate families were placing children in less than ideal conditions. In 1934, for example, the Home admitted a three-month-old baby 'in 'serious condition'. The father of the baby was a married man. According to Atwood, a lawyer 'to whom the term "shyster" would appear applicable' had threatened to send the man to prison if he did not sign a note for $1,200. One thousand was to be paid to 'a woman living in the vicinity of Bangor to dispose of the child'. The balance was to be paid to the doctor who made the arrangements with this woman. In a surprising denouement, the child's mother appealed to the wife of her erstwhile lover. The wife, in turn, appealed to the Good Samaritans who accepted the child as a boarder. The child's father agreed to pay for its board. The prospect is, Atwood noted, 'that he and his wife will bring it up in their own home'. A month later Atwood reported that the baby who had been admitted in 'such a pathetic condition' was making satisfactory improvement. It had, she said, gained in weight and 'lost much of its apparent fear when approached'. It had become 'much less nervous and wakeful'. That same month Atwood told the Board about the story behind a newspaper ad that offered an infant for adoption. The mother had come to the Good Samaritans but, unwilling to stay six months, had gone instead to a family who put her up. The family was offering the child to anyone who would pay fifty dollars. The money, Atwood suggested, was to pay for the expense of confinement. 'Undoubtedly the friends of the girl will be successful in placing it – but how desirably is a question', Atwood concluded.[33]

Slowly, faced with women who couldn't find the jobs that would enable them to support their children, with adoptive parents offering the opportunities a professional family with a secure income could provide, and the slipshod placement of children whose parents were desperate to find support for them, the Good Samaritans turned to adoption. Having done so, they took pride in doing it right. That meant conforming to 'all regulations' of the state welfare department.

Atwood noted in her annual report in 1937, that the Home worked to provide the 'best possible home' for the child and to 'select for placement only such children as have suitable background and are physically sound and mentally fit for such superior homes as are open to them'. The Home asked professional psychologists to test the children; they themselves recorded and studied the child's background. In addition, they relied on 'various social agencies outside of Maine' or on their own case committee to provide a thorough investigation of the adoptive families; and they required a one-year probationary period before they finalized an adoption. 'With the splendid co-operation and assistance in this work of baby specialists, psychiatrists, and lawyers, all leaders in their chosen professions, we believe we may feel justified in our satisfaction in this rapidly expanding department of our work'.[34]

Implementing professional child placing standards, however, had its disadvantages. The standards called for a strict screening of all children who were to be placed. This led to a number of women being unable to place their children. The Good Samaritan records and minutes are filled with notations about the children who were unsuitable for adoption for a wide variety of reasons: they were the result of incest or their fathers were unknown; they had an eye problem that could not be corrected for a year; or their mothers were 'mentally slow' or had epilepsy in their families. In addition, professional standards emphasized that children must be placed in families of the same faith as their natural families. This created a problem when the State Department insisted, as it began to do, that agencies limit their placements to Maine. Often the Good Samaritans faced a shortage of Catholic families; and they refused to even take on the responsibility of placing the child of a Jewish father.[35]

More significant to the women who might place their children for adoption, adoption required them to rely on strangers and to provide strangers with information on their family and lover. In 1938 Miss Fuger of the Bureau of Social Welfare suggested that the Good Samaritans try to learn more of the history and background of the men involved and to obtain a more detailed history of all of the Home's residents. Atwood responded that many of the girls came voluntarily and many came 'from homes of great ignorance and limitations and ... we are greatly handicapped by suspicions which such condition of ignorance breeds of any stranger or unfamiliar institutions'. The state might assume the fieldwork such investigation would require but Atwood was not confident of the results. 'We have the feeling ... that many of our girls might be fearful of such a procedure and believe that too much publicity was being given to their cases', she noted.[36]

Not only did the adoption encouraged by social workers involve a reliance on strangers, it also called for a new kind of information. This new information relied on professional evaluations of an individual rather than on the informal gossip of a community in which everyone knew everyone else and put an individual's behaviour into context. Professionals tended to gather information for adoptions unilaterally. Once they had put it into writing in formal reports it was not easily changed or contested. It also relied on tests designed to measure a child's intelligence and personality independent of the child's relations to others. Although professionals suggested a trial placement before the adoption was finalized, they urged the placement be made as early as possible for the sake of the child. Adopting parents, often professionals themselves, relied on a battery of tests as well as a thorough investigation of the child's parents' families to determine 'adoptability'.

This conflict between adopting parents' desire for proof of the adoptability of their children and traditional Maine values is reflected in Harriet's story. In 1934 Harriet, the daughter of a minister from the coast, gave up her child to the head of paediatrics in a Philadelphia hospital and his wife. At twenty-eight, Harriet was older than most of the women the Good Samaritans served. Her case was also atypical in that she, Atwood told the adopting parents, 'parted with her child from a sense of filial devotion and duty to her parents, and to protect them in their position in their community'. Contrary to its general practices, the Good Samaritans placed Harriet's child when the child was three months old. Nevertheless, the case makes clear the tension between 'professional adoption' and traditional Maine practices.[37]

The doctor and his wife were driven by the desire to know the background of the child they wished to adopt. 'I am perfectly willing to undertake all of the usual risks in raising a child', the doctor wrote. 'However if it should be shown that the paternal history is notable for the very high incidence of insanity, epilepsy and feeble-mindedness then do you think that the child is a suitable subject for adoption by anyone?' He urged Atwood to 'have several chats with the mother and see if more cannot be extracted from her' about the father. He did not, however, thoroughly trust what the mother would say as such information 'obtained too freely, is often false'. He proposed instead to use his hospital and agency connections to trace the father and the members of the father's family 'in a quiet way'. He was, he claimed, interested in any history of epilepsy, dementia praecox (early insanity), allergies, tendency to bleed, and the build of the father.[38]

Atwood chided him. Harriet's daughter had by this time been with the doctor and his family for several months. While Atwood was in deep sympathy with his desire to know more, she wrote, she was 'wondering how scientific we are in allowing her to visit your household, with the inevitable result of attachment formed for her and the distress if conditions found upon investigation should be unfavorable'. In what might have been a veiled threat, she told him that she had another family from Ohio that would be glad to adopt the girl.[39]

Atwood did, however, research the paternal background and send to the family a history of the father's work and family, but she was careful to place the boy's actions in context in the traditional Maine fashion. He had worked as a brake-

man, she found, 'which would indicate a record of sobriety'. He left school early
and though she didn't know why, it was 'probably for financial reasons as his was
a large family with not the best of management on the part of the mother'. The
family itself was in good standing, and the community considered the father
as reliable, upright, and industrious. Since leaving school, Atwood reported,
the boy had worked as a common labourer doing whatever came to hand for
unskilled labour. Though he did not have steady employment for any length of
time, she suggested this should not count against him 'under the present economic conditions'. In the tradition of those who referred women to the Good
Samaritans, Atwood pointed out his weak points but counterbalanced them
with other observations. 'He is irresponsible and apparently untruthful, but I
do not find any record of dissipation beyond being what he would perhaps term
being a "good fellow" as far as liquor is concerned'.[40]

Even though the Good Samaritans placed Harriet's child, they continued to
act as an intermediary for her. For the next few years they kept Harriet informed
about the development of her child.[41]

When Atwood provided information to the public on the new programme
of adoption, she took care to explain it in terms that the community could
accept. She repeatedly made clear that adoption was only used selectively, in
cases of economic need. She reported to the Board in 1937, 'We would not give
the impression that our children are being placed on a wholesale scale, far to the
contrary'. The Samaritans had placed only ten children in the last three years. She
also made clear that the adoption program was 'an outgrowth of the prevailing
economic conditions which have made it impossible for many of our girls entering domestic service when dismissed from the Home to earn a sufficient wage to
support themselves and children'.[42]

Economic pressures forced Atwood to turn to adoption, but she consistently maintained that it was the least desired option. In 1930 a reporter talked
about the new Good Samaritan adoption programme on the front page of the
Bangor Daily News. He commented on the requests for infants that came to the
Good Samaritans from all over the country, many from people 'blessed with this
world's goods'. In the following days, the Good Samaritans were 'swamped with
applications from Waterville to Canada'. Atwood inserted a story soon after to
make clear that the majority of women kept their children.[43]

Providing adoption as an option, professional social workers argued, required
casework that could only be provided by those with the right credentials. Coming as she did from a rural Maine community, Atwood understood and worked
to mediate the conflict between professional social workers and traditional
Maine practices. When Atwood died in 1941, the case committee attempted to
continue her practices. Although the chair of the case committee was a certified
medical social worker, she was also a volunteer and the daughter of a woman

who had been on the Board for over twenty years. The State Health and Welfare Department were not satisfied with this degree of professionalization and continued to push the Home to hire more trained social and caseworkers. At first Lena Parrot, head of the Children's Division of the Department, consulted with the Good Samaritans and urged them to hire a social worker. Later, Charles Downy, consultant to the Private Agencies of the State, visited the Home and 'made it very plain to the members present that the Home definitely needed a social worker, or at least a part time social worker'. When Mrs Reid explained that the Good Samaritans were, and always had been, 'very careful to choose people who have keen judgment to be on the case committee', he was not impressed. He threatened to hold up the Home's child-placement licence.[44]

The Home depended upon state funding, and it finally acquiesced to the Welfare Bureau's demands. In February 1950, Board members met with the Bangor Family Welfare Society and arranged to hire Mrs Tandy, the Society's licensed social worker part-time. Downy agreed to issue a licence to the Home when the agreement between the two agencies was signed. In March, Tandy assumed all of the casework for the Home.[45]

The newly-hired social worker pressed the Home to gather information about the mother and her family. She commented to a Children's Aid Society social worker that she had just assumed her job and that she 'felt it would be necessary to get more information than had previously been the custom'. She told the board that she hoped to interview each resident 'fairly early' when the resident came in. She planned to interview family members, write letters to doctors to get information on the family, and contact the fathers when possible.[46]

Tandy, like Eugenia Rugan her successor who became executive director in 1954, also cautioned women against arranging adoptions with people they knew. Both women emphasized the importance of severing all contacts between the adoptive family and the mother of the child. Rugan wrote in her case notes how she explained this to the mother:

> I said that if she knew where the child was, she would be wondering about it, and wantint [*sic*] to see it, and perhaps if she did see it, she would not be satisfied with the type of care it was getting, even though this might be the best of care. I said that the reason for this might well be that she would feel so badly that she was not caring for it that she could not see or accept another persons being called 'mother' by the child.[47]

In 1953 the Maine Legislature, with backing from the professional organizations in the state, legislated the complete separation of the birth mother from her adopted child when it ordered all future adoption records to be sealed.

While the Depression brought changes that led to acceptance of adoption and its concomitant, casework, a confluence of economic and cultural changes led to the end of the Home as an institution. Maud Morlock suggested in her talk to the Maine Social Work Conference in 1939 that private maternity homes such as the Good Samaritan Home may have 'outlived their need'. She called on the Good Samaritans to abolish their requirement that women remain in the Home six months after they deliver, admit the second offender, and consider replacing the institution with a network of foster homes. Each of these suggestions they ultimately accepted.[48]

World War 2 led directly to shortening the required length of the stay. During the Depression women remained in the Home often even longer than the required six months because there were no jobs for them to go to. With the War, however, high-paying jobs became available to women and residents began to want to leave early to take advantage of these jobs. A number of women applied for admission with money in hand only to decide they would prefer to go on their own to the hospital rather than submit themselves to the required length of stay. At the same time, hospitals and social agencies were pushing the Good Samaritans to shorten their length of stay requirement so that the Home could assist more women in labour. Superintendent Merrill quoted from *Modern Hospital* to emphasize how hospitals were struggling in their efforts to provide for all the care that was needed. The magazine made clear, she said, that local institutions 'must change overnight as the war steps up tempo and trends'. One change the Good Samaritans faced in order to 'take the bigger load off the shoulders of the remaining doctors, nurses and hospitals' was to shorten the stay so the Home could accommodate more women and so that more women would wish to come. In December 1942, the Board voted to reduce the required stay after delivery from six months to three. By 1949, it had reduced the stay to three weeks after delivery.[49]

Almost immediately after the War, the high-paying jobs available to women disappeared. At the same time, for a variety of reasons, the cost of maintaining the Home and its services continued to rise. In the first place, the residents who now remained only a short time did not have time to be trained in the operations of the Home. More significant, however, was the national culture's changing attitude toward young women. While rural communities still expected young women to work hard, popular culture and middle-class families identified the same young women as adolescents in need of time away from demands in order to mature. From 1931 to 1953 the Home offered the residents increasing opportunities for recreation. In December 1931 Gertrude Atwood recommended that the Board provide the girls with more opportunities for simple pleasures, especially during long winter evenings. Watching them, evening after evening, she had concluded that they were 'tremendously pathetic'. Acknowledging she might be considered a revolutionist, she suggested the Board allow the residents to play cards, sing songs and listen to records.[50]

Atwood apparently won her point for the minutes after that regularly record evening entertainment for the residents. They listened to music while they sewed, gathered around the piano, held evening parties with games and fortunetelling, took evening walks and ate quantities of popcorn.[51] The recreation described, however, was invariably in the evenings when the work of the day was done. It was also often productive. The women knitted and sewed or learned cooking. Gradually, however, the recreation became more diffused throughout the day and more geared toward pure entertainment. In 1940 the Board appointed a committee to plan for recreation. In 1943 the social committee congratulated its members for providing a diversified recreational programme. That year they had made the hours of recreation more interesting with a pool table in the basement and weekly excursions to the movies. In 1949 the Social Committee reported to the Board that the girls were 'restless at present, a young group. They need chaperoning for movies or any activity that would keep them occupied'. For the next decade the Social Committee brought in speakers and travel films. They arranged for lessons in stencilling, decorating tin-ware, Mexican beadwork and how to make flowers from stockings. They provided elaborate parties with decorations and baskets of candy for Easter, Halloween and birthdays as well as Christmas and Thanksgiving. Sometimes the recreation was 'educational'. Mr Dietrich of Bangor Family Welfare, for example, came to talk on the subject of mental hygiene and offered to show such films as 'Rejection' and 'Hostility'. For the most part, however, the recreation seemed geared to fill the residents' expanding leisure time.[52]

At the same time, the girls were doing increasingly less work. By 1942 the Board had added a cook and a laundress to the Home's staff. In 1943, it hired someone to take care of the yard and, finally, to do the spring-cleaning. In the early days of the institution, the women admitted to the Home did all the work of the Home under the supervision of a matron. By 1943, the staff had expanded to include two graduate nurses, a caseworker and ten other employees.[53] The superintendents explained to the Board that the reason additional help was needed was that the 'girls' in the Home were too young to do the hard physical labour.[54] The actual age of the residents (calculated by the average, median and modal age), however, remained fairly constant. Furthermore, the evidence suggests, they continued to work hard in their own homes, where they were expected to do both household and field labour. What had changed was the dominant society's attitudes towards these residents as the concept of adolescence gained social acceptance. New employees told the residents they were doing too much work, and one woman who had a series of disagreements with the staff complained to the Department of Health and Welfare that the Home worked them like slaves.[55]

Adolescence, according to the popular literature of the time, was a time in which girls were experimenting with growing up. They needed time, freedom from hard work, and understanding. The change in the attitudes towards the young women was reflected in the language used to describe them.

For over two decades Gertrude Atwood had maintained the traditional rural expectation that young women required supervision because they lacked judgment but that they were capable of doing, and in fact expected to do, hard physical work. She judged almost every woman in the Home as either 'satisfactory', 'very satisfactory' or 'not satisfactory'. If they did the work and got along with the others, she gave them her nod of approval.

In clear contrast, the two superintendents who followed Atwood identified the women they approved of not as 'satisfactory' but as 'nice'. While Atwood emphasized the work that the women did, Mary Hayward and Alice Merrill stressed the work that was required to deal with them. In 1936 Mrs Pearson, who had been the matron in the Home for ten years, lost her job when she could no longer adequately control the young women in the Home who were 'disobedient and unruly'. The Board made a conscious effort then to 'build up younger personnel as it appears older workers as have been employed in the past have not adequate strength and patience'.[56] From then on, the board members made it a point to hire young, single women when in the past they had hired exclusively older, married ones. Eight years later Hayward told the public, 'It takes hard strenuous work to re-establish these girls ... It takes time, encouragement, and much, much patience'.[57]

At the same time that changing attitudes forced the Home to hire more workers because the residents did less work, doctors were demanding their own costly changes. They had once delivered women in the Home free of charge. In 1951, they insisted that sound medical practice required them to deliver in the hospital. As the hospital at that time charged a fifty-dollar admission fee plus twenty-five dollars per week for board for the mother and child, the cost for a delivery rose substantially. In addition, if any complications arose the cost increased accordingly.[58]

The Home worked as it did because of the required length of stay and the institution. It offered the women an opportunity to work out their debts and to prove their worth with hard labour. Because the women provided work at no cost, the Home was able to provide inexpensive daycare and thus give residents an opportunity to continue to support their children as they settled into a job and found a husband. By working with the staff for six months, the residents could prove their value as workers and, therefore, earn recommendations that could help them obtain other jobs. In addition, the six-month stay provided women and their families a time in which to explore all the available options and avoid being forced into a quick decision. It also enabled women to blunt the edge of gossip and, if they so desired, to give up their children gradually.[59] Denied an opportunity to work out their fees and faced with the more costly service of hospitalization for a delivery that was not subsidized by women's labour, women from poor backgrounds found it impossible to earn their own way and, thus, to keep the self-respect that their communities attached to self-sufficiency.

The rising cost and decreasing length of stay led to an even more fundamental change. The Good Samaritans had always offered poor rural women economic support. Women rarely came to save their reputations but came, instead, for assistance in their delivery, room and board, and job placement. In exchange for these services, they offered their own labour. But the limited stay meant women did not have the time to work out their labour. In addition, not spending as much time in the Home meant that they were less well-known to the staff and therefore could not receive the same detailed references as earlier residents had. Having to hire more help, the Home had to charge more for its services. As a result women were faced with increasing charges at the same time as the Home was limiting the opportunity it had always offered to women to 'work out their fees'. Simultaneously, the increased costs and shortage of labour meant that the Good Samaritans had to cut back on the medical services they were providing.[60] With an increase in costs and a decrease in services the Home lost much of its appeal to poor rural women. It was forced to change its admissions policies.

From the time they first required women to sign rules before they entered the Home, the Good Samaritans made it very clear: 'On no consideration shall a girl be admitted to the Home a second time for the same offense'. Atwood regularly reported to the Board the applicants whom she had rejected and she invariably rejected the second offender. As she noted in 1933, 'Our policy regarding the admission of the second offender is so well known that we need not go into detail regarding it'.[61]

In addition to having a venereal disease, a second offence was the one reason why a woman would invariably be rejected for admission to Home. Married women, 'feeble-minded' women, older women and those who had been in the Women's Reformatory all had a harder time getting in than other applicants, but sometimes they were accepted. Women who had had several sexual partners were routinely accepted if they had community members to vouch for them. A second offender never was.

There was an important practical reason for this. Atwood excelled in public relations. Year after year she presented to the public an image of Good Samaritan 'girls' that reflected traditional community values. Each year she emphasized the girls' youth and their willingness to assume responsibility. The rural communities expected young girls (especially those without supervision) to have sexual encounters. They allowed them this indiscretion if they redeemed themselves by hard work and by assuming responsibility. While the communities could accommodate one child out of wedlock, however, it could not accommodate two.

By invariably rejecting the second offender, the Good Samaritans strengthened their argument that the women who found shelter with them were not bad, only unfortunate. Women grew, Atwood argued, when they gave birth and 'entered the portals of womanhood'.

The issue of the second offender turned on the interpretation of unwed motherhood. For the professional by this time, the unwed mother had become pregnant because she had a deep psychological need to do so.[62] This idea enabled the public to consider her with sympathy rather than fear. In Maine's rural communities, the idea that a young woman was unable for whatever reason to accept responsibility led the community to less sympathy.

Inherent in the two different interpretations were differing ideas of what the unwed mother needed in order to be returned to the community. Professional social workers argued that a woman needed counselling. Atwood and others argued that she needed to accept responsibility, most often including responsibility for her child. For professionals, the unwed mother had to change before she was like everyone else. For the Good Samaritans in the early years, she had to go on with her life. As Atwood wrote to one applicant, 'it is not so much what we have done as it is what we do in the future that really counts'.[63] The policy not to accept the second offender was critical to the Good Samaritan's public relations.

Professionals, who needed to find placements for the second offenders, pressured the Good Samaritans to take them. They repeatedly referred second offenders to the Home and made clear what a difficult time these women would have if the Good Samaritans did not take them in. 'Miss Parrot, Supervisor of Child Welfare Services in Augusta, called and spent an hour with me', Mary Hayward noted in 1942. 'She brought up the subject of the second offender and said so far unable to place this girl for confinement'.[64]

The newly hired social worker Tandy noted in 1951 that there had been increasingly fewer girls in the Home in the last two years and this had caused concern. The problem, she pointed out, was that more of the girls were going directly to the hospital for their delivery. While she attributed this to the fact that there was less stigma attached to illegitimacy, it is possible also that the services provided were not enough to attract the women. For Tandy, there was no difference between the second offender and the others except that the second offender might have been in more need of help. 'After all', she concluded, 'whether or not they will be an upsetting influence with the other girls is more a matter of individual personality than of whether they have been married or had a previous child'. That year, at her insistence, the Home began to admit the second offender, but even that was not enough to counteract the falling admissions. In 1954 the Board closed the Home and opened up a series of foster homes.[65]

In 1928 Atwood could reassure a sister of the resident that 'it has come to us, although we are strangers to her, to take the place of her own kin'. Overseen by women who understood the rural experience, filled with women who came from the same similar small communities, residents were reassured by what was familiar. Foster homes could not reassure a rural woman in the same way. One pregnant woman made clear her discomfort when Eugenia Rugan, the executive director, explained to her the new boarding home arrangement 'She found this very hard to accept', Rugan noted, 'and said that she had thought that when she came to Bangor she would live in a home with other girls'. Rugan explained that the Board had closed the Home and now placed girls in separate boarding homes, to little effect. 'This was very hard for her, as she did not want to go with strangers. I told her that I could place her in a home where there was another girl but this did not seem to be what she wanted'. The girl returned to her mother who was waiting in the car and insisted her mother take her back home.[66]

By 1956 the Good Samaritan Home had implemented most of what professional social workers defined as good social work practice, and it was totally transformed. An undated, unsigned report on the Home, written some time between 1950 and 1954, described a programme and philosophy that Gertrude Atwood would not have recognized. It described the girls as 'all disturbed, most of them from broken homes', a Home that provided 'as much entertainment as possible', and a belief that 'it seldom works out well for the mother or the child to have the mother keep her baby'. While the 'new' home was modelled on the latest social work standards, it did not meet the needs of the rural women who had turned to it in such great numbers in the previous decades.[67]

A sample of Good Samaritan case records from the 1940s and early 1950s makes clear the growing disparity between the professional services of the Good Samaritans, the traditional values of the community, and the way the women were caught in between.[68] While the Home's social worker urged women to be 'realistic' and place their children for adoption, neighbours and family members continued to encourage them to take care of their own. Those women who rejected the community values and placed their children for adoption risked having their children found unsuitable for adoption. When this happened, the same social service bureaucracy that had encouraged adoption and then found the child un-adoptable, forced the women to turn back to the communities they had rejected to find support.

Where once the Good Samaritans had offered the women a familiar but different space in which to negotiate new lives for themselves, it now offered them a service that was in conflict with their communities. The women could choose the adoption service of the Good Samaritans or accept responsibility for their children and their communities, but they could not do both. As a result, when the women found minimal economic support from the state, they rejected the option of adoption and returned to their communities with their children more dependent upon their families than before.

Throughout the period under study, the women had much in common with their earlier counterparts; they remained young, rural and poor. Although in later years the Home more regularly accepted women in their twenties and even thirties, the median and modal ages of those admitted remained seventeen and eighteen. The women also continued to come from the small townships or, if they came from the larger agricultural trading centres which now had populations of over 10,000, their fathers were farmers or woodsmen and their lovers, farm labourers.

Half of the one hundred and two women whose cases were consulted either identified themselves as poor or were identified by social service agencies as such. Only one had a father who was identified as a professional. A number came from families who were state paupers or from families who were relying on the town temporarily to help them through a time of sickness and unemployment. One woman went home for a visit and stayed because of the conditions she found there. 'To put it bluntly', she wrote, 'there isn't a penny coming in at home...Some one has to help out and since I used to send money home, I feel guilty for not having any to help. So I must go back to work'. In another case, the public health nurse wrote that the family could not take care of another child as there were nine other children in the family and their income was 'comparatively small'. 'We are poor', wrote one mother requesting admission of her daughter. 'We got burned out a year ago and lost all we had so we couldn't help too much'. Eugenia Rugan, investigating another request for admission, wrote in her notes that, while the home seemed adequate on the outside, inside it was very bare and cold. 'She has no money', Rugan noted, 'and she has no clothes which she felt she could wear while in a foster home'.[69]

For many, the combination of rural living and poverty meant isolation. Many could not afford cars and had to rely on others to get into town for social services. One mother apologized for the late payment of her bill. 'Please excuse the mistakes', she wrote, 'because I have to hurry – have to walk this morning about two miles. There is no early bus so have to ride with the mail man at six o'clock'. One resident wrote after she was married that she and her husband were moving to a house where the nearest town was seventeen miles away. 'So there won't be much excitement up there', she noted.[70]

As were the residents before them, the women were used to hard physical labour. A few were working to support themselves. In 1945, Cora wrote to the Good Samaritans, 'I am a girl of 17 all alone, expecting a baby in two months with no place to go and no money to pay my hospital bills but I could work till

	1930–41	1942–5	1946–50	1951–60
Institutional				
Number of Residents	53	16	31	63
Average Length of Stay (months)	9.8	6.1	3.7	3.3
Average Stay Prior to Delivery	1.7	2.7	2.2	2.5
Early Departure	0	1	2	18
Infant Deaths	8	1	1	0
Maternal Deaths	1	0	0	0
Population				
Average Age	19.5	18.6	19	19.6
Number Younger than 17	12	3	5	4
Marriage Impossible	14	1	8	16
Marriage Undesirable	16	14	12	26
Family of Poverty	20	1	4	10
Outcome				
Placement	16	1	4	3
Marriage	20	6	13	7
Settlement	9	2	6	2
Relative Adoption	2	2	1	9
Stranger Adoption	7	2	16	5
Baby Committed to State	0	0	4	6
Second o/w Pregnancy	3	0	0	0

These statistics are drawn from the record of every fifth woman admitted to the Good Samaritan Home between 1930 to 1960. The case records were provided by Debby Giguerre of the Good Samaritan Home Agency, 100 Ridgewood Drive,, Bangor, Maine.

It should be noted that information was not always available so the counts in any category may be underestimated

Those who leave early are either dismissed when it is discovered that they have a venereal disease or that this is the woman's second pregnancy or the women chose to ,leave within the first week or are noted as having run away.

When the amount of the settlements is included it ranges from $150 to $500.

Marriage is counted as impossible when it is a result of incest or the birth father (ad occasionally mother) is already married, in jail, or dead.

Marriage is counted as undesirable when it is noted that the parents object to a marriage, the birth mother and birth father are of different religions or race, or if the father is in the army.

I am sick and after the baby's born'. According to the case notes, Cora's mother deserted the family when Cora was two. At the time of Cora's application, her father had also left. Cora, Cora's sister and her brother were left to shift for themselves.[71]

Most, however, were either working to help support their families or helping to maintain their families when their mothers were sick or absent. In 1937, Emma, nineteen, was earning forty dollars a week as a telephone operator in Fort Kent. The reason she was unable to save more from her wages, the Director of the New England Home for Little Wanderers wrote, is 'the fact that she has been clothing all of the younger children in the family and in addition to this buying some much needed living room furniture for her parents'. Emma was the oldest of fourteen children.[72]

The families relied on the women for their help. One mother wrote in 1948 asking that the Home release her daughter early 'because I am sick and need her badly. I've had to overwork so much since she's been gone that I'm illin [*sic*] and all that fatigue has settled in my left ankle and the doctor bandaged me up and forbade me to walk on it'. Five days later she wrote again, 'If you were in my place you'd realize that I need her help badly as you must know there's no help to be had at any price for housework especially when there's so many to work and care for ... you know its quite a problem to do housework for nine of us including myself hobbling around on one leg'. A year later a sister of another resident wrote, 'Her father wants her to come right home as soon as she be able to come we need __ to take care for mother we can't afford a hired girl so please ... '[73]

While the families relied heavily on the labour of their daughters, the daughters were increasingly forced to depend on their families. What little opportunity they once had for independence was reduced even further when increasing costs of maternity services, restricted public assistance and new state laws requiring parental consent for institutional care all tied a young woman ever more closely to her family.

During the 1940s and 50s, the cost of the Good Samaritan services increased sharply even as the Good Samaritans stopped offering women an opportunity to work out their debts.[74] Board in a foster home and delivery in the hospital cost substantially more than did delivery in the Home where the other residents helped with the work. In 1930, a woman paid an entrance fee of $125 which covered her delivery, any medical costs and room and board for herself and her baby for at least six months after her delivery. She could work out this fee and, if she did, she took advantage of the free room and board for a longer period of time. By 1948, superintendent Mary Hayward was estimating that Good Samaritan services cost a woman $250. By 1955, women had to pay a hospital fee of fifty dollars plus twenty-five dollars a week board for herself and her child. Even though most women and babies stayed only a short time, bills quickly rose to over $300. If there were any complications in the hospital, the additional expense would fall on the woman. In addition, if the mother wished to place her child for adoption she had to pay for the baby's board until the foster parents took the child. If there were some question about the 'adoptability' of the child, the Good Samaritans might keep it in foster care for observation for up to six months.[75]

The Good Samaritans continued to offer to care for women who could not pay for the services and offered to help with the board when necessary, but the Agency could do nothing to defray the hospital expenses. Women could apply for Hospital Aid but in order to qualify, they had to prove that their parents could not afford to pay. While Hospital Aid paid 30 to 40 per cent of the hospital bill, the hospital required a fifty dollar medical deposit before the woman was admitted.[76]

Meanwhile, money from other sources was rarely adequate. The Good Samaritans were hesitant to charge adoptive parents any more than a processing fee of seventy-five dollars, though they did solicit contributions from them in 1953.[77] While almost one-quarter of the women relied on the traditional method of bastardy suits to force the men to help contribute financially and while the law continued to make it easy for a woman to win a suit, the amounts raised in bastardy suits were rarely enough to cover increasing costs. Furthermore, the Good Samaritans no longer actively pursued the suits as Atwood had but suggested that the woman obtain a lawyer and do so at her own cost.

Community members continued to expect a man to assume financial responsibility and supported those who sought informal as well as formal arrangements. Various family members as well as the woman herself sought the aid of a lawyer often before contacting the Good Samaritans; and lawyers led them to expect continued support in at least one case until the child was twenty-one.[78] The families were limited, however, in what they could obtain from a man who was often as poor as the woman herself. As one mother reported, her daughter got 'very little out of the father of the child because he didn't have any'. The parents of another father refused to pay bail when he was jailed for not paying his bastardy settlement; the man remained in jail for four months. In the end, the woman and her family accepted a private settlement 'for a small amount'. In a number of cases the families paid for a lawyer who obtained only the amount of the Good Samaritan bill, which at $250 was no small sum.[79]

Sometimes fathers and their families made informal arrangements. One woman wrote Hayward that she had seen her baby's father and reported that he had promised to send her five dollars a week 'towards bringing her up'. 'I don't know how long it will last', she conceded, 'but I hope to have it long enough to pay up my bills'. Another man accepted paternity and paid a settlement even though the woman had been institutionalized twice for mental illness and, the putative father claimed, there had been 'other men involved that night'.

Although another got married and left the state, her lover's parents, who were farmers, offered to help with the fees.[80]

Some fathers were not so available or so willing. As Eva Scates of the New England Home for Little Wanderers told Hayward in the case of a fifteen-year-old, there would be no settlement as the alleged father, was 'no good and has recently married someone else'. If a woman were married, her chances of winning a suit were slight.[81]

The court continued to rely on a signed statement that the woman had named that man in childbirth as proof that the man was the father of the child. Changing practices, however, meant that those who attended women in their delivery did not always pay attention to the need to obtain such a statement. Lawyers wrote asking the Good Samaritans to make sure that the woman gave a signed statement during childbirth. 'I have no doubt that you have had this sort of experience before', wrote a lawyer from Joly & Martin in Waterville in 1944, 'and I trust you will pardon the suggestion, but as you know it is a very important element in the case'. Eight years later, Harry C. McManus from Van Buren commented of the doctor who would deliver the child, 'I assume that he being familiar with these cases will probably put her on what is technically known as her discovery'. Nevertheless, he was writing to the Good Samaritans to ask them to make sure that the doctor did so. While lawyers and community members were fully aware of this requirement doctors in the hospital – many of them from out of state – were not. 'The doctors do not ask the girls the name of the alleged', Hayward answered the lawyer', but we do when they are in labor before they go to the hospital'. The Good Samaritans were unable to this, however, when residents boarded in foster homes.[82]

While the towns were still obliged to pay for the support of an unwed mother who had a settlement in the town and still in some cases paid for hospital costs, the practice became less common. In the first place families were more geographically mobile than they had been and less likely to have obtained a settlement. In addition, the community continued to place a high value on self-sufficiency. The Good Samaritans no longer made it possible for women to work out their indebtedness, and women who were unable to work to pay their bills often preferred not to ask for aid. One woman who had, according to Rugan, 'no money and no clothes', another who had been unable to work for two years, and a third whose mother 'had little money and was only earning twenty dollars a week', all suggested that they would rather borrow the necessary money than ask the town to pay the hospital bill.[83]

There were other forms of public assistance, most notably Aid to Dependent Children (ADC). The allotments were too small, however, to enable a woman to support herself and her child.[84] Most women had to supplement their welfare cheques with a job or family support. Furthermore, ADC was not available until the child was born, and, as Executive Director Rugan pointed out in 1954, would not pay for the hospital delivery or clothes for the baby.[85]

If public welfare did not pay enough to support a woman and child without additional support, it was increasingly hard for a woman to find the right combination of a job and childcare that would enable her to be independent. Until 1940, most of the women who were working independently before they came to the Good Samaritans were working as domestic servants or hired help and the Good Samaritans routinely 'placed' them in homes in the Bangor area at the end of their six-month stay. By the 1940s, the Good Samaritans had stopped the practice of placing women. They occasionally helped them find jobs, but they no longer routinely 'placed' them with members of the Board or their friends.

While this was most likely a mutually agreed upon change, it made the women more vulnerable to economic pressures. By this time, women had available an assortment of jobs that paid better and offered more independence as clerks, waitresses, nurses and beauticians. These jobs, however, lacked what domestic service did not – the opportunity for the women to keep their children with them as they worked. Because there were no daycare centres and because the Good Samaritans no longer offered to board children at a reduced rate, the women had to either find a reasonably-priced boarding home for their child or rely on family members to help. Most relied on family members. Those who went into homes as domestic servants without the supervision of the Good Samaritans ran the risk of gossip or of being taken advantage of.

If economics forced a woman to rely increasingly on her family, so did the law once women had stepped outside of the informal practices of the community. The law held parents responsible for young women until they married or reached the age of twenty-one. It required that her parents or her husband sign a permission to operate before she entered a hospital. If she were eighteen or younger and wished to place her child for adoption her parents had to sign the adoption papers. Furthermore, the law held the family responsible for the support of all its children. A woman could not obtain Hospital Aid if her family could afford to pay her expenses. At the same time, she could not commit an 'unadoptable' child to the state until the state made every effort to force her family to provide for the child's support.

The Good Samaritan case records make starkly clear the impact of all these changes. Once the Good Samaritans had changed its policies and before Aid to Dependent Children became readily available, adoption was the norm. Women who tried to keep their children struggled against insurmountable odds and found few alternatives other than committing their children to the state.

From November 1943, when the Good Samaritans reduced the time a woman had to remain in the Home, to August 1951, when the case records first noted a woman's plans to receive ADC, thirty-two women either placed their children for adoption or saw their children committed to the state. Overwhelmingly, the women or their families claimed that they were placing the children because they could not afford to do otherwise.

Most critical to their decision was the need for childcare. In making their plans, the women almost invariably named others – mothers, sisters, aunts, grandmothers and even landladies – who would help them out either by watching their children or by working to support them while they stayed home with the child. Women with no such support found it almost impossible to manage. Lauria, for example, was the first of two illegitimate children who had 'always been in the custody of the State'. Lauria had changed foster homes frequently. For the past six years she had lived with a couple in Ellsworth who were, according to the superintendent of the State Military and Naval Children's Home, 'the only people interested in her welfare'. Her mother was dead. When she applied to the Home she had forty-five dollars in savings, fifteen dollars in cash, and a three month's leave from the phone company.[86]

Lauria expressed a 'great desire to keep her baby if at all possible'. With the help of the Good Samaritans, Lauria placed her child in the University of Maine Home Economics Program which had supported babies from the Good Samaritan Home since 1927. The programme provided University of Maine students with a 'practice baby' in return for which the University provided the child with room and board for the academic year. In spite of this 'free care', Lauria fell behind on her payments to the Good Samaritans. 'To say that I am deeply disappointed in you is putting it mildly', Superintendent Merrill wrote Lauria when her baby was six months old.[87]

Merrill wrote Lauria several times asking her to pay her bill. Lauria finally wrote back that she had been thinking since the last letter and had come to the conclusion that the best thing for her daughter and herself was to give her up. Lauria wrote:

> I shall not be able to support her myself and I have no plans of getting married in the near future. Even if I did keep her I would have to board her out all the time and I know from experience that that is no life for a child … It is not what I really want but I think that it is the only right thing to do for her sake.[88]

Even when women had families, these families were often too poor to accept the additional burden of a child. Parents frequently wrote requesting that the Good Samaritans place their daughter's child. One woman's father wrote, 'This baby will have to be turned over to the state just as soon as it is borned [sic] because I am in no way able to take care of it and I am sure that __ can not...' The mother of another wrote, 'It can't be any other way. My husband has his mother's family as well as ours to keep'. And the mother of a third wrote, 'We are unable to care for her as neither mr. nor myself are well. She will be unable to care for her baby'.[89]

Five of the children in the sample were committed to the state instead of being placed. One was the baby of a state ward who actively fought to keep her child. The seventeen-year-old had been committed to the state for her care and protection when she was eight. Superintendent Eugenia Rugan noted in her records that the girl claimed she would never forget how the state agents took the child when she was feeding it. 'She did not feel the State was ever going to help her', Rugan wrote, 'because they took her baby without her wanting them to which seems to show that they have very little faith in her any way'. All Rugan could do was suggest the young woman tell her caseworker in the Department exactly what she thought.[90]

While Ella did not wish to give up her child, other women had their children committed to the care of the state only after professionals determined their children were not adoptable. Caseworkers made this decision for a variety of reasons that ranged from the child being the result of rape or incest to test results that suggested the child was limited in mental ability. When this happened, Maine's laws which required a family to support all its members and a town to support all its residents when the family couldn't, in some cases forced women who wished to become independent back into depending upon their families.

Catherine, for example, had moved to Massachusetts to live with her aunt in order to separate herself from her family. When she became pregnant, the Florence Crittenton Home in Massachusetts promptly notified the Good Samaritans that they were sending her back to her home state. Her story was recorded in a steady stream of letters between Catherine, the Superintendent of the Good Samaritans, and the Supervisor of the Child Welfare Services of the Maine Department of Health and Welfare. The letters reveal how Catherine was caught between the traditional Maine system of town-based care and the new professional social welfare reliance on adoption and public welfare.

Catherine agreed to go to the Good Samaritans only under compulsion from the Florence Crittenton staff. She was, a staff member wrote, without funds and her aunt was unable to help her. In addition, she 'did not want her parents to know of her situation and said they were unable to help her'. When her parents were contacted they confirmed what Catherine had claimed: They 'did not want to accept any state aid'.[91]

Catherine gave birth to a daughter at the Good Samaritans in September 1941. Three months later she released her daughter to the Good Samaritans for placement in an adoptive home. Ten days after she returned to her aunt's home an x-ray showed that her daughter, Elsie, had 'recult' spina bifida. Elsie was, the doctor concluded, 'placeable but not adoptable'. Mrs Merrill, superintendent of the Home, notified Catherine that although at the moment her daughter was 'normal in every way ... at some future date in her life she may have some difficulty there'. Merrill wrote to ask what Catherine wanted to do with her child. 'As she cannot be put out for adoption of course someone must pay her board, either you or some member of you family', she told Catherine. For the next year, Merrill, Catherine and Lena Parrot, Supervisor of Child Welfare Services of the Maine Department of Health and Welfare, negotiated to find some solution for the child.[92]

Catherine was very clear about her situation. 'If I could of kept that baby I certainly never would not of put her out for adoption. I have no means myself. I'm not working and my family has no way of paying board for her ... If my aunt could have means she would have let me had her here with me'. Furthermore, Catherine was very clear that she did not want her family to have anything to do with the baby. 'This is my trouble', she asserted, and she would rather not have her hometown know. 'If you can't put her out as she is for adoption the only way is to put her out on the State. I hate to have it that way but it is the only way out for me'.[93]

Parrot was as clear that Catherine could not give up her child. 'I'm afraid', she wrote to Merrill, '[Catherine] will not find it as easy to dispose of the responsibility of her baby as her letter indicated'. In order for Catherine to put her baby on the state, Parrot informed Merrill and Catherine, the state would have to bring a charge of wilful neglect or failure to provide for the child in the local court. It would then have to prove that the mother was an 'improper guardian' and had willfully failed 'to provide the child with suitable food, clothing and privileges of education'. Furthermore, once the child was committed, the Department of Health and Welfare had the authority to charge the town where the mother had a settlement for two-thirds of the cost of the child's care. 'Since your settlement would be that of your parents, the town where they have a settlement would be billed for part of the support of your child'. Parrot noted that Catherine seemed to want to keep this matter from her parents. 'If the child is committed and the town pays part of the expense, it is more than likely that your parents will hear about it'.[94]

In further letters Parrot made clear to Catherine that the family's responsibility for an 'un-adoptable' child did not end when the family's town of settlement accepted financial responsibility for its care. 'I wonder', she wrote, 'if you have overlooked your moral responsibility to this child, and who is going to give her the love and affection that every child must have in order to develop to his full capacity?' A foster home, she pointed out, would not give the child the feeling of belonging to a family group. 'If you are unable to think of yourself as being a mother to this child, we will be anxious to know whether or not the maternal grandparents or other maternal relatives may have affection and interest to offer the child that will be more satisfying to her than any foster family can offer'.

Sooner or later, Parrot concluded, the Department will want to 'explore all possibilities of placement with people in her own family before we consider placing her with strangers'.[95]

Parrot wanted Catherine to come to Maine to discuss the situation, but Catherine was adamant. 'The child has to be in a place where I have no means of caring for her and my family hasn't. I have to do this problem the way it is'. Furthermore, she didn't have the money to do so. 'As it is now I'm not working. My aunt hasn't the means to give the money to me as she has all she can do for themselves [*sic*]'.[96]

Eventually Catherine gave permission to the Department to send a staff member to interview her parents. She was insistent, nevertheless, that the Department not place the burden of her child on her parents. 'I'd rather have the child out among strangers than have the burden of my child on them', she wrote. Her parents were separated, and she recommended that the staff see her father. 'He will understand my problem better ... I know my mother wouldn't take the child ... My father would liked of had the child but he has no means of caring for the child, no more than I have myself'. She told Parrot that when she got work she would give a certain amount towards her child's cost so that her father wouldn't have to. 'He has enough to look out for his trouble without mine. My father is very proud of the baby, but he would have to put that child in a place just as I am trying to do now. He can't take the place of a mother'. She would write to him and 'explain why I had to do this, so he will understand'.[97]

The following year, Catherine wrote to the Good Samaritans one last time. She had received the warrant to appear in court. 'I told you as soon as I could I would pay so much to you for the baby when you found a home for her', she wrote. 'It takes money to go to court and I certainly haven't got it'. She offered to pay five dollars a month for the child until the child was eighteen. 'Or I could pay about seven dollars but I can't afford to pay any more because I haven't got it ... I have no means and my folks haven't'.[98]

Those who kept their children and tried to remain independent showed the struggle that this choice required when small Maine communities offered few opportunities. One who left her baby to board in the Home when she went back to Ashland wrote to apologize for not keeping up with the payments. 'At present it's quite hard for me to send any more than five dollars. I have no help from no one, I have to work everything out myself the best way I can'. She was hoping to go to Hartford, Connecticut, where she heard that factories were opening up and the wages might help her to make ends meet. 'As long as I stay here', she acknowledged, 'I will not get ahead, I'm just working hard for almost nothing'.[99]

Women found difficulties both in bringing their children to domestic situations when it was no longer the accepted norm and in boarding their babies while they worked at higher paying jobs in the larger cities. Doris experienced both. Although she had a friend 'willing to help in a small way', she was extremely vulnerable under the new conditions, as her story suggests. Doris applied to an employment agency when her time in the Home was up, and the Agency found her a job in a small town caring for a man and his three children. The man allowed Doris to bring her baby, but within six months Doris had lost her job because people in the small town 'were talking'. She moved to Bangor and took a job as a waitress at the Brass Rail.[100]

Doris wrote to the Samaritans asking who she could see about getting Mother's Aid (ADC) for her son. 'It is difficult to get everything he needs on my wages', she wrote. 'He is well fed and well clothed, but in the near future it will be harder and he will need many new things'. It would be a help to get any amount, she added, no matter how small.[101]

Doris had obtained a bastardy settlement from the father of her child, but she fought with the Good Samaritans who had, as was their practice, taken much of the settlement to pay for Doris's debt to the Home. 'She seems to feel', the health officer wrote, that 'because she worked at your Home, she does not have any further obligation to you. I tried to explain ... that whatever she was able to do while there did not relieve her of financial obligation'. The lawyer who had arranged for the settlement refused to release the money to Doris until she had agreed to pay her bill.[102]

Doris had been bright in school, had skipped second grade, and joined the outing club, chorus and girl scouts. She showed ambition when she left her job as a nurse's aid to work in a factory where she could get more money. But caring for her child with little support seemed to unbalance her. The Good Samaritan social worker noted when she visited Doris's boarding room that Doris 'was heard to scream a lot at the child, place dirty, looked like she'd been sick a lot in bed'. Her behaviour became increasingly erratic or at least irresponsible. She lost her job because she didn't show up for work. She borrowed clothes and money from her friends and went with other men, possibly getting money from them as well. She finally returned to Auburn where she got pregnant again; the Welfare Department took both children. She may have been emotionally unstable, but she was also faced with extreme economic difficulties.

While the economic difficulties of supporting a child on one's own were almost insurmountable, the women found support for keeping their children within their families and communities. As soon as funds through ADC were generally available, women began to keep their children rather than place them for adoption. In a complete reversal from the previous decade, from August 1951, when the first woman wrote that she was on Mothers Aid with her child, till the end of 1958, forty-four out of fifty-three women kept their children. Of the nine who did not, seven were either state wards who had no control over the commitment of their children, already had one child out of wedlock, or were married and had husbands who insisted on the placement. Only two chose to place their children without being forced to by external forces. One was the oldest of fourteen children and gave most of her salary as a telephone operator to help support the family.[103]

One woman who placed her child for adoption offers such a contrast with the other women that her story is worth relating. Kay consistently showed a combination of personal ambition and a drive to protect her reputation. She was twenty years old when she told her boyfriend, an airman at Loring Air Force Base, that she was pregnant, and he dropped her. Kay came to Bangor in order to earn the money for her hospital bill, and she took great care to hide the fact of her pregnancy. She was the only one, for instance, of whom it was mentioned that she wore a wedding ring. And she told her employer that she was married, but her husband was in the army. She was, Rugan noted, 'quite ambitious for herself and has wanted very much to go on beyond high school and I feel that she has been somewhat discouraged because this has not been possible'. When Rugan suggested to Kay that she do housework, Kay responded that she knew she could do better, and Rugan agreed. Kay placed her child for adoption, obtained a job with the phone company, and married her next-door neighbour.[104]

In the other forty-four cases, the records reveal that once Aid to Dependent Children had taken the economic pressure off families, members of the woman's family and her community actively pressured her to keep her child. In case after case, women struggled with the question of whether or not to keep their children. The social workers consistently urged them to be 'realistic' and place their children. Just as consistently, family members, friends, and women in the community encouraged them to keep them.

Their families offered the women emotional and child care support, and their communities placed pressure on the women to accept the support and to keep their children. The women, having to choose between the adoption services offered by the Good Samaritans and the support offered by their communities, most often chose the support of their communities. In doing so, they chose to remain in the communities where they were relegated to isolation, hard work and gossip with the additional burden (and the additional dependence that that burden entailed) of a child.

Some women applied to the Good Samaritans hoping, they claimed, to keep their pregnancy from their families or hoping to save their families from embarrassment. Many found, however, that their families were more accepting than they had expected. The reason one woman had applied to the Good Samaritans, health officer Shirley Davis wrote to the Home, was to protect her grandparents who would be extremely embarrassed should her condition become known to the rest of the family. 'Now she has her child living there with them', Davis reported later, 'and they seem to have had a complete change in their attitude'.[105]

Another woman, a twenty-year-old telephone operator who lived on her own and who did not want the father of her child, 'a navy man', to know about her pregnancy, planned to place her child for adoption. Her father would be furious if he knew, she claimed. After her baby was born, however, she changed her mind. Her mother agreed to help her out, and she decided to keep the child. 'I saw my parents when I got back', she wrote, 'I wanted to keep it from my Dad but he knew it all along. So I guess it'll work out a lot better that he does'. She must have received enough support for her child to make keeping it possible, for, three months later, she wrote, 'I feel sure I made the right decision in keeping him. I love him so much now, I'd never give him up'.[106]

Families also encouraged women to keep their children. One mother did not even want her daughter to place her child in a foster home, for even that 'seemed to mean "giving the child up" to them' a social worker wrote to the Good Samaritans. The mother came to the office to tell the social worker that if she did not help her daughter keep the child she would feel considerable guilt. 'For', Krick explained, 'she said she had always helped her other children with their children and felt perhaps she should for __ with her baby'. In another case, the Good Samaritan's social worker noted that a nurse was 'having trouble with her mother about placing her baby for adoption. Mother thinks she should keep her'.[107]

In numerous other cases, women made clear that they kept their children in part because the community encouraged them to do so. In 1951, Tandy noted that the minister of one woman approved of her leaving her boyfriend and keeping the baby. The woman herself, Tandy noted, wanted to keep the baby because she knew of a girl in a nearby town who kept hers and 'had no difficulty in being accepted'.[108]

Another woman chose not to tell the father of her child that she was pregnant. Her mother supported her in this, for she did not want the couple to marry if they did not care for each other. The sixteen-year-old considered giving up her child so she could support herself, but, she told the caseworker, her big concern was that the community 'would hold it against her if she did not take the baby and bring it up and she could not do this and work'. Both women kept their children.[109]

Letha considered giving up her child because she could not possibly take care of it herself and her parents, unable to help her, would worry about her and the child if she kept it. Rugan noted:

> She realized this was going to be hard because everyone knew about it. She thought, however, that she would just go home and try to make the best of it, and that when she did not bring the baby home, perhaps they would understand that she had tried to do the best for her baby. She knew that there would be some who would ask her why she did not bring it home and she felt that she was just going to be honest about it and say that she could not give a baby a good home.[110]

As with many other cases, Letha kept her child.

At times, the community even actively interfered to see that the woman kept her child. In 1958, Lura wavered on whether to give up her child or not. Before its birth she had claimed that she 'wasn't remotely interested' in her son and 'didn't even want to know the color of his hair or eyes'. Lura signed an adoption consent form but then, finding she had to go before a judge, changed her mind. Finally, her minister, her cousin, and the woman for whom her mother worked all came into the Good Samaritan office. This last woman, the social worker noted, 'seemed to be extremely aggressive and at one point said that pressure had been put on Lura to place the baby for adoption'. The baby went home with Lura and her entourage.[111]

The social workers accepted these choices with resignation. Miss Krick wrote to Regina Rugan of an eighteen-year-old who decided to keep her child at the family farm. 'It is a good community and perhaps the child will be accepted and things work out better than we usually expect'. Besides, she added with resignation, 'If Anna wants to take the baby, there is little we can do to prevent it'.[112]

That the family coerced the women to keep their children was often the case, but the coercion was not solely to punish the women for having a child out of wedlock. A number of women made a deliberate choice not to marry the father of their child because they did not like him enough or he was planning to move out of state. They chose instead to be unwed mothers.

The decision to return home with a child born out of wedlock was not necessarily, however, an easy one, as some of the above quotations suggest. For all, it meant remaining within a community where they experienced isolation, hard work and community scrutiny. The Good Samaritans stopped recording marriages of past residents, and so there is no way of telling how many eventually married. Many did, however, write to the Good Samaritans of their desire to return to Bangor.

As one wrote in 1953, 'It seems good to be home after four months but I have a lot of lonesome moments. My mother is starting to work all day instead of just afternoons ... so it gives me a lot of time to be alone'. Another seventeen-year-old wrote, 'I wish I was back down there because I miss it. I work harder now than I did when I was down there'. In another letter she noted, 'I am just beginning to appreciate what Mrs. Merrill & you did for me. Remember when I was down there, well in the afternoon I didn't have to work but I am telling you I have to work afternoons now and I mean work too'.[113] A number wrote requesting jobs at the Good Samaritans. As one wrote, 'I really miss the place a lot so that's why I like to work there'.[114]

The conflict that the girls felt between their local communities and a larger world, between the work and isolation of their home towns and the promise of something else in the larger cities, was reflected by one woman who wrote:

I miss the girls awfully there isn't any girls up here that are of my age now. They are
married or gone away ... Just been to town three times. Can't go when your picking
you get so tired you like to go to bed as soon as possible ... There are a lot of potatoes
yet to be dug.

Two months later she wrote, 'I wanted to come here awfully bad when I was
down there. Now I'm kinda lonesome for Bangor. There isn't much doing here.
No movies or anything'.[115]

The emphasis on local community support and individual responsibility
extended well into the twentieth century. While it promised women at least the
minimal support necessary to survive, it reinforced their dependence on their
families and their communities. In the first half of the twentieth century, when
educational opportunities were expanding for women nationwide, it worked
primarily to limit their options.

CONCLUSION

There has been a sea-change in the United States in society's attitude toward unwed mothers. First of all, they are more likely now to be called single mothers because the vast majority raise their children. Ann Fessler estimates that in 1960 40 per cent of white single women gave up their children to adoption; today that percentage has dropped to only 1.5 per cent. When they do choose to surrender their children, single women often do so in open adoptions that enable birth mothers to stay in touch with their children.[1]

There has been a corresponding recognition that the middle-class consensus of the past half-century was damaging to young single women. As early as 1964 a Canadian conference on out of wedlock pregnancy noted in its final report that there was a general feeling that 'these Homes for Unmarried Mothers should not be so cut off from the community and so isolated that no one knows about them.' Dr May Taylor urged her colleagues to fact facts. 'For generations social workers have been strongly encouraging girls who were pregnant out of wed-lock to place their children for adoption and we have done this with the very best intentions [but] we are faced at this moment with the need to re-evaluate this advice...'[2] In 1997 the Australian Association of Social Workers Ltd issued a statement of apology for the lifelong pain they inadvertently had caused many women who had relinquished their children. In 1998 the Tasmanian Parliament held public hearings in which it concluded 'In hindsight, it is believed that if knowledge of the emotional effects on people was available during the period concerned ... witnesses and respondents, who include some adopted children, would not therefore be experiencing the pain and suffering which continues to influence their lives'.[3]

In the United States, the sea-change began with different members of the adoptive triad who began grassroots movements to provide emotional support for one another and to provide assistance to those who wanted to search for those from whom they had been separated. In 1971 those who had been adopted formed the Adoptees Liberty Movement Association. In 1976 those who had placed their children for adoption organized the Concerned United Birthpar-ents. Today approximately one-third of the states provide some non-identifying information to members of the adoptive triad and some help facilitate reunions. Bastard Nation, an adoptees' rights organization provides a full list of state disclosure laws and the National Adoption Clearinghouse provides details on the various state laws.

Tennessee was the home of one of the early and best-known search organizations. In 1978 Denny Glad, who had a relative who had been adopted, formed Tennessee's Right to Know. She spent the next three decades assisting adopted children and their birth parents search for one another and fighting to provide them access to their birth certificate information. She gathered all the information she could on Georgia Tann and the Tennessee Children's Home Society Memphis Branch. With Caprice Ease she formed the Coalition for Adoption Reform. The Coalition was instrumental in persuading the Tennessee legislature to investigate Tennessee's adoption practices. Today Tennessee adoptions records are open to all but those whose births were a result of rape or incest.

Maine became the fifth state in the Union to provide complete open access to adoption records in 2009. The Good Samaritan Association is still active and offers single mothers childcare and a high school education.

While these changes have meant that the number of white women who surrender their children to adoption has dropped dramatically, the number of couples seeking infants to adopt has not. Many couples have now turned to other countries where poverty has left many infants vulnerable. In 2006, for example, there were 8,000 orphan visas obtained from China alone, with Russia, Guatemala, South Korean, Ukraine and Kazakhstan together providing many more.[4]

A century ago a changing economy forced a mass migration of rural populations into the urban areas of the United States. We are now at the beginning of another century and in the midst of another information revolution. The internet has made global communication instantaneous and carried the separation of space from place to an entirely new level. At the same time, mass migration has become a global phenomenon as the growth of global corporations undermines the local communities' abilities to survive. Today new technologies and mass migration are drawing rural areas around the world into a global community. Now, as then, the changes have reflected dramatic economic disparities. As Barbara Raymond has pointed out, some Americans have paid as much $40,000 to adopt a child in countries where the average income is $1,800. Also in parallel to the past, Governments and the United Nations are working to ensure that the children who are adopted are 'legitimately eligible' and that formal procedures are followed.[5]

While mothers in isolated areas around the world do not share the concept of unwed-motherhood so pronounced in the United States at the turn of the last century, similar economic inequalities raise troubling questions. In seeking answers, we must now, as in the past, understand how the rural is implicated in the urban or global.

Scholars of globalization have emphasized the importance of paying attention to the rural communities in this global shift. Arjun Appadurai notes, 'Globalization has shrunk the distance between elites, shifted key relationships between producers and consumers, broken many links between labor and family life, obscured the lines between temporary locales and imaginary national attachments'. He cautions, however, that

> one of the most problematic legacies of grand Western social science ... is that it has steadily reinforced the sense of some single moment – call it the modern moment – that by its appearance creates a dramatic and unprecedented break between past and present. Reincarnated as the break between tradition and modernity and typologized as the difference between ostensibly traditional and modern societies, this view has been shown repeatedly to distort the meanings of change and the politics of pastness.[6]

Barbara Ching and Gerald W. Creed also argue for the importance of recognizing the distinctiveness of the rural. Noting both the invisibility and the denigration of the rural they call for maintaining its visibility and vitality, 'not only for the sake of the food supply but also for the analytical possibilities opened up by attention to life at the rustic margin'. They argue that 'despite the significance of the rural/urban distinction, contemporary cultural research and theory have focused little attention on it'. Often, they note, the idea of place is used metaphorically and yet they 'argue instead for a theoretical middle ground in which "place" can be metaphoric yet still refer to a particular physical environment and its associated socio-cultural qualities'. They published a collection of essays which, they note, 'insists on marking the conceptual and experiential difference between the country and the city by uncovering and extending the longstanding discourse which constructs these differences'.[7]

These scholars argue for the importance of the rural in understanding the impact of modernity on identity. My hope is that this work will encourage scholars to focus on the rural and the implications of the rural/urban split when they explore issues related to mothers and their children.

NOTES

Introduction

1. J. Keith, *Country People in the New South* (Chapel Hill, NC: University of North Carolina Press, 1995), p. 4; R. Condon, 'Living in Two Worlds, Rural Maine in 1930' *Maine History*, 25, pp. 58–87.

2. See for example M. J. Morton, *And Sin No More: Social Policy and Unwed Mothers in Cleveland, 1855–1990* (Columbus, OH: Ohio State University Press, 1993); S. Brandenstein, 'The Colorado Cottage Home', *Colorado Magazine*, 53:3 (1976), pp. 229–41; S. Ruggles, 'Fallen Women: The Inmates of the Magdalene Society Asylum of Philadelphia 1836–1908', *Journal of Social History*, 16 (Summer 1983), pp. 65–82.

3. L. M. Friedman, *A History of American Law*, 2nd edn (New York: Simon and Schuster, 1985), p. 590.

4. R. Lane, *Murder in America: A History* (Columbus, OH: Ohio State University Press, 1997), pp. 193 and 184.

5. D. Massey, *Space, Place, and Gender*, 5th edn (Minneapolis, MN: University of Minnesota Press, 1994), p. 167.

6. V. E. Bynum, *Unruly Women: The Politics of Social and Sexual Control in the Old South* (Chapel Hill, NC: University of North Carolina Press, 1992), p. 6.

7. J. R. Beniger, *The Control Revolution* (Cambridge, MA: Harvard University Press, 1986), pp. 14 and 15; O. Zunz, *Making America Corporate, 1870–1920* (Chicago, IL: University of Chicago Press, 1990), p. 7.

8. R. W. Wiebe, *The Search for Order, 1877–1920* (New York: Hill and Wang, 1967), p. 112.

9. Ibid., p. 130.

10. D. B. Danbom, *Born in the Country: A History of Rural America* (Baltimore, MD: Johns Hopkins University Press, 1995), p. 86. See also J. Butler, 'A Family & Community Life in Maine, 1783–1861', in R. W. Judd et al. (eds), *Maine: The Pine Tree State from Prehistory to the Present* (Orono, ME: University of Maine Press, 1994), pp. 217–41; Keith, *Country People*; L. Beam, *A Maine Hamlet* (1957; Augusta, ME: Lance Tapley, 1985).

11. R. Fuchs, *Gender and Poverty in Nineteenth-Century Europe* (Cambridge: Cambridge Univ. Press, 2005), pp. 56, 57, and 156.

12. This description is taken from Danbom, *Born in the Country*, pp. 5–13.

13. D. Kemmis, *Community and the Politics of Place* (Norman, OK: University of Oklahoma Press, 1990), p. 71.

14. N. Cott, *Public Vows: A History of Marriage and the Nation* (Cambridge: Harvard University Press, 2000), p. 29; US Congress Senate *Report on the Condition of Women and Child Wage Earners in the United States*, doc. no. 645 61st Cong. 2nd sess., 1911, p. 92; A. T. Bingham, 'Determinants of Sex Delinquency in Adolescent Girls' *Journal of Law and Criminology*, 13 (February 1923), p. 70, as quoted in R. Kunzel, *Fallen Women, Problem Girls* (New Haven, CT: Yale University Press,1993), p. 61.

15. See for example J. Ladner, *Tomorrow's Tomorrow: The Black Woman* (New York: Doubleday, 1973) and C. Stack, *All Our Kin: Strategies for Survival in a Black Community* (New York: Harper & Row, 1974).

16. J. J. Brumberg, 'Ruined Girls: Changing Community Responses to Illegitimacy in Upstate New York, 1890–1920', *Journal of Social History*, 18 (1984–1985), pp. 247–72, p. 249.

17. B. J. Bledstein, *The Culture of Professionalism* (New York: Norton & Co., 1976), p. 3.

18. A. Fessler, *The Girls Who Went Away* (New York: Penguin, 2006), pp. 134, 16, 36, 80, and 102.

19. Ibid., pp. 293, 147; *Gone to an Aunt's: Remembering Canada's Homes for Unwed Mothers* (Toronto: McClelland & Stewart, 1998).

20. A. C. Wiggins, 'The Migrant Girl' (unpublished thesis for Vanderbilt University, 1933), pp. 13 and 17.

21. D. S. Smith, 'The Long Cycle in American Illegitimacy and Prenuptial Pregnancy', in P. Laslett et al. (eds), *Bastardy and Its Comparative History* New York: Cambridge University Press, 1980).

22. Interview with Donna Lemieux, 25 January 1996; Letter from William S. Silsby to Good Samaritan Agency, 27 May 1981.

23. D. B. Rutman, 'Assessing the Little Communities of Early America'. *The William and Mary Quarterly*, 3d ser., 43:2 (April 1986), pp. 164–78.

24. R. G. Fuchs, *Poor & Pregnant in Paris: Strategies for Survival in the Nineteenth Century* (New Brunswick, NJ: Rutgers University Press, 1992), p. 5.

25. Massey, *Space, Place, and Gender*, p. 5.

26. Ibid., pp. 153 and 167.

1 Rural Communities and Regional Differences: Maine and Tennessee

1. R. E. Corlew, *Tennessee: A Short History*, 2nd edn (Knoxville, TN: University of Tennessee Press, 1990), p. 340; Judd et al. (eds), *Maine*, 356–7; J. W. Davidson et al., *Nation of Nations: A Narrative History of the American Republic* (New York: McGraw Hill, 1990), p. 611.

2. Judd et al. (eds), *Maine*, pp. 164 and 235.

3. M. J. McDonald and J. Moldowny, *TVA and the Dispossessed: The Resettlement of Population in the Norris Dam Area* (Knoxville, TN: University of Tennessee Press, 1982), p. 37

4. M. J. Hagood, *Mothers of the South: Portraiture of the White Tenant Farm Woman* (1939; NY: Greenwood Press, 1969), pp. 170–2.

5. McDonald and Moldowny, TVA and the Dispossessed, p.37.

6. Judd et al. (eds), *Maine*, pp. 254, 255.

7. McDonald and Moldowny, *TVA and the Dispossessed*, p. 38.

8. T. E. Terrill and J. Hirsch (eds), *Such As Us: Southern Voices of the Thirties* (New York: W. W. Norton, 1978), p. 3; I. A. Newby, *Plain Folk in the New South: Social Change and Cultural Persistence 1880–1915* (Baton Rouge, LA: Louisiana State University, 1989), p. 184.

9. Beam, *A Maine Hamlet*; Keith, *Country People*, p. 26.

10. Beam, *A Maine Hamlet*, p. 87.

11. J. B. Killibrew, *Resources of Tennessee* (Nashville, TN: Tavel, Eastman & Howell, 1874), p. 354 as quoted in McDonald and Moldowny, *TVA and the Dispossessed*, p. 27; Hagood, *Mothers of the South*, 158.

12. Good Samaritan Case Records, #297–125: Letter from Gertrude Atwood to IRS, 12 October 1928

13. US Department of Labor, Children's Bureau, Publication No. 120: Maternity and Infant Care in a Mountain County in Georgia (1923 as quoted in Newby, *Plain Folk*, p. 294.

14. J. T. Kirby, *Rural Worlds Lost: The American South, 1920–1960* (Baton Rouge, LA: Louisiana Sate University Press, 1987), pp. 156 and 157. Beam noted that her grandmother began housekeeping at 11 when her mother died. Beam, *A Maine Hamlet*, p. 12.

15. Kirby, *Rural Worlds Lost*, pp. 156 and 157.

16. Newby, *Plain Folk*, p. 105.

17. L. T. Ulrich, *A Midwife's Tale: The Life of Martha Ballard, Based on Her Diary, 1785–1812* (New York: Knopf, 1990) , pp. 147–60.

18. L. Pope, *Mill Hands and Preachers* (New Haven, CT: n.p., 1942), p. 66 as quoted in Newby, *Plain Folk*, p. 339; H. White, 'Our Rural Slums', *Independent*, 8 October 1908, in *The Annals of America* vol. 13 edited by W. Benton (Chicago, IL: Encyclopedia Britannica, 1968), p. 151.

19. Hagood, *Mothers of the South*, p. 112.

20. Beam, *A Maine Hamlet*, p. 175.

21. W. T. Couch (ed.), *These Are Our Lives* (Chapel Hill, NC: University of North Carolina Press, 1939), p. 46; J. R. Robinson, *Living Hard: Southern Americans in the Great Depression* (Washington, DC: University Press of America, 1981), p. 74.

22. Good Samaritan Case Records, check Letter from ___ to Good Samaritans, 31 May 1920.

23. Kirby, *Rural Worlds Lost*, 173; Cott, *Public Vows*, pp. 24 and 29.

24. Terrill and Hirsch, *Such as Us*, pp. 126 and 124.

25. Hagood, *Mothers of the South*, pp. 112, 134, 148.

26. It cannot be confirmed that every suit was brought by a rural woman, but in Maine, where their towns are identified, they are almost exclusively small towns. In Tennessee, the towns weren't often named but often the record reports that they were 'out in the country' or 'country girls'.

27. *Parker v. Meek*, 35 Tenn 30 (*Franklin v. McCorkle*, 1 Southwest, 250

28. *Franklin v. McCorkle*, 1 Southwest 251.

29. *Thompson v. Glendenning*, 1 Head 295

30. *Mann v. Maxwell*, 83 Maine 146; *Palmer v. McDonald*, 92 Maine 125; *Drew v. Shannon*, 105 Maine 565; *Ferguson v. Moore*, 90 Tenn. 341.

31. *Thompson v. Clendening*, 1 Head 289; *Love v. Masoner*, 65 Tenn 29 ; *Graham v. McReynolds*, 18 Southwestern Reporter 122.

32. *Messer v. Jones*, 88 Maine 349.

33. *Baker v. Bates*, 4 Higins 176. See also *Heggie v. Hayes*, 141 Tenn. 221. *Kaufman v. Fye*, 42 Southwest 25; *Love v. Masoner*, 65 Tenn 25; *Ferguson v. Moore*, 39 Southwestern 41.

34. These changes and the rural response to them are clearly described in M. S. Hoffschwelle, *Rebuilding the Southern Community: Reformers, Schools, and Homes in Tennessee, 1900–1930* (Knoxville, TN: University of Tennessee Press, 1998); Keith, *Country People*; L. M. Kyriakoudes, *The Social Origins of the Urban South: Race, Gender, and Migration in Nashville and Middle Tennessee, 1890–1930* (Chapel Hill, NC: University of North Carolina Press, 2003); and H. S. Barron, *Mixed Harvest: The Second Great Transformation in the Rural North, 1870–1930* (Chapel Hill, NC: University of North Carolina Press, 1997).

35. Judd, et al. (eds), *Maine*, p. 249. See also footnote 34. For accounts of the mass out-migration of rural people in Maine and Tennessee see H. S. Barron, *Mixed Harvest*, Kyriakoudes, *The Social Origins of the Urban South* and McDonald and Muldowny, *TVA and the Dispossessed*.

36. M. Walker, 'The Changing Character of Farm Life: Rural Southern Women' in M. Walker, J. R. Dunn, and J. P. Dunn (eds.), *Southern Women at the Millennium: A Historical Perspective* (Columbia: University of Missouri Press, 2005), p. 147.

37. Judd et al. (eds), *Maine*, p. 187–90.

38. E. Abbott, *Public Assistance: American Principles and Policies* (Chicago, IL: University of Chicago Press, 1940), Reprint ed. (New York: Russell and Russell, 1966) p. 3. Most states required only a year's residence to obtain a settlement.

39. *Inhabitants of Hiram v. Pierce*, 45 Maine 367.

40. Abbott, *Public Assistance*, p. 26; *Hall v. Clifton*, 53 Maine 60; *Inhabitants of Portland v. Inhabitants of New Gloucester*, 16 Maine 427.

41. Overseers of the Poor of Bangor Records, 1830–1925 (not complete), unlabelled box, Bangor City Hall.

42. J. F. Hankins, 'A Cage for John Sawyer: The Poor of Otisfield, Maine,' *Maine History*, Fall 1994, p. 115.

43. Trattner suggests that the county-based system of poor relief in the Southwest grew out of the parish system and the Northwest Ordinance. W. Trattner, *From Poor Law to Welfare State: A History of Social Welfare in America*, 2nd edn (NY: Free Press, 1979), p. 17; Corlew, *Tennessee*, p. 166.

44. The degree of separation of the poor from their communities that existed in Tennessee is suggested by an appellate court case in 1884 which determined that if the commissioners of the poor inhumanly neglect to supply the poor under their charge with food and shelter, they might be indicted. Two residents had died a short way from the county's poor farm. *State v. West*, 82 Tenn 38.

45. J. B. Vickery et al., 'Maine Agriculture, 1783–1861', in Judd et al. (eds), *Maine*, pp. 250–252, 259.

46. D. L. Winters, *Tennessee Farming, Tennessee Farmers: Antebellum Agriculture in the Upper South* (Knoxville, TN: University of Tennessee Press, 1994), p. 108.

47. Winters found that most farmers in his study owned 50–100 acres. Winters, *Tennessee Farming*, p. 108.

48. Historians of other Southern states have analyzed the compromises developed as a result of similar competing economic interests. See for instance S. Hahn, *The Roots of Southern Populism: Yeoman Farmers and the Transformation of the Georgia Upcountry, 1850–1890* (New York: Oxford University Press, 1983) and A. Kulikoff, *Tobacco and Slaves: The*

Development of Southern Cultures in the Chesapeake, 1680–1800 (Chapel Hill, NC: University of North Carolina Press, 1986).

49. As quoted in Vickery et al., 'Maine Agriculture' in Judd et al. (eds), *Maine*, p. 256.
50. The right of inheritance was not made an option in adoption until 1880. *Bunker v. Mains*, 139 Maine 231; *Tabor v. Douglas*, 101 Maine 363; *Wilder v. Wilder*, 116 Maine 389.
51. Ulrich, *A Midwife's Tale*, ch. 6.
52. Winters, *Tennessee Farming*, p. 135. There was a similar parallel with regard to legitimation. In Maine, a father could legitimate his child by taking it into his home. In Tennessee, a man could legitimate his child only by guaranteeing the right of inheritance to his child. See below.
53. It must be stressed that these are the assumptions of only the elite. There is evidence that poor southerners crossed over the race line when support was necessary.
54. H. D. Krause, *Illegitimacy: Law and Social Policy* (New York: Bobbs-Merrill, 1971), p. 485.
55. E. Freund, *Illegitimacy Laws of the US and Certain Foreign Countries* (Washington, DC: GPO, 1919), p. 27.
56. J. Perley, *Powers and Duties of Justices of Peace with the Necessary Forms Particularly Adapted to the Laws of Maine*. 2nd edn (Hallowell: Glazier, Masters, & Co., 1829), p. 60.
57. *Blake v. Junkins*, 34 ME 237. See also *Woodbury v. Yeaton*, 135 Maine 147.
58. *Blake v. Junkins*, 34 Maine 238; *Beals v. Furbish*, 39 Maine 473; *Wilson v. Woodside*, 67 Maine 249.
59. *Harmon v. Merrill et al*, 18 Maine 150; *Keniston v. Rowe*, 16 Maine 38; *Low v. Mitchell*, 18 Maine 372.
60. *Woodward v. Shaw*, 18 Maine 304, 307.
61. *Burgess v. Bosworth*, 23 Maine 573.
62. *Boisvert v. Charest*, 135 Maine 220.
63. *Woodward v. Shaw*, 18 Maine 307.
64. *Low v. Mitchell*, 18 Maine 372; *Harmon v. Merrill*, 18 Maine 150.
65. *Mariner v. Dyer*, 2 Maine, 171.
66. *McLaughlin v. Whitten*, 32 Maine 21; *Brett v. Murphy*, 80 Maine 358.
67. Overseers of the Poor of Bangor Log Book, 1830–1925, not complete, in the basement of Bangor City Hall.
68. It was invariably other women who testified that the woman named the father of the child during travail, even when a doctor attended the birth. See for example *Wilson v. Woodside*, 67 Maine 244 and *Mann v. Maxwell*, 83 Maine 146.
69. Perley, *Powers and Duties of Justices of Peace*, p. 61.
70. *State v. Kirby*, 57 Maine 30.
71. *State v. Kirby*, 57 Maine 36.
72. Seduction laws provided families with compensation for the theft of their daughter's virginity and the depreciation of her marriage value. A daughter did not have to be pregnant in order for the family to bring suit. Appellate court records suggest that the vast majority of women involved in seduction suits were pregnant.
73. This was true even if the mother married some one else before the baby was born. The husband, the court concluded, might disinherit the child by swearing to his illegitimacy, or he might be a pauper, or he might die and leave his property to others. *Edmonds v. State*, 24 Tenn 94, 95; *State v. Ingram*, 5 Tenn 221.

74. *State v. Coatney*, 16 Tenn 210.
75. *State v. Howard*, 1 Swan 133; *Kirkpatrick v. State*, 19 Tenn 124; *State v. Howard*, 1 Swan 133.
76. *State v. Elijah Jameson*, 50 Tenn 108. It is significant that the one case identifying a woman of color occurred in 1871, six years after an amendment to the state constitution emancipated the slaves and at the tail end of Reconstruction.
77. B. F. Reskin, 'Bringing the Men Back In: Sex Differentiation and the Devaluation of Women's Work,' *Gender & Society* 2:1 (March 1988), pp. 58–81.
78. Shannon's Code Sec. 4186.
79. B. Wyatt-Brown, *Honor and Violence in the Old South* (New York: Oxford University, Press, 1986), pp. 188 and 198.
80. As late as 1920 a father had the right to consent to or forbid an adoption of his child while the consent of the mother was not required. E. N. Clopper, *Child Welfare in Tennessee: An Inquiry by the National Child Labor Committee for the Tennessee Child Welfare Commissioner* (Nashville, TN: Tennessee Industrial School, 1920), p. 26.
81. *McReynolds v. McCallie*, 69 Tenn 260; *McKamie v. Baskerville*, 86 Tenn 459.
82. The legitimation laws enabled some unwed mothers to claim large inheritances through their children when the father and child had both died. See for example see *McCormick v. Cantrell*, 7 Yerge 615; *McReynolds v. McCallie*, 69 Tenn 260; *Murphy v. Portrum*, 95 Tenn 695.
83. In 1895 Victor Beaudette of Maine brought a seduction suit against Narcisse Gagne. In proof he asserted he had taken his daughter to a distant city for an abortion and that she was sick for three weeks following. The court responded that Beaudette could not base the action upon the commission of sexual seduction alone, no matter how wrongfully done. If the daughter were of age, 'some act of service is necessary on the part of the daughter to enable the father to maintain the action.' *Beaudette v. Gagne*, 87 Maine 534. See also *Tabor v. Douglass*, 101 Maine 363 and *Bunker v. Mains*, 139 Maine 185.
84. *Wallace v. Clark*, Overton II, 93. The court confirmed that 'The parent ... has no direct remedy at common law for the debauching of a daughter. He has to resort, therefore, to what has been denominated "but little more than matter of fiction" –the relation of master and servant assumed to exist between parent and child – in order to redress this wrong.' *Parker v. Meek*, 35 Tenn 29.
85. *Godall v. Thurman*, 1 Head 209.
86. *Conn v. Wilson*, 2 Overton 234.
87. *Conn v. Wilson*, 2 Overton 234; *Godall v. Thurman*, 1 Head 209. In an inheritance case regarding a woman who had four children by one man and who claimed she was named in his will, the contestants claimed that the woman, being an unmarried mother was a 'woman devoid of virtue' and therefore not worthy of being believed. *Morris v. Swaney*, 54 Tenn 601.
88. *Goddard v. State*, 10 Tenn 98, 99.
89. *Thompson v. Clendening*, 1 Head 288; *Love v. Masoner*, 6 Baxt. 25.
90. See for example *Wallace v. Clark*, Overton 92, *Godall v. Thurman*, 1 Head 209; *Graham v. McReynolds*, 18 SW 272.
91. *Thompson v. Clendening*, 1 Head 300. The court also made this distinction in bastardy suits. Although the law required the court to place the child of a woman who had brought a bastardy suit when the child was three, faced with a woman who had then married into money the court queried, suppose if a woman 'has a large landed estate and is very wealthy,' would the county court have the power to take her child from her at

its discretion? ... The idea that such a child could be taken from its mother, and bound apprentice to any mechanical employ the county court chose, has not occurred to one man who is a member of the county court.' *Lawson v. Scott*, 9 Tenn 92.

92. *Maguinay v. Saudek*, 37 Tenn 146.
93. *Bradshaw v. Jones*, 103 Tenn 331, 52 SW 1073, 1074. The court however maintained the social distinction determined by class. G. A. Jones had asked for $10,000. The jury awarded him $5,000; and the judge reduced the compensation to $2,500.
94. *Lea v. Henderson*, 1 Coldwell 147.
95. *Love v. Masoner*, 65 Tenn 24.
96. *Franklin v. McCorkle*, 1 SW 250.
97. *Kaufman v. Fye*, 99 Tenn 145, 42 SW 30.
98. *Finch v. Gibson*, 140 Tenn 134, 203 SW 759
99. *Finch v. Gibson*, 140 Tenn 134, 203 SW 760, 761.

2 Tennessee: Maintaining Hierarchies of Race and Class.

1. As quoted in Corlew, *Tennessee*, p. 328.
2. The sample included all the bastardy suit files found in the Washington County Court records that have been transferred to the Sherrod Library of the University of Tennessee-Johnson City. The court records were submitted to the archives in a jumbled fashion and the archivist had isolated all the bastardy suits that she could find.
3. *State v. Hyder*, 4 February 1878. Hyder, an African-American, quoted the law *verbatim* when he challenged the accusation.
4. *State v. Mohler*, 10 November 1879.
5. *State v. Green*, 1882.
6. *State v. Sliger*, 1 March 1869.
7. *State v. Ford*, 2 July 1872.
8. *State v. Little*, 9 April 1878.
9. *State v. Mohler*, 10 November 1879.
10. A. M. Plane, 'Colonizing the Family: Marriage, Household and Racial Boundaries in Southeastern New England to 1730' (unpublished dissertation Brandeis University, MA, 1996), p. 62.
11. *State v. O'Brien*, 28 June 1886.
12. *State v. Crosswhite*, 28 June 1870.
13. *State v. Bacon*, 4 October 1869. Bacon too was wealthy enough to hire a lawyer.
14. *State v. McCracken*, 28 February 1885. The power of the court to take a child away once a bastardy suit is initiated is reflected in the case of African Americans Ellen Lane Bayless and James Hill. Hill contested the case but was found guilty and paid in full. Nevertheless relatives of both Hill and Bayless bound themselves 'to the county ... that a bastard child born of said Ellen Jane Bayless shall never become chargeable to said county as a pauper. If it should we will pay all such expenses and charges as soon as they are incurred to the trustee of said county'. *State v. Hill*, 29 November 1871.
15. Clopper, *Child Welfare in Tennessee*, p. 90. Although Clopper was writing in 1920, ninety dollars was a relatively small amount at the end of the nineteenth century. In Maine in 1888, for example, the court ordered Edgar Murphy to pay Cora Brett $125 immediately and then two dollars a week for maintenance of the child until a further court order. *Brett v. Murphy*, 80 Maine 350.

16. In Knoxville, the fourth major city, women would organize a home in 1896 'after many years of unsatisfactory effort to do something for unfortunate women'. Photocopy of p. 545 from *History of Knoxville, Tennessee* provided by the Knoxville Florence Crittenton Association, July, 1996.

17. N. F. McConnell and M. M. Dore, *Florence Crittenton Services: The First Century*. (Washington, DC: National Florence Crittenton Mission, 1983), p. 82.

18. Ibid., p. 241; *Memphis Commercial Appeal*, 14 February 1895, 'Woman's Edition'.

19. M. Morlock and H. Campbell, *Maternity Homes for Unmarried Mothers: A Community Service* (Washington, DC: US Dept of Labor, 1946), p. 4.

20. Kunzel, *Fallen Women, Problem Girls*, pp. 2 and 13. See also Morton, *And Sin No More*; Brandenstein, 'The Colorado Cottage Home'; and Ruggles, 'Fallen Women'.

21. *Tennessean*, 6 February 1898.

22. Jane Turner Censer found a similar response in her study of white privileged women in Virginia and North Carolina. Even as, she notes, some white women critiqued their society and looked for alternative models of mores and manners, they came 'increasingly under attack in the 1890s, as more virulent strains of racism and Confederate celebrations took a new, aggressively martial form'. See J. T. Censer, *The Reconstruction of White Southern Womanhood 1865–1895* (Baton Rouge, LA: Louisiana State University Press, 2003), p. 9.

23. See above, Chapter 1. For a discussion of honour in the south see P. Bardaglio, *Reconstructing the Household: Families, Sex, and the Law in the Nineteenth-Century South* (Chapel Hill, NC: University of North Carolina Press, c. 1995), B. Wyatt-Brown, *Honor and Violence in the Old South* (New York: Oxford University Press, 1986).

24. M. Vicinus, *Independent Women: Work and Community for Single Women, 1850-1920* (Chicago, IL: University of Chicago Press, 1985), p. 76.

25. *Memphis Commercial Appeal*, 3 October 1863; Convent of the Good Shepherd, *Fifty Years of Service* (hereafter *Fifty Years of Service*), p. 1.

26. 'The Work of the Home of the Good Shepherd', undated clipping in the Convent of Good Shepherd file in the Memphis Public Library. Excerpts from this report were printed in *Women's Work in Tennessee* (Federation of Women's Clubs. Memphis: Jones-Briggs, 1916), p. 233.

27. 'Work of the Home...'; *Fifty Years of Service*, pp. 12 and 13; *Memphis Commercial Appeal*, 10 October 1932; *Commercial Appeal*, 31 October 1939. There were convents for the penitential order in New Orleans, Chicago and Milwaukee.

28. *Fifty Years of Service*, p. 13.

29. P. J. Giddings, *Ida: A Sword Among Lions* (New York: Harper Collins, 2008), p. 43; W. D. Miller, *Memphis During the Progressive Era* (Memphis, TN: Memphis State University Press, 1957), pp. 3–7; R. Biles, *Memphis in the Great Depression* (Knoxville, TN: University of Tennessee Press, 1986), p. 3.

30. H. G. Gutman, *The Black Family in Slavery and Freedom, 1750–1925* (New York: Random House, 1976), p. 24; Biles, *Memphis*, p. 10; W. J. Cooper, Jr and T. E. Terrill, *The American South* (New York: McGraw-Hill, 1991), p. 400; Miller, *Memphis*, pp. 3–7.

31. T. B. Alexander, *Political Reconstruction in Tennessee* (1950; New York: Russell & Russell, 1968), p. 53; Works Projects Administration, *Tennessee: A Guide to the State* (New York: Viking Press, 1936), p. 207.

32. Miller, *Memphis*, pp. 91, 92 and 26; Biles, *Memphis*, p. 15. The Prudential Insurance Company found that the homicide rate for Memphis was 47.1 per 100,000 compared to the average rate of 7.2 per 100,000 for cities over 25,000.

33. M. Wedell, *Elite Women and the Reform Impulse in Memphis, 1875–1915* (Knoxville, TN: University of Tennnesse Press, 1991), p. 14. Wedell thoroughly examines the women's reform movement in Memphis following the Civil War.

34. She was a friend of the judge and clerk of elections and no action was taken against her. This is an indication of the status of the women who were organizing in Memphis at this time. Wedell, *Elite Women*, p. 24.

35. Both Johnson and Meriwether – leaders in the reform movement and among the founders of the unwed mother's home – were born in the south in the 1830s, attended Emma Willard or Emma-Willard-influenced schools, and began their organized reform efforts several years after their last children were born. Wedell contends that their work during the Civil War encouraged their social activism by showing them they could cope with emergencies, survive without men and connect with other women. Both were also staunch supporters of the southern cause and thus 'could affect change without casting themselves in a radical position'. Wedell, *Elite Women*, pp. 12, 25, 28, 65, 67, and 31–4.

36. Prominent among these was the Nineteenth Century Club which was founded in Memphis and became the South's foremost women's organization. Wedell, *Elite Women* pp. 85 and 87; 'Woman's Edition,' *Memphis Commercial Appeal*, 14 February 1895.

37. *History of the Women's and Young Women's Christian Association of Memphis*, 1892, p. 1.

38. *Memphis Commercial Appeal*, 23 February 1875, p. 4.

39. *Memphis Daily Appeal*, 23 February 1875, p. 4.

40. This class definition owes much to the discussion on class in G. E. Gilmore, *Gender & Jim Crow: Women and the Politics of White Supremacy in North Carolina, 1896–1920* (Chapel Hill, NC: University of North Carolina Press, 1996).

41. Wedell, *Elite Women*, p. 149, #22.

42. *History of the Women's and Young Women's Christian Association of Memphis*, p. 2; *Memphis Commercial Appeal*, 6 March 1881, p. 4.

43. L. Meriwether, *Soundings* (Memphis: Boyle & Chapman, 1872), frontispiece.

44. Ibid., pp. 147, 41, and 97.

45. Ibid., p. 151.

46. Her sister-in-law Elizabeth Johnson also stressed this point. In a talk she gave to the National Woman's Christian Association she pointed out that God saved the life of the harlot Rehab of Jericho because 'she was the only one that had faith to be saved'. *Memphis Daily Appeal*, 22 January 1882.

47. *Memphis Commercial Appeal*, 14 April 1889, p. 10.

48. Ibid., pp. 13, 14, and 27.

49. *Memphis Daily Avalanche*, 14 April 1889, p. 10.

50. Meriwether, *Soundings*, pp. 165–7.

51. See above, footnotes 17 and 18.

52. 'In the past several decades, the presence of large numbers of girl migrants in city populations has become a significant social fact and social problem. These girls are not transients or wanderers but are girls who leave the country-side or small town to find employment in the urban centers'. Wiggins, 'The Migrant Girl', p. 1.

53. E. Scott, *Background in Tennessee* (New York: Robert McBride, 1937), p. 224; 'I'd Rather Die' in Couch (ed.), *These Are Our Lives*, p. 248. We don't have as much information as to how the rural women saw the urban women though Maureen Murphy gives us an idea of what it might be when she talks about her arrival in Memphis. 'We didn't have a lot of fancy food in the country, but Mother was a fiend about germs. She'd have died off

if she had seen how the trade gobbled up stuff she'd thrown out the kitchen door to the chickens. I ate it too and it didn't kill me'. Ibid., pp. 343, 344.

54. A. M. Duster (ed.), *Crusade for Justice* (Chicago, IL: University of Chicago Press, 1970), p. 44. The date of this encounter is never explicitly stated but I have extrapolated the date from other events. For an excellent biography of Wells see Giddings, *Ida*, p. 56.

55. *Memphis Commercial Appeal*, 19 June 1883, p. 3.

56. *Memphis Daily Avalanche*, 14 April 1889, p. 10.

57. *Memphis Daily Appeal*, 1 June 1984.

58. *WCA Annual Report*, 1893; *Appeal*, 19 July 1881 and 26 March 1881, p. 2. In 1878, the *Appeal* announced that a Mrs Dr Cutter would give a free lecture in the Navy Yard Mission on the anatomy and physiology of the human body illustrated with a life size mannequin. *Appeal* 26 January 1878.

59. *Memphis Daily Appeal*, 17 June 1984; *Daily Memphis Avalanche*; 6 March 1881, p. 6.

60. *Memphis Daily Avalanche*, 19 July 1881.

61. *Memphis Commercial Appeal*, 26 March 1881 and 26 March 1881.

62. *Memphis Daily Appeal*, 17 June 1884; *Gleaner* #8 (June, 1891), p. 123.

63. *History of the Women's and Young Women's Christian Association of Memphis*, p. 31.

64. *Annual Report*, 1904, p. 17.

65. *Tennessean*, 6 February 1898; *Gleaner*, March, 1892.

66. That Lillie put herself beyond the bounds of the white society is made clear by the fact that she was named. No other residents ever were. The story of Lillie is recorded in *Selected Works of Ida B. Wells-Barnett*, ed. T. Harris (New York: Oxford University Press, 1991), pp. 203–4.

67. Anon., letter, 'Woman's Edition,' *Memphis Commercial Appeal* (14 February 1895)

68. *History of the Women's and Young Women's Christian Association of Memphis*, p. 70; *Memphis Commercial Appeal*, 15 June 1881, 19 July 1881 and 28 February 1875.

69. *Memphis Daily Appeal*, 17 June 1884.

70. *Memphis Daily Avalanche*, 19 June 1883, p. 3, and 17 June 1884.

71. *Memphis Daily Appeal*, 17 June 1984.

72. In 1881, the Mission reported it had twenty women and twenty-five children in the Home. Seven of the children were infants. In 1884, while the laundry brought in $242 and sewing, $379, the boarding children brought in $581. In the same report, the WCA commented that as the sewing was less profitable than had been hoped, the WCA was going to try a new industry – rug making. There is no further mention of the rug making. *Memphis Daily Appeal*, 26 March 1881, pp. 2 and 6, and 17 June 1884.

73. *Memphis Daily Appeal*, 26 March 1881, p. 2, and 15 June 1881. This public relations approach was effective. In March the *Appeal* published a frontpage editorial praising the Mission's work. *Memphis Daily Appeal*, 26 March 1881, p. 1.

74. *Memphis Appeal*, 15 June 1881.

75. *Gleaner*, March 1892; *History*, p. 16.

76. *Gleaner*, March 1892.

77. *Annual Report*, 1891–2.

78. It was not only Maud's father's judgeship that revealed her class. Her father wrote that she had received 'every advantage of education,' including one year of college in Detroit. *Memphis Commercial Appeal*, 28 July 1881.

79. The story that follows is reported in the *Memphis Commercial Appeal*, 19 July 1881 and 28 July 1881.

80. *Memphis Daily Appeal*, 19 June 1883.

81. It is possible that William Meisner was Jewish, in which case another social distinction was maintained in this process.
82. *Appeal*, 23 January 1880.
83. The women who managed the Mission were well-educated (see above). As the newspapers reported on seduction hearings almost daily they would have been able to inform themselves of successful seduction cases.
84. *Appeal*, 18 June 1882.
85. *Appeal*, 15 June 1882.
86. Ibid.
87. *Tennessean*, 6 February 1898.
88. Statistics derived from data collected in the Archives and Museum of Tuskegee University and Tuskegee National Center for Bioethics as cited in C. Arnold-Zourie, "'A Madman's Deed – A Maniac's Hand": Gender and Justice in Three Maryland Lynchings', *Journal of Social History* (Summer 2008), pp. 1031–45.
89. See above, footnote 88.
90. R. Wiegman, 'The Anatomy of Lynching', *Journal of the History of Sexuality*, 3:3 (1993), p. 461. Ida B. Wells, impelled to investigate the facts behind lynchings in the south when three of her friends were lynched in Memphis in 1892, was the first to explore the reality behind the myth. In her research she found that only one-third of the men who were lynched were accused of sex offences. Of this third, many were falsely accused or were involved in consensual sex with a white partner. In the majority of cases, white men hanged and mutilated black men for a wide variety of non-sex related incidents that ranged from hog-stealing and quarrelling to being 'saucy' to whites. I. Wells-Barnett, *Selected Works of Ida B. Wells-Barnett*, ed. T. Harris. (New York: Oxford Univ. Press, 1991), pp. 61–2, 184, 140, 201.
91. *Selected Works*, pp. 184, 140, and 201.
92. *Appeal*, 27 April 1881. Ida B. Wells would be thrown off a train in similar fashion two years later. At issue for her was the first class ladies car. Giddings, *Ida*, ch. 2; N. I. Painter, 'A Prize Winning Book Revisited', *Journal of Women's History* 2:3 (Winter 1991), p. 133.
93. *Appeal*, 2 October 1898.
94. *Appeal*, 24 April 1881.
95. *Appeal*, 15 July 1881
96. *Appeal*, 19 April 1881, p. 2, 28 July 1881
97. Miller, *Memphis*, p. 91; *Appeal* 7 June 1904.
98. As quoted in Wells-Barnett, *Selected Works*, pp. 32–3.
99. *Avalanche*, 27 June 1878; *Appeal* 15 January 1881.
100. Meriwether, *Soundings*, p. 162–3.
101. *Appeal*, 15 June 1881. The homes for unwed mothers in Chattanooga and Nashville suffered also from a severe lack of funds. Both of these home remained open only by becoming affiliated with, and receiving major donations from, the Florence Crittenton Association O. Wilson, *Fifty Year's Work with Girls, 1883-1933: A Story of the Florence Crittenton Mission* (1933; New York: Arno Press, 1974), pp. 63, 74, 351.
102. As reported in *Appeal*, 22 January 1882; *Gleaner*, June 1892, #8, v. 11.
103. *Appeal*, 17 March 1880, 19 June 1883, and 15 June 1881. The Mission claimed only once to have placed women in domestic positions.
104. *Appeal*, 29 June 1881.
105. *History of the Women's and Young Women's Christian Association of Memphis*, p. 16.

106. *Commercial Appeal*, 14 February 1895; *Daily Memphis Appeal*, 28 February 1875; *Annual Report*, 1891–2. That they were preparing them for the occupations available to women in Memphis at the time is suggested by Lisa Duggan who notes that of the 8,200 women employed, the 'vast majority were employed as servants and laundresses, and another large proportion worked as dressmakers and seamstresses'. L. Duggan, *Sapphic Slashers* (Durham, NC: Duke University Press, 2000), p. 45.

107. *Annual Report*, 1891–2, 1902–3, 1904–5, and 1902–3, p. 31.

108. *History of the Women's and Young Women's Christian Association of Memphis*, p. 16; *Commercial Appeal*, 24 December 1972.

109. Woman's Edition', *Appeal*, 14 February 1895.

110. *History of the Women's and Young Women's Christian Association of Memphis*, p. 11; *Annual Report* 1902-1903, p. 14; Interview with Denny Glad, 5 June 1994.

3 Maine: Preserving Resources: Hard Work and Responsibility.

1. The Maine State Prison had held women ever since it was established in 1824. The first time a court committed a woman to the prison for life, however, was in 1867 when a Washington County Court sentenced Mary Elliot to be hanged for poisoning her daughter-in-law. See E. O. Schriver, 'Female Prisoners at the Maine State Prison, 1864–1887' (Unpublished paper, University of Maine, 1993).

2. *Oxford Democrat*, 3 April 1877.

3. Letter from Amos L. Allen, to Governor Frederick Robie 10 April 1885 in pardon file of Sarah P. Whitten. See also the pardon files of Sophronia J. Libby, Iantha A. E. Morgan and Sally Morrisey.

4. Judd et al. (eds), *Maine*, p. 352.

5. Judd et al. (eds), *Maine*, pp. 358, 404, and 405. On the economic transformation see chapter 18 generally. The impact of the out-migration which began with the Civil War is suggested by the town of Aurora which in 1880 had an adult population of 124. Of the twenty-six men who left to fight during the war only four returned. Of those that chose to move west, the historian stated, 'There wasn't enough room for them in a standstill economy'. As small as it was, Aurora sent representatives to the Maine Legislature fourteen out of ninety-eight sessions. H. T. Silsby, *A History of Aurora, Maine* (Ellsworth, ME: Hancock County Publishing, 1958), pp. 80 and 60.

6. P. C. DeRoche, '"These Lines of My Life": Franco-American Women in Westbrook, Maine, the Intersection of Ethnicity and Gender in 1884–1984' (MA Thesis, University of Maine 1994), p. 23. The Irish, also Catholic, came in large numbers earlier, but they often came as individuals and assimilated more quickly. Judd et al. (eds), *Maine*, p. 465

7. Judd et al. (eds), pp. 463, 465, and 466.

8. On economic conditions for women in Maine see *Maine Bureau of Labor, Research and Statistics* (Augusta, ME: State of Maine).

9. *Daily Eastern Argus*, 14 January 1882, p. 1.

10. *Eastern Daily Argus*, 21 January 1882.

11. *Daily Eastern Argus*, 12 January 1882, p. 2.

12. Rev. Stat. 1916 c. 144 sex. 20 as amended by Laws of 1921, c. 55 as reported in 'Juvenile Delinquency in Maine' (US Department of Labor: Children's Bureau Publication 201), p. 20. This reason for commitment was first defined when the school was created.

13. The history of the training school is based on J. P. Blaisdell (compiler), 'History – Stevens School, Hallowell Maine 1875–1920' (Unpublished manuscript).

14. Blaisdell, 'History', p. 2. The state later raised the age of women committed to the training school to sixteen. Women in a similar situation who were slightly older were committed to the Reformatory for Women, established in 1916. The Reformatory's second biennial report reported that of forty-four inmates, one was committed for assault, six were committed for larceny and two for neglect of children. The rest were committed for sexual offences. A full twenty-six were committed for being 'idle and disorderly' and others, for adultery, common night walking, wanton and lascivious conduct, and incorrigibility. Almost half, nineteen out of forty-four, were identified as something other than white American. The report noted of the unmarried mothers, 'In many instances the parental homes are not suitable places at all for the young women to return to'. As of July 1919, there were twelve babies in the institution. *Second Biennial Report of the Reformatory for Women at Skowhegan* (Waterville, ME: Sentinel Publishing Co., 1920), pp. 12, 15, 16, and 17.

15. Blaisdell, 'History', pp. 8, 3 and 19.

16. Letter from Edith G. Cram to Frances Scoboria, 17 November 1923, #236-65.

17. In 1930 the Children's Bureau concluded in its study of Maine that the care for pregnant women was 'so much more adequate' for pregnant women at the Reformatory than at the Training School that the state often sent girls to the Reformatory for their confinements. The advantage to the Reformatory was that the girls and women could receive confinement care in the institution and could keep their babies with them for two years. The Children's Bureau noted that while 'there is some question as to the desirability of keeping children who are over nine months of age in a penal institution', the Reformatory prevented the 'undesirable early separation of the babies from their mothers that occurs at the State School for Girls' ibid, p. 72.

18. A study of every third adoption record filed in Penobscot County uncovered only two out of 112 prior to 1900 adoptions of an infant whose mother was not known to the adoptive parent. Those who adopted young children had generally taken care of the children for some time as relatives, friends, or paid boarding mothers. See Chapter 5.

19. An 1821 Maine law empowered Overseers of the Poor to bind out without the consent of the parents any children whose parents became chargeable to the town or whose parents were thought to be unable to maintain the children. Unlike a similar Tennessee statute, the law does not specifically mention illegitimate children. W. D. Barry, *The History of Sweetser-Children's Home: A Century and a Half of Service to Maine Children* (Portland, ME: Anthoensen Press, 1988). pp. 5, 6 and 14.

20. Prior to the discoveries in bacteriology, physiology and nutrition at the end of the nineteenth century, there was no adequate substitute for breast milk. Historians have estimated that as many as 90 per cent of infants placed in foundling homes or asylums died. This was also the case in baby farms 'discovered' in the 1880s and much discussed in the newspapers of the time. These were private homes where women could place their infants for a nominal fee. I have not identified any in Maine. R. D. Apple, *Mothers and Medicine: A Social History of Infant Feeding, 1890-1950* (Madison, WI: University of Wisconsin Press, 1987), p. 18; V. A. Zelizer, *Pricing the Priceless Child: The Changing Social Value of Children* (New York: Basic Books, 1985), p. 177.

21. These were the Female Orphan Asylum, the Bangor Female Orphan Asylum, and St Elizabeth's Orphan Asylum. Barry, *The History of Sweetser-Children's Home*, pp. 44, 50 and 256. *Argus*, 12 October 1881, p. 3.

22. This and the following account of Rose's story come from *Daily Eastern Argus*, 30 January 1896 and 31 January 1896.

23. The Governor pardoned Mrs Dolley in 1905, a practice that was common in infanticide cases. See above. *Argus*, 10 August 1905.

24. The Good Shepherd Convent opened the third home, St Andres, in Biddeford in 1940. Although Good Shepherd nuns came to Biddeford in 1882, seven years after they immigrated to Memphis and started a home for unwed mothers there, the Maine convent did not open such a home until 1940. The Florence Crittenton Home Association noted in its history that J. Grenville Harvey of Old Orchard Beach left a legacy of $15,000 and his home to the national organization in 1911. His wife opened their home to unwed mothers but, the history notes, 'on a very restricted scale', suggesting only a handful of women ever took advantage of the free service. O. Wilson, *Fifty Years' Work with Girls* (1933; New York: Arno Press, 1974), p. 388; 'A Brief History of St. Andres Home, Inc'. available through St Andres Home.

25. *Temporary Home Annual Report* 1899 and 1913. In the Maine State Archives. It is interesting to note that the women of the board had the first option to hire the residents when they left. The Temporary Home eventually shared many features with the Good Samaritan Home. It adhered to its practices less stringently, however, and regularly attracted far fewer women than the Good Samaritans.

26. In 1913 the Home admitted thirty-one women who came from every county in the state. *Annual Report*, 1913.

27. This was true even though the Temporary Home provided similar services at less cost and with less stringent requirements. It should be noted, however, that much of the information on the Temporary Home comes from comments made by Good Samaritan Board members who, in the nature of competition, may have highlighted the negative aspects of the Temporary Home. Nevertheless the Board of the Temporary Home visited the Good Samaritan Home a number of times to learn its techniques and commented periodically on the disparity in the numbers. See Superintendent's Report, January 1934 and May 1938. Beginning in 1905 the state legislature regularly voted to fund the Home and in addition individuals, businesses, and organizations from around the state regularly contributed to its maintenance. See below. *Annual Report*, 1915.

28. *Annual Report*, 1920. Two of the women on the first board may have had direct experience with infanticide. Mary Glyn, sentenced to life for killing her daughter's child, had worked for a Mrs Bragg. When the police came to her home looking for the child, Mrs Glyn told them that Mrs Bragg had taken the child. Later Mrs Bragg was called to testify in the trial. In the trial, Mr. Merrill was counsel for the defence. Both a Mrs Merrill and a Mrs Bragg were long-term members of the Board. *Bangor Daily Commercial*, 26 February 1882.

29. Good Samaritan Agency, '90th Anniversary Historical Review', 1992; *Bangor Daily Commercial*, 28 May 1923.

30. *Bangor Daily Commercial*, 15 January 1913.

31. *Annual Report*, 1915; *Bangor Daily Commercial*, 22 January 1924 and 28 January 1941.

32. Ibid.

33. *Annual Report*, 1915; *Bangor Daily Commercial*, 28 August 1935. Religion continued to play a role in the Home, albeit a diminishing one. While Frances Scoboria who was hired in 1907 was not a deaconess, she saw religious instruction as part of her job. She told the press at the end of her tenure that while many mothers came without knowing the Ten Commandments, they left knowing a lot of the Bible. And Alice Harden, secretary in 1920, spoke in religious terms when she noted in the annual report that the Home's work was rescue work, for God the Good Shepherd came 'to save that which was lost'.

The Home, she said, required every girl to stay six months after delivery 'in order that she may be brought under the uplifting influence of a good, Christian home'. The rules also required residents to attend religious services in the Home and to attend church on a Sunday. By the 1920s, however, the religious services were limited to a Mrs. Grace Cole coming once a week to lead the group in hymns and prayer. If the residents went out to church services there is no mention of it in the copious minutes. *Bangor Daily Commercial*, 19 August 1925; *Annual Report*, 1920, pp. 6 and 8.

34. This information comes from basic information recorded in the Good Samaritan Log Book and made available by Good Samaritan Association staff.

35. The boarding babies provided good public relations and a regular income. *Annual Report*, 1920, p. 9.

36. *Annual Report*, 1920, p. 5.

37. #173, 'Good Samaritan Home Rules'. The rules were not substantially changed until the 1940s though the entrance fee was gradually raised to $125. See Chapter 5.

38. Case Committee Report, December 1931.

39. The Bangor Public Library has an extensive index and clippings file with information on many Bangor families. See for example *Bangor Daily News*, 13 September 1941, p. 12, 16 February 1961, p. 27, 15 July 1953, 24 July 1950, p. 14, 7 July 1949, 6 November 1954, p. 1, 3 January 1950, p. 3, 8 December 1953, p. 5, 4 April 1959, p. 22, 3 July 1969, 6 November 1954, p. 1, 17 October 1952, p. 16, 1 June 1929, 29 June 1942, p. 15, 9 September 1944, p. 5, 11 September 1916, 28 July 1925, 16 March 1938, 14 November 1924, p. 1, 26 June 1948, p. 1 and 7, 6 June 1965, p. 1, 13 June 1939, 12 July 1949, p. 3, 19 January 1955, p. 2; *Bangor Daily Commercial*, 18 April 1930, 28 July 1925, 2 November 1917, and April 1926.

40. Perhaps as a result of the family's desire to advance economically and socially and of its commitment to education, seventeen of the twenty-four of the original long-term members who can be identified had two or fewer children and only two had more than three. Four had none. One of those who had more than three was E. G. Merrill who became prominent in the banking world in New York City. He would have had less need to limit his family as he had money enough to give all his children a good education.

41. *Bangor Daily News*, 20 December 1980; Bangor Public Library Clippings File 974. 131. b267, vv1, p. 28.

42. Bangor Public Library Clippings File, 974. 1c65m, vol. 3, p. 238.

43. *Bangor Daily Commercial*, 1 June 1929.

44. *Bangor Daily Commercial*, 12 April 1926.

45. *Bangor Daily News*, 25 January 1933 and 13 September 1941.

46. *Bangor Daily News*, 8 January 1941. Gertrude requested to be paid for her work at the Good Samaritan Home when her husband died and the Board agreed, noting her straightened circumstances Executive Committee Report, 9 June 1932.

47. *Bangor Daily News*, 13 September 1941, p. 12, and 25 January 1933.

48. Residents' log provided by the Good Samaritan Association.

49. *Annual Report*, 1920 and 1922.

50. From #77 to #105 eleven babies out of twenty-eight died. The case records suggest that it was the poor health of the mothers, rather than the medical care they received, that led to the deaths. At least from 1906 on, established doctors with good reputations in the community had delivered the babies. The women, however, were paupers or very young. In many cases the babies were born with deformities. The mother of one baby who died, for example, was thirteen. Her mother was noted as insane; the girl was pregnant by her

brother. Her delivery was a breach case in which the baby's hip was broken. Another baby was born with a double harelip and cleft palate. It was operated on at Eastern Maine General Hospital by a Dr Smith of Portland but died when it was six weeks old. (#109 and #104) There are no deaths of children reported for the first six years when the Home was under the management of a Deaconess. During this time the women stayed a shorter period of time and less is recorded about what happened to them. The lack of death may be a reflection of a different recordkeeping system or the possibity that they were not pregnant when they came.

51. *Annual Report*, 1920 and 1925.
52. *Annual Reports*, 1925, 1926, 1933 and 1935.
53. #357-185 Letter from Atwood to __, 9 November 1931; #196-24 Letter from __ to Atwood, 3 December 1920.
54. Superintendent's Report, February 1938.
55. Superintendent's Report, November 1939, February 1938, and January 1937.
56. #428-256 Letter from Atwood to Eva Scates, 10 February 1934.
57. Superintendent's Report, April 1934. 'This ordeal of annual spring cleaning is quite a strain on the tempers of both girls and workers in the Home, with nerve tension and high tempers much in evidence. This has resulted in more or less arguments, necessary disciplinary measures, apologies, and diplomacy of a high order'. Superintendent's Report, April 1935.
58. Case Committee Report, November 1932.
59. Superintendent's Report, February 1939.
60. Case Committee Report, March 1931.
61. Case Committee Report, Summer 1930.
62. Case Committee Report, September 1931.
63. Case Committee Report, February 1930.
64. Superintendent's Report, November and December 1936.
65. Ibid.
66. Superintendent's Report, 10 May 1938, October 1935, January 1936 and February 1936. The Home eventually released Mildred but the records do not make clear what happened to her baby. Three years later Mildred applied again to the Home 'in an exceedingly destitute condition'. She had had, she told Atwood, only eight meals during the month of November. The Home took her in and in one month she had gained seventeen pounds. The Home then found her employment. Superintendent's Report, December 1939 and 16 January 1940.
67. *Annual Report*, 1930.
68. This and the following discussion on community responsibility is taken from the *Annual Report*, 1924, pp. 6–7.
69. Ibid, p. 7.
70. Superintendent's Report, 1935.
71. Glenna Stearns lasted only one year as superintendent, but the fact that the Board hired her suggests that the majority endorsed her philosophy. Several weeks previously Frances Scoboria, who had been the superintendent for seventeen years, gave an exit interview to the *Bangor Daily Commercial*. She pointed with pride to the fact that a number of the children born under her care were later baptized and that many mothers came without knowing the first commandment but left knowing a lot of the Bible. Scoboria's departure, on account of a 'nervous collapse' marks the end of the religious influence on the Home. *Bangor Daily Commercial*, 19 August 1925 and 1 August 1925.

72. Superintendent's Report, April 1934, May 1935, December 1935 and January 1937.
73. Superintendent's Report, January 1936; *Annual Report*, 1937 and 1938.
74. Superintendent's Report, January 1939.
75. Case Committee Report, February 1931.
76. Superintendent's Report, October 1938 and January 1939.
77. Superintendent's Report, September 1936.
78. #586-405 Letter from Atwood to __, 16 December 1940.
79. *Annual Report*, 1915, pp. 8, 11, and 12.
80. 'Infinite Pathos' (Bangor: Thomas W. Burr, 1920) pp. 4, 5; *Annual Report*, 1924, p. 17; *Annual Report*, 1925, p. 6. The same language was used repeatedly in annual reports from 1915 (the earliest extant) to 1941.
81. *The Revised Statutes of the State of Maine*. Passed 22 October 1840 (Augusta, 1841), 686. As noted in J. Mohr, *Abortion in America: The Origins and Evolution of National Policy* (New York: Oxford University Press, 1978), p. 41.
82. *State v. Charles D. Edmunds*, Bangor Municipal Court, 19 January 1925. Edmunds testified that though Anna Stairs had a high fever he sent her away, afraid to be mixed up in an abortion.
83. 'Juvenile Delinquency in Maine'. Children's Bureau Publication #201. (US Dept. of Labor, Washington, DC: GPO, 1930).
84. Interview with Donna LeMieux, 4 April 1997.
85. Clippings file at the Good Samaritan Association.
86. Of the fourteen who ran before they gave birth, five entered the Home in its first six years. The Home dismissed fifteen before they delivered, mostly for health reasons.
87. There were nine whose ages were unknown.
88. These figures are gathered from the admissions log of the Good Samaritan Association copied by members of its staff.
89. The annual report of the Skowhegan Women's Reformatory reported that the women in the Reformatory preferred factory to domestic work because the wages were better and there was more freedom. *Second Biennial Report of the Reformatory for Women at Skowhegan* (Waterville, ME: Sentinel Publishing, 1920).
90. #348-176 and #404-232.
91. That this was not just a legal fiction is made clear by the Bangor City records which include over 1,000 letters sent to towns notifying them that one of their town members was in need of aid and the town should send transportation home for this individual or Bangor would provide aid and bill the town. See above, Chapter 1. 'Death of a Hired Hand' in *The Poetry of Robert Frost*, ed. E. C. Lathem (New York: Holt, Rinehard and Winston, 1969): p. 38.
92. #287-115.
93. #207-36. See also #287-115.
94. #188-16 Letter to Good Samaritans from William Waldron, 16 July 1919.
95. #196-24 Letter from Lamoine to Atwood, 31 May 1920, 3 December 1920, and 1 June 1922.
96. #240-69 Letter from Richmond to Atwood, 5 March 1928. Another couple promptly adopted the child.
97. #392-220, Letter from Eva Scates to Atwood, 6 March 1934.
98. #178-6 Letter from __ to Auntie, 2 February 1920.
99. #195-23.

100. #297-125 Letter from Atwood to Immigration, 20 September 1928 and 12 October 1928.
101. #196-24 Letter from __ to Good Samaritans, 31 May, 1920; *Annual Report*, 1923.
102. Executive Committee Report, 28 October 1936; #297-125, Letter from Atwood to Immigration Service, 27 March 1928.
103. #257-85 Letter from __'s husband to Atwood, 19 November 1925.
104. #187-15 Letter from Laura Klippel to Atwood, 18 October 1921.
105. #201-30 Letter from __ to Frances Scoboria, 1 November 1921.
106. #215-44 Letter from Scates to Atwood, 7 October 1922.
107. #207-36 Letter from Sawyer to Atwood, 6 October 1921; Letter from Alfred G. Davis to Atwood, 1 November 1921.
108. #179-7 Letter from __ to Scoboria, 19 October 1920; Letter from ___ to Scoboria, 7 February 1921.
109. #195-23 Letter from __ to Scoboria, 13 June 1920.
110. Superintendent's Report, February 1938. The Depression increased the number of very poor women into the Home and widened the gap between the managers of the Home and the women. See Chapter 5.
111. #196-24 Letter from __ to Atwood, 31 May 1920; #317-145 Letter from __ to __ 26 June 1029. For more on adoption see below.
112. #195-25, Letter from __ to Scoboria, 26 November 1920.
113. Superintendent's Report, Summer 1933 and October 1933.
114. #327-155 Letter from __ to Atwood, 24 October 1929; #513-341, Letter from __ to Atwood, 23 November 1937.
115. #180-8 Letter from __ to Scoboria, November 1918; #292-120. One was the daughter of a foreman in a paper mill and of a music teacher. She entered Gilman Business College when she left the home. The other was an orphan with a small inheritance.
116. #184-12 Letter from __ to Scoboria, 17 June 1919; #473-301; #586-405.
117. #256-84 Letter from Atwood to __, 23 November 1925.
118. #177-5 Letter from __ to Scoboria, 29 September 1919; #453-281 Letter from __ to Mrs. Pearson, 21 December 1934. These are only the marriages that were identified in the records. There no doubt were others.
119. Superintendent's Report, January 1934. The fact that six of these lost their children suggests that they came from poverty and had not had appropriate pre-natal care.
120. #342-170.
121. #600-419 Letter to Atwood from __, undated; #342-170 Letter to Mrs. Pearson from __ undated; #600-419 Letter to Mrs. Herlihy, undated.
122. #377-205 Letter to Mrs Pearson from __ 2 December 1932.
123. #195-23 Letter to 'My Dear Friend' from __, 1 June 1920. There is no record of what later happened to the child.
124. #600-419 Letter to the Home, undated; #212-41 Letter from O. L. Keyes to Scoboria, 9 February 1922 and from Assistant to Special Agent to Scoboria, 23 June 1922.
125. #377-165 Letter to Good Samaritan Home from T. D. Pelletier, 11 June 1930; T. D. Pelletier to Atwood, 23 March 1931.
126. #498-326 Letter from Eva W. Scates to Atwood, 8 February 1937.
127. #498-326 Letter from Atwood to Scates, 22 January 1938; Letter from Scates to Atwood, 20 January 1938.

128. #468-296 Letter from Atwood to Sister Genevieve, 7 January 1937; Letters from __ to Atwood, 17 September 1936 and 13 October 1936. This was the only time Atwood ever referred to a mother as domineering.
129. #571-400 Letter to the Good Samaritan Home from Dr. Taylor, 21 September 1940; Superintendent's Report, September 1940.
130. #236-65 Letter from Edith G. Cram to __ 21 March 1923; Letter from Adella Rouibold to __ 24 April 1923; Letter from Rouibold to Miss Scoboria, 17 November 1923.
131. #246-75 Letter from Atwood to Mrs. Craig, 19 November 1925, 24 November 1925, and 1 March 1926; Letter from __ to Mrs. Garcelon, 16 April 1927.
132. #272-100 Letter from Atwood to __ 22 September 1926; #468-296, #493-321, and #478-306; Superintendent's Report, March 1936.
133. #282-110 Letter to 'My Dear Mrs. __' from __ 12 September 1928.
134. #191-19 Letter from __ to Scoboria 15 January 1922 and 27 December 1920; Letter from 'professional man (not a doctor)' to Scoboria, 11 August 1922.
135. #433-261 Letter from __ to Atwood, undated.
136. #492-320 Letter from Atwood to __, 13 May 1938 and 7 June 1937; Letter from __ to Atwood, 15 April 1938 and 14 May 1938.
137. #492-320, Letter from __ to Atwood, 18 December 1940; Letter from Atwood to __, 8 February 1941. By 1940 Fern had a second child, married a man who was not the father, divorced the man and kept her child. Although her husband 'wasn't the type of person I thought he was or hoped he'd be' Fern reported that 'I am very happy because I have another daughter'.
138. Superintendent's Report, September 1936; #240-69 Letter from Atwood to __, 12 March 1927.
139. There were only two others who became pregnant out of wedlock a second time, and both had been married and deserted. #240-69 and #397-225.
140. #297-125 Letter from __ to Atwood, 2 March 1929 and 23 July 1930.
141. #287-115, Letter from Atwood to Immigration Service, 19 June 1928; Case Committee Report, May 1931.
142. #292-120; Case Committee Report, March 1931.
143. #302-130.

4 Professional Standards in Tennessee: Only Perfect Children Will Do

1. R. L. Taylor, 'Report to Governor Gordon Browning on the Shelby County Branch Tennessee Children's Home Society' (Nashville, TN: Tennessee Department of Human Services, 21 May 1951), pp. 24, 25, 45, and 53. B. B. Raymond, *The Baby Thief: The Untold Story of Georgia Tann, the Baby Seller who Corrupted Adoption* (New York: Carrol & Graf, 2007), p. 115; Taylor, 'Report to Governor Gordon Browning', p. 80. Tann's fascinating tale is told in Raymond, *The Baby Thief*, and L. T. Austin, *Babies for Sale: The Tennessee Children's Home Adoption Scandal* (Westport, CT: Praeger, 1993).
2. Raymond, *The Baby Thief*, p. 6.
3. Ibid., p. 28; Taylor, 'Report to Governor Gordon Browning', pp. 62–3.
4. Taylor, 'Report to Governor Gordon Browning', pp. 62–3, 320; G. Mangold, 'Unlawful Motherhood'. *Forum*, 53 (February 1915), 338. As quoted in Kunzel, *Fallen Women, Problem Girls*, p. 67.

5.   M. Walker, J. R. Dunn and J. P. Dunn (eds), *Southern Women at the Millennium: A Historical Perspective* (Columbia, MO: University of Missouri Press, 2005), p. 6; Wiggins, 'The Migrant Girl', p. 61.

6.   C. E. Lively and C. Auber, *Rural Migration in the United States* (DC: US Government Printing Office, 1939), p. 122.

7.   Jonathan Daniels, *A Southerner Discovers the South* as excerpted in *Annals of America*, 15 1929–1936 (London: Encyclopaedia Britannica, 1968), p. 551.

8.   Kyriakoudes, *The Social Origins of the Urban South*, p, 111.

9.   W. A. Dromgoole, 'The Age of Consent in Tennessee', *Arena*, 11 (January 1895), pp. 207–9.

10. This and the following story is reconstructed from the *State v. Alonzo Ball: Pardon File*. Board of Pardons and Paroles, Lonnie Ball. In the Tennessee State Library and Archives.

11. Mr Collins reportedly tracked Lonnie down twice and brought him back.

12. Wiggins found in her study that out of one hundred girls in subsidized boarding homes only five came from out of state. 55 per cent came from within sixty-five miles of Nashville. Wiggins, 'The Migrant Girl' p. 11.

13. In 1920–1, women made up 40 per cent of the profession. By 1930 they made up seventy per cent. Kunzel, *Fallen Women, Problem Girls*, pp. 40 and 45.

14. F. G. Wickware (ed.), *The American Year Book: A Record of Events and Progress* (New York: D. Appleton and Co., 1917), p. 410; Wiebe, *The Search for Order*, pp. 120–1 Kunzel, *Fallen Women*, p. 38.

15. M. B. Katz, *In the Shadow of the Poorhouse: A Social History of Welfare in America* (New York: Basic Books, 1986), p. 121; L. Gordon, *Pitied But Not Entitled: Single Mothers and the History of Welfare* (New York: Free Press, 1994), pp. 91 and 92.

16. In 1880 the federal government created a death registration area that by 1900 included ten states, many more cities, and over 40 per cent of the population. In 1902 Congress created the Bureau of Census as an independent and permanent agency. R. A. Meckel, *Save the Babies* (Baltimore, MD: Johns Hopkins University Press, 1990), pp. 104–5.

17. In 1919 the Children's Bureau held major conferences in Chicago and New York. Approximately one hundred and twenty judges, lawyers, caseworkers, city officials, and delegates representing thirty-five cities, twenty-one states, and Canada met to discuss the issue. By then two-thirds of the states were involved in some effort to improve child welfare legislation that specifically addressed the needs of illegitimate children E. O. Lundberg and K. F. Lenroot, *Illegitimacy as a Child Welfare Problem* (Washington, DC: Government Printing Office, 1920), p. 8.

18. *Standards of Legal Protection for Children Born Out of Wedlock: A Report of Regional Conferences* (Washington, DC: Government Printing Office, 1921), p. 54.

19. Ibid., p. 41.

20. Ibid., p. 25.

21. Ibid., p. 4.

22. For a thorough discussion of the growing influence of the professionals on maternity homes see Kunzel, *Fallen Women*, ch. 5.

23. For these cultural shifts see Kunzel, *Fallen Women*; J. Berebitsky, *Like Our Very Own: Adoption and the Changing Culture of Motherhood, 1851–1950* (Lawrence, KS: University Press of Kansas, 2000); and R. Solinger, *Wake Up Little Susie: Single Pregnancy and Race Before Roe v. Wade* (New York: Routledge, 1992).

24. See Berebitsky, *Like Our Very Own*, p. 134. E. F. Peck, *Adoption Laws in the United States*, U. S. Children's Bureau Publication No. 148 (Washington, DC: GPO, 1925).

25. Berebitsky, *Like Our Very Own*, p. 137.

26. K. F. Lenroot, 'Social Responsibility for the Care of the Delinquent Girl and the Unmarried Mother', *Journal of Social Hygiene*, 10 (1924), pp. 78, 81 and 82. Lenroot would become the director of the Children's Bureau in 1933.

27. V. Ashcraft, *Public Care: A History of Public Welfare Legislation in Tennessee* (Knoxville, TN: University of Tennessee, 1947), pp. 37–41. It should be stressed that while Maine law sought to keep women with their children this did not necessarily protect immigrant women and their children. See above, ch. 3.

28. Ashcraft, *Public Care*, pp. 5, 15, 37–9.

29. Meriwether, *Soundings*, p. 142.

30. J. C. Ferris, *Homes for the Homeless or Fourteen Years Among the Orphans* (Nashville: ME Church, South, 1895), p. 30.

31. *Commercial Appeal*, 14 April 1907, art sec. p. 2. It is interesting to note that in two of these cases the baby was at first cared for by an African American woman. The fact that the white women involved did not have to provide infants with direct care may have been a factor in the widespread use of infant adoption.

32. Clopper, *Child Welfare in Tennessee*, p. 597.

33. 'A Century of Service' and minutes, Protestant Orphan Asylum, Tennessee State Archives, Box 19, file 2.

34. Letter from Mary J. Lockett to the Asylum, 18 April 1884. Ibid.

35. Protestant Orphan Asylum (POA) Minutes, June 1905 and November 1900, ibid. POA Minutes, September 1903 and March 1904.

36. POA Minutes, October 1901.

37. POA Minutes, 7 June 1938.

38. 'A Century of Service'.

39. Ferris, *Homes for the Homeless*, p. 293.

40. Ibid., 92.

41. Tennessee passed a Mother's Pension Law in 1915 that specifically stated that to receive funds a mother must be a 'proper person morally, mentally, and physically for rearing a child'. A 1921 amendment allowed counties to give aid to unwed mothers but only two counties out of ninety-five actually provided aid under the statute. When Tennessee implemented Aid to Dependent Children it had a similar stipulation. Ashcraft, *Public Care*, p. 26.

42. *Mr. Evelyn Mary Blalock v. TCHS* #48261. Shelby County Courthouse.

43. Ibid.

44. Other sections of the bill prohibited private individuals from placing children; allowed judges to sign adoption papers in the case of all foundlings or abandoned children; and, in this last case only, required all records to be sealed and placed in archives where they could be opened only on judicial order. Ashcraft, *Public Care*, pp. 23, 20 and 21; E. McCauley, 'A Study of Legal and Social Aspects of Adoption in Tennessee'. (Manuscript, Nashville School of Social Work, 1947), p. 6.

45. Department of Institutions, 'Welfare Division Report Covering First Eleven Months of Its Existence 8/1/25–6/30/26;' 'Biennial Report, 1925–1926', 11 and 18.

46. Department of Institutions, 'Biennial Report 1930–1932'.

47. Ashcraft, *Public Care*, p. 85; McCauley, 'A Study', pp. 59 and 60.

48. Clopper, *Child Welfare in Tennessee*, p. 612.

49. See for example McCauley, 'A Study', p. 114; Memorandum from Mrs. Vallie S. Miller to Commissioner J. O. McMahon, 28 April 1952, Box 157, File 3, Tennessee State Archives.
50. E. Oppenheimer, *Infant Mortality in Memphis*, US Children's Bureau Publication #233 (Washington, DC: Government Printing Office, 1937), p. 67.
51. McCauley, 'A Study', pp. 55, 124 and 125. The Department could not even identify all the adoptions that occurred in six months.
52. Ashcraft, *Public Care*, p. 83.
53. McCauley, 'A Study', p. 15.
54. Clopper, *Child Welfare in Tennessee*, pp. 609–13.
55. Ibid., p. 201.
56. *Memphis Press Scimitar* 2 July 1935, p. 10, and 15 September 1950, pp. 1, 4. Raymond, *The Baby Thief*, p. 5
57. *Memphis Press Scimitar*, 2 July 1935, p. 10.
58. *Memphis Press Scimitar*, 2 July 1935, p. 10.
59. C. Kelley, *Delinquent Angels* (Kansas City, MO: Brown-White-Lowell Press, 1947), p. 6.
60. Ibid, p. 24.
61. K. Neill, 'Adoption for Profit: Conspiracy and Cover-Up', *Memphis Magazine*, 3:7 (October 1978), p. 52.
62. Gilkey was the author of numerous stories on the TCHS and may have found much of her news at the TCHS. *Memphis Press Scimitar*, 2 December 1937, 1, and 25 December 1941.
63. See for example *Memphis Press Scimitar*, 11 March 1929 and 5 November 1940 and 'Greetings', TCHS Shelby County Division, 1946, 1947 and 1948. In the TCHS file in the Memphis Room of the Main Branch of the Memphis Public Library.
64. 'Greetings', 1946.
65. 'Greetings', TCHS Shelby County Division, 1946, 1947 and 1948.
66. Neill, 'Adoption for Profit', p. 51.
67. Ibid, p. 51; Taylor, 'Report to Governor Gordon Browning', p. 80.
68. Taylor, 'Report to Governor Gordon Browning', p. 6; *Commercial Appeal 10 July 1991*, *p. 31*.
69. Letter from A. Waldauer to Mrs. Thorne Deuel, 9 March 1943.
70. Tann claimed that the League was only acting on personal disagreements with her and the local press did not report the expulsion. *Nashville Tennessean*, 18 September 1950.
71. Ibid.
72. Neill, 'Adoption for Profit', p. 25.
73. Austin, *Babies for Sale*, pp. 77–105.
74. *Commercial Appeal*, 30 September 1979.
75. Taylor, 'Report to Governor Gordon Browning', pp. 24, 25, 45, and 53.
76. Ibid., 55–6.
77. Juvenile Court Judge Camille Kelley approved adoptions of children in Care and Protection cases. Taylor suggested that the state had never adequately explored her involvement in the scandal. Kelley resigned from the court immediately after the scandal broke. See Taylor, 'Report', p. 14; Neill, 'Adoption for Profit', p. 52.
78. Taylor, 'Report to Governor Gordon Browning', p. 6; Letter from Mary Owens to Mrs. O'Connor 21 May 1940 as quoted in Raymond, *The Baby Thief*, p. 85.
79. The doctor who for years delivered babies at the Woman's Christian Association Refuge in Memphis served on the Board of the TCHS and was a personal friend of Tann.

The Florence Crittenton Home in Nashville invited the TCHS to visit regularly to talk with women who wished to give up their children. The Salvation Army in Nashville provided emergency assistance to unwed mothers. It sent the women to its own maternity home in Louisville, Kentucky, and then these mothers 'often relinquished' their children to the TCHS. The state's Welfare Division noted in its report for 1929 that the cases of unwed mothers who were 'unable or unwilling to keep their own babies', were handled by the TCHS, and a Children's Bureau study of infant mortality conducted in Memphis in 1933 concluded that many women gave up their children through the TCHS. L. Young, 'Unmarried Mothers in Nashville and Davidson County: A Study of Requests for Service and Its Availability to Unmarried Mothers in Nashville and Davidson County, Tennessee' (Nashville, TN: Council of Community Agencies, July, 1949), p. 56; 'Biennial Report: Welfare Division', 1929–1930, pp. 21 and 19; Oppenheimer, *Infant Mortality* (Washington, DC: G. P. O., 1937), p. 66.

80. Cotton prices rose in 1922 but fell steeply again during the Depression. See M. Walker, *Country Women Cope With Hard Times: A Collection of Oral Histories* (Columbia: University of South Carolina Press, 2004), pp. xxiii, xxiv and Kyriakoudes, *The Social Origins of the Urban South*, pp. 49 and 50. The Fair Labor Standards Act of 1938 made child labour illegal. Keith, *Country People*, pp. 18 and 34.

81. W. C. Holley, et al, *The Plantation South* DC: US Government Printing Office, vol. xxii, 1940), p. xxi; Keith, *Country People*, p. 179.

82. See the 'Uprising of '34' video (New York, NY : First Run/Icarus Films, 1995) for a vivid portrayal of the strict control mill owners maintained over the behaviour of their workforce.

83. The two counties were Knox and Shelby. Ashcraft, *Public Care*, pp. 25,26, and 29.

84. *Adoption Edward Dallas Gibson*, #41001 January 7 1939.

85. Clopper, *Child Welfare in Tennessee*, pp. 614 and 586; *Nashville Banner*, 11 October 1974.

86. Beulah Home was the other. See below. Clopper, *Child Welfare in Tennessee*, p. 586.

87. *Tennessean*, 6 February 1898 and 26 May 1918.

88. The Chattanooga Home reported having twelve women in 1930 and fourteen in 1931. Having had two fires, they were in straightened circumstances, living in 'three veritable shacks', but they did find room to house eleven babies for the Tennessee Children's Home Society. *Tennessean*, 15 January 1930, p. 6, and unclear date, 1955.

89. Community Chests had their beginnings in the first decades of the twentieth century as social services struggled to coordinate services to the poor. Finding a model in community war fund campaigns that were developed by the Red Cross and others during World War I, social service agencies united to coordinate fund raising and to evaluate and implement 'best practices'. Within forty years 450 cities would have some form of community chest or fundS. Kravitz and F. K. Kolodner, 'Community Action: Where Has It Been? Where Will It Go?' *Annals of American Academy of Political and Social Science* 5: 385 (Sept. 1969), pp. 30–40.

90. 'MOTHER'S DAY', dated May, 1936. Ella Oliver Clippings File.

91. Interview, Denny Glad, 5 June 1994. Memphis Room, Memphis Public Library.

92. See for example Oppenheimer, 'Oppenheimer', and *TCHS Guardian of Person Baby Sherrer*, #29138 Shelby County Courthouse.

93. Ibid.

94. Ibid.

95. *Commercial Appeal*, 8 October 1932, 10 January 1933, 12 March 1934, and 4 May 1936. *Commercial Appeal*, 4 May 1936 and 17 June 1937; 'Mother's Day'.
96. *Press Scimitar*, 25 January 1937. He also had five daughters and one foster daughter.
97. Scrapbook, Bethany Home, 901 Chelsea St., Memphis. Clopper reported in 1920 that the home urged women to keep their children and that while 77 women were served during the year only 5 children were adopted. Clopper, Child Welfare, p.551.
98. He also unsuccessfully sued the Bethany board for forcing him out. Bethany Scrapbook.
99. *Commercial Appeal*, 23 January 1937; *Press Scimitar*, 25 January 1937. The strike lasted thirty-eight days.
100. *Press Scimitar*, 27 January 1937.
101. Bethany Home staff believed that he destroyed records when he was forced to leave Bethany. Visit to Bethany Home, June 6, 1994.
102. Several decades later the superintendent of the Good Samaritan Home, struggling to understand why so many young women kept their children, suggested that it was because so many were Pentecostalists. This religious aspect of unwed mothers had yet to be fully explored.
103. The Bethany Board might have paved the way to professionalization. One of the original board members, Mrs. Charlotte Cameron Mitchell, was 'loved and respected for her work with many social service organizations in Memphis, some of which she was instrumental in founding'. Another early board member, Mrs. Edna Watkins Royal, operated the Doctor's Service Bureau for ten years. Unidentified Clipping, 29 July 1957 and 8 June 1940. Bethany Home Clipping File, Memphis Room, Memphis Public Library.
104. L. Ware, 'History of Bethany Home' and Press Scimitar 16 May 1931. From the Bethany Scrapbook.
105. Ibid.
106. 1951 Unidentified Clipping, Bethany Scrapbook.
107. *Exchange Newsletter* 1950, 1955, and 1956, Bethany Scrapbook.
108. *Memphis Press Scimitar*, 15 July 1935.
109. Unidentified clipping, 9 April 1941, Bethany Home File; *Exchange Club Bulletin*, 1949 and 1954.
110. *Commercial Appeal*, 9 July 1935.
111. *Press Scimitar*, 11 May 1943.
112. Ibid..
113. Ibid..
114. *Exchange Club Bulletin*, 1944, 1948, and 1951.
115. Unidentified Newspaper Clipping, 14 October 1959, Bethany Scrapbook.
116. I. Clements, 'Enlightened Society Now Aids Unmarried Mothers in City In Facing Problems of Life', *Commercial Appeal* (4 October 1951). The same ideas were repeated in *Appeal*, 14 October 1959.
117. Unidentified Clipping, 8 September 1949, Bethany Scrapbook.
118. *Press Scimitar*, 8 October 1946.
119. There was another Mary, the paper continued, 'daughter of respectable Shelby county parents who took her to the home in order to protect her and themselves from the stigma of attending her condition'. Unidentified Newspaper Clipping, October 1953, Bethany Scrapbook.
120. Unidentified Clipping, 1948, Bethany Scrapbook.

121. *Press Scimitar*, 1 April 1948; *Commercial Appeal*, 10 September 1951; *Press Scimitar*, 31 January 1957. As records for Bethany Home are not available, we do not know if these reports were accurate. The only indication that the women in the Home were more consistently middle class was that in 1959 the Exchange noted that they had not found 'the right girl' to use the scholarship that they offered. This might suggest that no one was in a position to need it. *Exchange Club Bulletin*, 1959.
122. L. Ware, 'History of Bethany Home' in the Bethany Home Files.
123. Ibid.
124. Unidentified Newspaper Clipping October 1953, 1951, and 1954, Bethany Scrapbook; Exchange Club Bulletin, 1952.
125. *Press Scimitar*, 1 April 1948; Unidentified Newspaper Clipping, 20 November 1957, Bethany Scrapbook.
126. *Press Scimitar*, 1 April 1948; Unidentified Newspaper Clipping 1948 and 8 September 1949.
127. Newspaper Clipping, 51 January 1960. Bethany Home Scrapbook.
128. *Exchange Club Bulletin*, 1952.
129. *Exchange Club Bulletin*, 1956.
130. By 1966 Chattanooga, which reported serving twelve women in 1930 and 14 in 1932, had to turn away seventy-eight women in 1966 and and 177 in 1968. All the women who entered gave up their children to adoption. L. Young, 'Unmarried Mothers', p. 56. In 1959, Memphis had the third highest illegitimacy rate of the nation's largest cities, and in 1962, Shelby County had the highest illegitimacy rate of any county in the state. *Commercial Appeal*, 3 March 1962 and 14 October 1959.
131. *Exchange Club Newsletter*, 1949, Bethany Scrapbook.
132. *Tennessean*, 25 November 1942, 5, and 25 March 1945, 5.
133. Abe Waldauer to Honorable G. C. Moreland, 5/23/35, to a lawyer representing a father who protesting the placement of his child. As quoted in Raymond, *The Baby Thief*, p. 55.
134. In at least several cases the TCHS did retake the child either because the adoptive parents left the state, divorced, and 'failed to show any fundamental interest whatsoever' in the child, or were living in open adultery and were 'physically and morally unfit and unable to care for' the child. See *TCHS v. Robert Love*, #34661, 4 May 1933; *TCHS in re Paula Thompson* #32829, 46017, and 24 June 1931; *TCHS v B. A. Nolen and Lillian Nolen Cummins* #36632 26 May 1935. *Press Scimitar* 12 December 1938 as quoted in Raymond, *The Baby Thief*, p. 162.

5 Professional Standards in Maine: Relying on Strangers

1. Superintendent's Report, September 1939 and December 1939.
2. *Annual Report*, 1939.
3. Superintendent's Report, December 1939.
4. *Annual Report*, 1924, 1926 and 1928.
5. *Annual Report*, 1933.
6. The Board of Health was created in 1885, the Board of Charities and Corrections, in 1913, and the Board of Mother's Aid, in 1917. 'Agencies of Government, 1820-1971' (Augusta: 1971).
7. Superintendent's Report, May 1935 and December 1935.

8. Superintendent's Report, February 1935. Atwood reported that Miss Fuger inspected the case record system, by-laws, patient register, and birth and death register and expressed 'great satisfaction' that the work was being conducted on 'a very high plane'. Superintendent's Report, January 1937.

9. Superintendent's Report, February 1938, February 1945, and February 1946; *Annual Report*, 1946; Executive Director's Report, October 1947.

10. *Annual Report*, 1936 and 1946; Superintendent's Report, February 1945.

11. Bangor developed a Bangor/Brewer Community Fund in 1938. Almost immediately the Good Samaritans had conflicts with the Community Chest Board which was mostly male and 'evidently not entirely in sympathy with our request'. Appearing before the Chest for the first time was, Atwood reported, 'a most unpleasant' experience. The Chest, by determining how public donations would be spent, limited the Good Samaritans' ability to draw on the support of the public which it had cultivated so well for so long. By 1946, however, the superintendent was able to report that the Home was able to operate without asking money from the Community Chest. Instead it relied on state funds, a healthy endowment, and admissions fees. Minutes, 13 September 1938; Superintendent's Report, September 1946.

12. The discussion is based on an analysis of a sample (every fifth record) of the adoption records arranged alphabetically in the Penobscot County Courthouse from 1857 to 1953.

13. Probate #138. 88, Penobscot County Courthouse.

14. #196-24 Letter from __ to Atwood, 31 May 1920.

15. This discussion is based on a sample of case files from the Good Samaritan Home. The sample comprised of the first six records of 1918 and every fifth record in chronological order of admission after that. The husbands of four other women may have adopted their wives' children, but there is no indication in the records that they did.

16. All the names of the parties involved were deleted from the case records. I have provided fictive names to make the narrative flow more naturally. In the case of quotes, however, I have retained the blanks that were in the documents.

17. In one case, it was the wife of the father of the child who insisted that her husband adopt the child. Superintendent's Report, February 1934; #508-336 Letter from __ to Atwood, 27 September 1939.

18. #191-19. Almost thirty years later one woman wrote that her child was placed in her hometown and that she could see her child whenever she wanted to. #805-610.

19. Neither did the New England Homes For Little Wanderers, the other child placing agency in the state. It was only the Maine Department of Welfare that required a woman to sign that she did 'hereby agree and pledge not to interfere with the custody, control, care or management of said child in any way or encourage or allow anyone else to do so'. Probate #6989, 1945.

20. #179-7 Letter from __ to Atwood, 27 February 1920.

21. #173-1 Letter from __ to Scoboria, 9 January 1918; #195-23 13 June 1920.

22. See above, ch. 4. For the history of adoption see Berebitsky, *Like Our Very Own*; W. E, Carp, *Family Matters: Secrecy and Disclosure in the History of Adoption* Cambridge: Cambridge University Press, 1998; and B. Melosh, *Strangers and Kin: The American Way of Adoption* (Cambridge, MA: Harvard University Press, 2002).

23. When the Depression hit three-fifth's of Maine's population still lived in rural areas. For Maine's response to the Depression see Judd, et al., *Maine*, pp. 506–29, 524 and 507.

24. Superintendent's Report, November 1933; Case Committee July, 1931; Superintendent's Report, April 1934; Minutes, 12 September 1933; Superintendent's Report, October 1933.
25. Superintendent's Report, April 1933.
26. Report to Trustees, 6 March 1933; *Annual Report*, 1938.
27. Fern was unusual in that she was married and Atwood took her husband to court. It is unclear from the record whether the baby was her husband's or not. Superintendent's Report, April 1934.
28. #571-400.
29. Hers was not an isolated case. The Good Samaritans were keeping Melvina so they could work out a plan for her when her mother demanded her immediate return to pick potatoes. 'The unwholesome condition of poverty and squalor existing in Melvina's home when she arrived there...was so upsetting to her that she is unwilling to remain at home or to leave her child there and she is now willing to comply with any plan made for her'. Superintendent's Report, Summer 1937. In spite of the squalid conditions, Atwood hesitated to attribute the bad conditions to the mother. Perhaps, she observed, 'in a family the size in which many of them are being reared, we should not expect much from a mother whose time must of necessity be spent in seeing that the family is fed and whose strength must have already been spent in giving birth to a child every year'. Superintendent's Report, February 1935, September 1937 and October 1937.
30. Superintendent's Report, Summer 1934 and October 1937. While Atwood described the advantages of the adopting parents, she did not stress the natural mother's poverty and low social status. Elsewhere, she reported that a fifteen-year old from Hall's Quarry 'with all that name implies', had placed her child. But when she reported the adoption to the Board, she stressed the youth of the girl and the inappropriateness of her living with grandparents 'both over seventy'.
31. Superintendent's Report, December 1938, January 1939, and December 1935; *Annual Report* 1934. It should be noted that even in these years the Good Samaritans placed relatively few children: four in 1935, three in 1936, and three in 1937. Superintendent's Report, Summer 1937.
32. The Good Samaritans had turned to adoption in cases where the mother had died or abandoned her child. They had also placed for adoption babies who had been boarded in the Home. See for example Minutes, 8 April 1930. Superintendent's Report, March 1935, May 1935 and Summer 1934; *Annual Report*, 1934.
33. Superintendent's Report, March 1934.
34. *Annual Report*, 1937.
35. Superintendent's Report, Summer 1940.
36. Superintendent's Report, February 1938.
37. #433-261.
38. Ibid., Letter from __ to Atwood, 4 August 1934 and 27 August 1934. The doctor strengthened his argument by referring to the advice and expertise of his friend, Dr. Bond, of the Mental Hygiene Institute.
39. Ibid. Letter from Atwood to __, 31 August 1934 and 8 December 1934.
40. Ibid. Letter from Atwood to __, 8 December 1934.
41. Ibid.
42. Superintendent's Report, Summer 1937; *Annual Report* 1937.
43. Oscar Shepard, article, *Bangor Daily News*, 23 October 1940; undated newspaper clipping in Good Samaritan Association newspaper collection.

44. Minutes, 14 September 1948, 14 October 1949, and May 1950; *Annual Report*, 1949.
45. Case Committee Report, 7 February 1950. 'It would have been impossible for our Home to have functioned but for State Aid', Atwood noted in 1939. Budget figures confirm that the $4-6,000 the Good Samaritans received annually from the state was critical to its operation. *Annual Report*, 1939.
46. #820-625, Letter from Tandy to Miss Alice Boyden, Vermont Children's Aid Society, 16 May 1950; Case Committee Report, 13 June 1950.
47. #865-670 Letter from Miss Krick to Mrs Tandy, 15 October 1951; #982-787 Case Notes, 24 August 1954.
48. In later conferences, state and national experts continued to stress the hazards of group homes, and Linwood Brown, Consultant for Private Agencies and Institutions, reminded the Good Samaritans that institutions were 'black eyes'. Executive and Budget Committee Report, 18 September 1946.
49. Even then the newly-shortened stay was longer than professionals recommended. The Temporary Home in Portland was astounded that the Good Samaritans had as many as thirteen residents willing to stay three months. The Temporary Home required a stay of six weeks after delivery, and still it could attract only one resident. Not only did the Board decrease the amount of time that a woman was required to stay, but it decreased the time a baby had to stay. This was in part in response to the demands of adopting parents who wanted a child in its infancy. By 1951 the Board was discussing the problem of women leaving their babies in the Home too long, and Lena Parrot offered to investigate the women who left babies for six months or more. 'Families would not like to have babies 'already used', she suggested.
50. Case Committee Report, December 1931.
51. See for example Minutes, 14 March 1933 and 13 March 1934; and Superintendent's Report, January 1936.
52. Minutes, 13 April 1943, Annual Report of Social Committee, January 1944; Social Committee Report, 10 May 1949; Executive Director's Report, February 1949, October 1951, February, April and October 1952; Minutes, 13 February 1951.
53. Superintendent's Report, December 1942; *Annual Report*, 1943; Minutes, 11 May 1943; Superintendent's Report, May 1942; *Bangor Daily News*, 24 August 1943.
54. Atwood bought a washing machine in 1934 explaining, 'This appeared necessary as our girls at present are so very young that it did not seem wise for them to do such heavy work'. In 1943, Hayward explained that they needed to hire someone to do the yard work by commenting, 'Our slogan at the Home regarding grass cutting is now, 'They're either too young or too old'. That year the staff also relied on firemen to do the shoveling. Superintendent's Report, December 1934; *Annual Report* 1943; Social Committee Report, 1943
55. Superintendent's Report, February 1944; Executive Director's Report, October 1950.
56. Executive Committee, 28 October 1936; Minutes, 13 April 1937.
57. *Annual Report*, 1944 and 1945.
58. #988-793 Letter from Rugan to __, 9 March 1955; #890-695 Letter from Hayward to __ 30 November 1951; #945-740 Letter from Hayward to Rubinoff, 7 October 1953.
59. The gossip in rural Maine communities reinforced the obligation the young women had to work hard and support their children. See below.
60. In 1950, for example, they had to cut out the services of one of three nurses. *Annual Report*, 1950.

61. #173-1 'Rules'. These rules were in use at least from the time the Home was on 105 Third Street. Case Committee Report, 1933. The Good Samaritans sometimes helped the second offender unofficially.
62. Regina Kunzel discusses the shift from seeing the woman as feeble-minded or sex delinquent to psychologically damaged. See Kunzel, *Fallen Women*, ch. 5.
63. #212-41 Letter from Atwood to __, 16 December 1940.
64. Executive Director's Report, Summer 1942.
65. Social Worker Report, 1951. Good Samaritan Agency, *90th Anniversary Historical Review*.
66. #297-125 Letter from Atwood to __, 2 April 1928. #1042-849 Case Notes.
67. Undated and unsigned report, Good Samaritan Association Files.
68. The sample includes every fifth case of the Good Samaritan Association records for that time.
69. #865-670 Letter from __ to Hayward, undated; #760-563 Letter from Shirley Davis, RN, to Hayward, 7 January 1948; #988-793 Letter from __ to Good Samaritans, undated; #997-801 Case Notes, 26 April 1955.
70. #617-436 Letter from __ to Mrs. Merrill, 1 January 1944; #685-690 Letter from __ to Hayward, 11 April 1953.
71. Not only were these women working independently at an early age, they were also taking care of themselves. Cora, only seventeen, had already contacted a lawyer about a bastardy suit when she contacted the Good Samaritans. #495-323 Letter from __ to Good Samaritans, undated.
72. #1072-901 Letter from Mrs. Edith Anderson to Eugenia Rugan, 29 April 1957.
73. #498-326 Letter from Eva Scates to Atwood, 8 February 1937; #573 Letters from __ to Hayward, 6 and 11 June 1948.
74. The Good Samaritans offered women the opportunity to earn money in work foster homes but as Rugan noted in 1956, the Good Samaritans could not be responsible for the work homes as they hadn't had good luck with them in the past. #1048-855 Case Notes, 31 July 1956 to 24 January 1957.
75. #785-588 Letter from Hayward to Edward I. Gross, 10 November 1948; #988-793 Letter from Eugenia Rugan to __, 9 March 1955; #890-695 Letter from Hayward to __, 30 November 1951; #945-740 Letter from Hayward to Leah S. Rubinoff, 7 October 1953. In the last case the woman owed $203. 81 for an extended hospital stay and hospital aid would pay no more than sixty dollars of this.
76. #840-645 Letter from __ to Mrs Tandy, 1 May 1952; #896-695 Letter from Hayward to __ 30 November 1951; #877 Letter from Rugan to __ 19 March 1957; #1035-842 Letter from Rugan to Dr. Desjardin, 26 April 1956.
77. #840-645 Letter from __ to Mrs Tandy, 1 May 1952.
78. In 1954, one woman reported to Rugan that Judge Gross had informed her that the boy would pay weekly. In 1951, another resident reported that her lawyer had said that she could get the father to pay until the child was twenty-one. #982-787 Superintendent Notes, 19 July 1954; #890-695 Superintendent Notes, 4 March 1952.
79. See for example #760-563, #785-588, #805-610 and #840-645. #988-793 Letter from __ to Rugan, undated (1955); unnumbered (Admission date 8 January 1959) Case Notes, 6 January 1959 to 29 April 1959.
80. #815-620 Superintendent's Notes, 14 March 1950; #810-615 Superintendent's Notes, March 1950; #380.

81. Many of the bastardy suits that were initiated involved men in the Air Force and many of these men were from out of state. #755-558 Letter from Scates to Hayward, undated (1953).
82. #465 Letter from Joly & Marden to Merrill, 14 November 1944; 915-720 Letter from Merrill to Harry C. McManus, 27 January 1953.
83. #915-720; #941-776; #997-801 Case Notes.
84. The allotments were $64 a month in 1952.
85. #982-787 Case Notes, 19 July 1954.
86. #775-578 Letter from Helen L. Webber to Merrill, 8 July 1948.
87. #775-578 Letter from Merrill to __, 8 February 1949. Tennessee had a similar program though it may not have lasted as long as the program in Maine did. *Memphis Press Scimitar*, 4 December 1929.
88. Ibid, Letter from __ to Merrill, 15 May 1949.
89. #735-538 Letter from __ to Hayward, 18 July 1947; #720-523 Letter from __ to Hayward, undated (1946); #785-588 Letter from __ to Hayward, 21 February 1949.
90. The state during this time and through 1958 routinely took into its custody the children of women committed to its care. #976-781 Case Notes, 13 September 1954.
91. #595-414 Letter from Mrs Marjorie P. Anderson to 'Madame', 26 August 1941.
92. Ibid, Record, unidentified; Letter from Merrill to Miss __, 7 April 1942. Elsie was deemed un-adoptable due to the fact that the doctors could not be certain that she would develop normally. When she was one-year-old, Dr. Albert Fellows conducted a second exam and concluded that she was doing well. 'No evidence of damage to the nerves of the legs. Normal child except' as found in the first examination, the 'nodule at the end of the inter-gluteal fold'. Letter from Merrill to Parrot, 19 August 1942.
93. Ibid, Letter from __ to Mrs Merrill, 8 April 1942.
94. Ibid, Letter from Parrot to Merrill, 9 May 1942; Letter from Parrot to __, 20 July 1942.
95. Ibid, Letter from Parrot to __, 31 July 1942. In a memo to the social worker asking her to contact Catherine's parents, Parrot makes clear that if the baby is not adoptable, 'it is doubly important for us to preserve the family ties she has. Commitment may be necessary in order to provide support for the child, but we can handle commitment in such a way that Elsie's mother and other relatives can still feel that she is their child to love and plan for'. Memo from Parrot to Miss Hall, 13 August 1942.
96. Ibid, __ to Parrot, 21 July 1942.
97. Ibid, Letter from __ to Parrot, 3 August 1942.
98. Ibid, Letter from __ to Mrs. Stearns, 20 March 1943. The child was committed. Six years later the Aid to Dependent Children Division of the Overseers of the City of Boston wrote to the Good Samaritans requesting information about Catherine who wanted to place a child in care. The record is silent on whether Catherine had a second child or was taking Elsie back.
99. #830-635 Letter from __ to Hayward, 19 August 1950.
100. #850-655.
101. Ibid. Letter from __ to Merrill, 30 December 1950.
102. #850-655 Letter from Davis to Merrill, 6 July 1951; Social Worker's Notes, undated.
103. #1072-901 Case Notes, 29 April 1957 to October 7 1957.
104. #1048-855 Case Notes, 31 July 1956 to 24 January 1957.
105. #850-655 Letter from Shirley Davis to Merrill, 6 July 1951.
106. #1014-821 Case Notes, 8 July 1955; Letters from __ to Rugan, 14 July 1955 and 28 October 1955. Hazel's decision to give up the child and then to keep it was complex.

As with so many of the other women, Hazel explained that she wanted to give the child up because she knew she could not care for it and she did not see how her parents could because they had a large family. Hazel's mother had left school to marry and it is possible that Hazel did not want to follow in her mother's footsteps. Rugan, however, suspected that the father was a married man and that he was paying her bill. 'It was very hard for __ to see the baby go', Rugan noted right after it was born '...and I felt as I watched her that she had not made up her mind'.

107. #967-772 Letter from Krick to Rugan, 4 August 1954; #935-740 Case Note, 27 July 1953.

108. #885-690 Case Notes, 9 August 1951

109. #1004-811 Case Notes, 23 March 1955.

110. #1035-842 Case Notes, 1 May 1956 to 18 September 1956.

111. #1089-926, Case Note, 27 February 1958.

112. #967-772, Letter from Miss Krick to Rugan, 4 August 1954.

113. #940-745 Letter from __ to Hayward, 2 December 1953; #705-512 Letters from __ to Mrs. Lovitt, 22 December 1946 and 11 January 1947.

114. #758-561 Letter to Merrill from __ 20 June 1948.

115. It was also reflected in the large number of women who returned home only to ask the Good Samaritans for a job. Letters from __ to Hayward, 21 October 1943 and 7 December 1943.

Conclusion

1. Today black women give up their children at the same rate as do white women. Historically, however, they did so at a much lower rate. Fessler found that between 1952–1972 white women surrendered their children ten times more often than black women. Fessler, *The Girls Who Went Away*, pp. 108 and 110.

2. A. Petrie, *Gone to Aunt's: Remembering Canada's Homes for Unwed Mothers* (Toronto: McLelland and Stewart, 1998), pp. 222 and 224.

3. Parliament of Tasmania, Joint Select Committee, 1999, 'Adoption and Related Services: 1950–1988', 10 and 11 as quoted in Fessler, *The Girls Who Went Away*, p. 293

4. B. B. Raymond, *The Baby Thief: The Untold Story of Georgia Tann, the Baby Seller Who Corrupted Adoption* (New York: Carrol & Graf, 2007), p. 248.

5. Raymond, *The Baby Thief*, p. 248 and 251.

6. A. Appadurai, *Modernity at Large: Cultural Dimensions of Globalization* (Minneapolis, MN: University of Minnesota Press, 1996), pp. 9, 10, 2 and 3.

7. B. Ching and G. W. Creed, 'Recognizing Rusticity: Identity and the Power of Place' in *Knowing Your Place: Rural Identity and Cultural Hierarchy* edited by Ching and Creed (New York: Routledge, 1997), pp. 5 and 7.

WORKS CITED

Newspapers

Bangor Daily News

Bangor Daily Commercial

Chattanooga Times

Daily Eastern Argus

Gleaner, June 1891–June 1892 (Publication of the Memphis Woman's Christian Association)

Memphis Commercial Appeal

Memphis Evening Scimitar

Memphis Press Scimitar

Memphis Daily Avalanche

Memphis Daily Appeal

Memphis Appeal-Avalanche

Tennessean

Archives

Bethany Home, 901 Chelsea Avenue, Memphis, TN 38107.

Charles C. Sherrod Library, East Tennessee State University, Lake Street and Seehorn Road, Johnson City, TN 37614-1701.

Good Samaritan Agency, 100 Ridgewood Drive, Bangor, ME 04401.

Maine State Archives, 84 State House Station, Augusta, ME 04333.

Memphis and Shelby County Room, Memphis Public Library: Central Branch 3030 Poplar Avenue, Memphis, TN 38111-3527

Nashville Public Library, 615 Church Street, Nashville, TN 37211.

Tennessee State Library and Archives, 403 7th Avenue, Nashville, TN 37243.

Primary Sources

Ashcraft, V., *Public Care: A History of Public Welfare Legislation in Tennessee* (Knoxville, TN: University of Tennessee Press, 1947).

Clements, I., 'Enlightened Society Now Aids Unmarried Mothers in City In Facing Problems of Life', *Commercial Appeal* (4 October 1951).

Clopper, E. N., *Child Welfare in Tennessee: An Inquiry by the National Child Labor Committee for the Tennessee Child Welfare Commissioner* (Nashville, TN: Tennessee Industrial School, 1920).

Ferris, J. C., *Homes for the Homeless or Fourteen Years among the Orphans* (Nashville, TN: M.E. Church, South, 1895).

Freund, E., *Illegitimacy Laws of the US and Certain Foreign Countries* (Washington, DC: GPO, 1919).

Hagood, M., *Mohers of the South* (1939; New York: Greenwood Press, 1969).

Holley, W., C. E. Winston, and T. J. Woofter, Jr, *The Plantation South: 1934–1937*, vol. 22, Research Monograph (Washington, DC: US Government Printing Office, 1940).

Kelley, C., *Delinquent Angels* (Kansas City, MO: Brown-White-Lowell Press, 1947).

Killibrew, J. B., *Resources of Tennessee* (Nashville, TN: Tavel, Eastman & Howell, 1874).

Lively, C. E., and C. Aeuber, *Rural Migration in the United States*, ed. Works Progress Administration, vol. 19, Research Monograph (Washington, DC: US Government Printing Office, 1939).

Lundberg, E. O., and K. F. Lenroot. 'Illegitimacy as a Child Welfare Problem' (Washington, DC: Government Printing Office, 1920).

McCauley, E., 'A Study of Legal and Social Aspects of Adoption in Tennessee' (Nashville, TN: School of Social Work, 1947).

Meriwether, L., *Soundings* (Memphis, TN: Boyle & Chapin, 1872).

Perley, J., *Powers and Duties of Justices of Peace with the Necessary Forms Particularly Adapted to the Laws of Maine*. 2nd edn (Hallowell: Glazier, Masters, & Co., 1829).

Scott, E., *Background in Tennessee* (New York: Robert McBride, 1937).

Wilson, O., *Fifty Years' Work with Girls, 1883–1933* (Alexandria, VA: National Florence Crittenton Mission, 1933).

Young, L., *Unmarried Mothers in Nashville and Davidson County: A Study of Requests for Service and Its Availability to Unmarried Mothers in Nashville and Davidson County, Tennessee* (Nashville, TN: Council of Community Agencies, 1949).

Secondary Sources

Abbot, E., *Public Assistance: American Principles and Policies*, reprint (New York: Russell and Russell, 1940).

Alexander, T. B., *Political Reconstruction in Tennessee* (1950; New York: Russell & Russell, 1968).

Appadurai, A., *Modernity at Large: Cultural Dimensions of Globalization* (Minneapolis, MN: University of Minnesota Press, 1997).

Apple, R. D., *Mothers and Medicine: A Social History of Infant Feeding, 1890-1950* (Madison, WI: University of Wisconsin Press, 1987).

Arnold-Zourie, C., '"A Madman's Deed – A Maniac's Hand": Gender and Justice in Three Maryland Lynchings', *Journal of Social History* (Summer 2008), pp. 1031–45.

Austin, L. T., *Babies for Sale: Tennessee Children's Adoption Scandal* (Westport, CT: Praeger, 1993).

Bardaglio, P. W., *Reconstructing the Household: Families, Sex, & the Law in the Nineteenth-Century South*, ed. T. A. Green and H. Hartog, Studies in Legal History (Chapel Hill, NC: University of North Carolina Press, 1995).

Barron, H. S., *Mixed Harvest: The Second Great Transformation in the Rural North 1870–1930*, ed. J. T. Kirby, Studies in Rural Culture (Chapel Hill, NC: University of North Carolina Press, 1997).

Barry, W. D., *The History of Sweetser-Children's Home: A Century and a Half of Service to Maine Children* (Portland, ME: Anthoensen Press, 1988).

Beam, L., *A Maine Hamlet* (1957; Augusta, ME: Lance Tapley, 1987).

Beniger, J. R., *The Control Revolution: Technological and Economic Origins of the Information Society* (Cambridge, MA: Harvard University Press, 1986).

Berebitsky, J., *Like Our Very Own: Adoption and the Changing Culture of Motherhood, 1851–1950* (Lawrence, KS: University Press of Kansas, 2000).

Berkeley, K. C., 'Elizabeth Avery Meriwether, "an Advocate for Her Sex": Feminism and Conservatism in the Post-Civil War South', *Tennessee Historical Quarterly* 63 (1984), pp. 390–407.

Biles, R., *Memphis in the Great Depression* (Knoxville, TN: University of Tennessee Press, 1986).

Blaisdell, J. P. (compiler), 'History – Stevens School, Hallowell Maine 1875–1920' (Unpublished manuscript).

Bledstein, B. J., *The Culture of Professionalism: The Middle Class and the Development of Higher Education in America* (New York: Norton & Co., 1976).

Brandenstein, S., 'The Colorado Cottage Home', *Colorado Magazine*, 53:3 (1976), pp. 229–41.

Brumberg, J. J., 'Ruined Girls: Changing Community Responses to Illegitimacy in Upstate New York, 1890–1920', *Journal of Social History*, 18 (1984–1985), pp. 247–72.

Butler, 'A Family & Community Life in Maine, 1783–1861', in R. W. Judd et al. (eds), *Maine: The Pine Tree State from Prehistory to the Present* (Orono, ME: University of Maine Press, 1994), pp. 217–41.

Bynum, V. E., *Unruly Women: The Politics of Social and Sexual Control in the Old South* (Chapel Hill, NC: University of North Carolina Press, 1992).

Carp, E. W., 'The Sealed Adoption Records Controversy in Historical Perspective: The Case of the Children's Home Society of Washington, 1895–1988', *Journal of Sociology and Social Welfare*, 19 (June 1992), pp. 27–58.

Censer, J. T., *The Reconstruction of White Southern Womanhood 1865–1895* (Baton Rouge, LA: Louisiana State University Press, 2003).

Ching, B., and G. W. Creed, 'Recognizing Rusticity: Identity and the Power of Place' in *Knowing Your Place: Rural Identity and Cultural Hierarchy* edited by Ching and Creed (New York: Routledge, 1997).

Condon, R. H., 'Nearing the End: Maine's Rural Community, 1929–1945', *Maine History*, 25, pp. 58–87.

Cooper, W. J., Jr and T. E. Terrill, *The American South* (New York: McGraw-Hill, 1991).

Corlew, R. E., *Tennessee: A Short History*, 2nd edn (Knoxville, TN: University of Tennessee Press, 1990).

Cott, N. F., *Public Vows: A History of Marriage and the Nation* (Cambridge, MA: Harvard University Press, 2000).

Couch, W. T. (ed.), *These Are Our Lives* (Chapel Hill, NC: University of North Carolina Press, 1939).

D'Emilio, J., and E. B. Freedman, *Intimate Matters: A History of Sexuality in America* (New York: Harper & Row, 1988).

Danbom, D. B., *Born in the Country: A History of Rural America*, ed. P. Daniel and D. K. Fitzgerald, Revisiting Rural America (Baltimore, MD: Johns Hopkins Univ. Press, 1995).

DeRoche, P. C., '"These Lines of My Life": Franco-American Women in Westbrook, Maine, the Intersection of Ethnicity and Gender in 1884–1984' (MA Thesis, University of Maine 1994).

Dromgoole, W. A., 'The Age of Consent in Tennessee', *Arena*, 11 (January 1895), pp. 207–9.

Duggan, L., *Sapphic Slashers: Sex, Violence, and American Modernity* (Durham, NC: Duke University Press, 2000).

Duster, A. M. (ed.), *Crusade for Justice* (Chicago, IL: University of Chicago Press, 1970).

Fessler, A., *The Girls Who Went Away: The Hidden History of Women Who Surrendered Children for Adoption in the Decades before Roe v. Wade* (New York: Penguin Press, 2006).

Friedman, L. M., *A History of American Law*, 2nd edn (New York: Simon and Schuster, 1985).

—, *Crime and Punishment in American History (New York: Basic Books, 1993)*.

Fuchs, R. G., *Gender and Poverty in Nineteenth-Century Europe*, ed. W. and T. C. W. Blanning Beik, New Approaches to European History (Cambridge: Cambridge University Press, 2005).

—, *Poor & Pregnant in Paris: Strategies for Survival in the Nineteenth Century* (New Brunswick, NJ: Rutgers University Press, 1992).

Giddings, P., *Ida: A Sword among Lions* (New York: Harper Collins, 2008).

Gilmore, G. E., *Gender & Jim Crow: Women and the Politics of White Supremacy in North Carolina, 1896–1920* (Chapel Hill, NC: University of North Carolina Press, 1996).

Gordon, L., *Pitied but Not Entitled: Single Mothers and the History of Welfare, 1890–1935* (Cambridge, MA: Harvard University Press, 1994).

Grossberg, M., *Governing the Hearth: Law and the Family in Nineteenth-Century America* (Chapel Hill, NC: North Carolina Press, 1985).

—, 'Guarding the Alter: Physiological Restrictions and the Rise of State Intervention in Matrimony'. *The American Journal of Legal History*, 26:3 (1982), pp. 197–226.

Gutman, H. G., *The Black Family in Slavery and Freedom, 1750–1925* (New York: Random House, 1976).

Hahn, S., *The Roots of Southern Populism: Yeoman Farmers and the Transformation of the Georgia Upcountry, 1850–1890* (New York: Oxford University Press, 1983).

Hodes, M., 'The Sexualization of Reconstruction Politics: White Women and Black Men in the South after the Civil War', *Journal of the History of Sexuality*, 3:3 (1993), pp. 402–17.

Hoffschwelle, M. S., *Rebuilding the Southern Community: Reformers, Schools, and Homes in Tennessee, 1900–1930* (Knoxville, TN: University of Tennessee Press, 1998).

Judd, R. W. et al. (ed.), *Maine: The Pine Tree State from Prehistory to Present* (Orono, ME: University of Maine Press, 1995).

Katz, M. B., *In the Shadow of the Poorhouse: A Social History of Welfare in America* (New York: Basic Books, 1986).

Keith, J., *Country People in the New South*, ed. J. T. Kirby, Studies in Rural Culture (Chapel Hill, NC: University of North Carolina Press, 1995).

Kemmis, D., *Community and the Politics of Place* (Norman, OK: University of Oklahoma Press, 1990).

Kirby, J. T., *Rural Worlds Lost: The American South, 1920–1960* (Baton Rouge, LA: Louisiana State University Press, 1987).

Krause, H. D., *Illegitimacy: Law and Social Policy* (New York: Bobbs-Merrill, 1971).

Kulikoff, A., *Tobacco and Slaves: The Development of Southern Cultures in the Chesapeake, 1680–1800* (Chapel Hill, NC: University of North Carolina Press, 1986).

Kunzel, R. G., *Fallen Women, Problem Girls: Unmarried Mothers Ande the Professionalization of Social Work, 1890–1945* (New Haven, CT: Yale University Press, 1993).

Kyriakoudes, L. M., *The Social Origins of the Urban South: Race, Gender, and Migration in Nashville and Middle Tennesee, 1890–1930* (Chapel Hill, NC: University of North Carolina Press, 2003).

Ladner, J., *Tomorrow's Tomorrow: The Black Woman* (New York: Doubleday, 1973).

Lane, R., *Murder in America: A History* (Columbus, OH: Ohio State University Press, 1997).

Laslett, P, K. Oosterveen and R.M. Smith, *Bastardy and Its Comparative History* (Cambridge, MA: Harvard university Press, 1980).

Massey, D., *Space, Place, and Gender*, 5th edn (Minneapolis, MN: University of Minnesota Press, 1994).

McCauley, E., 'A Study of Legal and Social Aspects of Adoption in Tennessee'. (Manuscript, Nashville School of Social Work, 1947).

McConnell, N. F., and M. Morrison Dore, *1883–1983: Crittenton Services: The First Century* (Washington, DC: National Florence Crittenton Mission, 1983).

McDonald, M. J., and J. Muldowny, *Tva and the Dispossessed: The Resettlement of Population in the Norris Dam Area* (Knoxville, TN: University of Tennessee Press, 1982).

Meckel, R. A., *Save the Babies* (Baltimore, MD: Johns Hopkins University Press, 1990).

Melosh, B., *Strangers and Kin: The American Way of Adoption* (Cambridge, MA: Harvard University Press, 2002).

Miller, W. D., *Memphis During the Depression Era* (Memphis, TN: Memphis State University Press, 1957).

Mohr, J., *Abortion in America: The Origins and Evolution of National Policy* (New York: Oxford University Press, 1978).

Morton, M. J., *And Sin No More: Social Policy and Unwed Mothers in Cleveland, 1855–1990* (Columbus, OH: Ohio State University Press, 1993).

Neill, K., 'Adoption for Profit: Conspiracy and Cover-Up', *Memphis Magazine*, 3:7 (1978).

Newby, I. A., *Plain Folk in the New South: Social Change and Cultural Persistence 1880–1915* (Baton Rouge, LA: Louisiana State University Press, 1989).

Painter, N. I., 'A Prize Winning Book Revisited', *Journal of Women's History* 2:3 (Winter 1991).

Pascoe, P., *Relations of Rescue: The Search for Female Moral Authority in the American West, 1874–1939* (New York: Oxford University Press, 1990).

Petrie, A., *Gone to an Aunt's: Remembering Canada's Homes for Unwed Mothers* (Toronto: McClelland & Stewart, 1998).

Plane, A. M., 'Colonizing the Family: Marriage, Household and Racial Boundaries in Southeastern New England to 1730' (unpublished dissertation Brandeis University, MA, 1996).

Raymond, B. B., *The Baby Thief: The Untold Story of Gerogia Tann, the Baby Seller who Corrupted Adoption* (New York: Carroll & Graf, 2007).

Reskin, B. F., 'Bringing the Men Back In: Sex Differentiation and the Devaluation of Women's Work', *Gender & Society* 2:1 (March 1988), pp. 58–81.

Robinson, J. L., *Living Hard: Southern Americans in the Great Depression* (Washington, DC: University Press of America, 1981).

Ruggles, S., 'Fallen Women: The Inmates of the Magdalen Society Asylum of Philadelphia, 1936–1908', *Journal of Social History*, 16 (1983), pp. 65–82.

Rutman, D. B., 'Assessing the Little Communities of Early America'. *The William and Mary Quarterly*, 3d ser., 43:2 (April 1986), pp. 164–78.

Schriver, E. O. 'Female Prisoners at the Maine State Prison, 1864–1887' (Unpublished paper, University of Maine, 1993).

Silsby, H. T., *A History of Aurora, Maine* (Ellsworth, ME: Hancock County Publishing, 1958).

Smith, D., 'The Long Cycle in American Illegitimacy and Prenuptial Pregnancy', in P. Laslett et al. (eds), *Bastardy and Its Comparative History* New York: Cambridge University Press, 1980).

Solinger, R., *Wake up Little Susie: Single Pregnancy and Race before Roe v. Wade* (New York: Routledge, 2000).

Stack, C., *All Our Kin: Strategies for Survival in a Black Community* (New York: Harper & Row, 1974).

Taylor, R. L., 'Report to Governor Gordon Browning on the Shelby County Branch Tennessee Children's Home Society' (Nashville, TN: Tennessee Department of Human Services, 21 May 1951).

Terrill, T. E., and J. Hirsch, *Such as Us; Southern Voices of the Thirties* (Chapel Hill, NC: University of North Carolina Press, 1978).

Trattner, W., *From Poor Law to Welfare State: A Hisory of Social Welfare in America*, 2nd edn (New York: Free Press, 1979).

Ulrich, L. T., *A Midwife's Tale: The Life of Martha Ballard, Based on Her Diary, 1785–1812* (New York: Knopf, 1980).

Vicinus, M., *Independent Women: Work and Community for Single Women, 1850-1920* (Chicago, IL: University of Chicago Press, 1985).

Walker, M., *All We Knew Was to Farm: Rural Women in the Upcountry South, 1919–1941*, ed. P. Daniel and M. C. Neth, Revisiting Rural America (Baltimore, MD: Johns Hopkins Univ. Press, 2000).

—, *Country Women Cope with Hard Times: A Collection of Oral Histories*, ed. C. Bleser, Womens Diaries and Letters of the South (Columbia, SC: University of South Caolina Press, 2004).

Walker, M, J. R. Dunn and J. P. Dunn (eds), *Southern Women at the Millennium: A Historical Perspective* (Columbia, MO: University of Missouri Press, 2005).

Walker, M., and R. Sharpless. *Work, Family, and Faith: Rural Southern Women in the Twentieth Century* (Columbia, MO: University of Missouri Press, 2006).

Wedell, M., *Elite Women and the Reform Impulse in Memphis, 1875–1915* (Knoxville, TN: University of Tennessee Press, 1991).

Wells-Barnett, I., *Selected Works of Ida B. Wells-Barnett*, ed. T. Harris (New York: Oxford University Press, 1991).

Wickware (ed.), F. G., *The American Year Book: A Record of Events and Progress* (New York: D. Appleton and Co., 1917).

Wiegman, R., 'The Anatomy of Lynching', *Journal of the History of Sexuality*, 3:3 (1993), p. 461.

Wiebe, R. H., *The Search for Order, 1877–1920* (New York: Hill and Wang, 1967).

Wiggins, A. C., 'The Migrant Girl' (unpublished thesis for Vanderbilt University, TN, 1933).

Wilson, O., *Fifty Years' Work with Girls* (rpt. 1933, New York: Arno Press, 1974).

Winters, D. L., *Tennessee Farming, Tennessee Farmers: Antebellum Agriculture in the Upper South* (Knoxville, TN: University of Tennessee Press, 1994).

Wyatt-Brown, B., *Honor and Violence in the Old South* (New York: Oxford University Press, 1986).

Zelizer, V. A., *Pricing the Priceless Child: The Changing Social Value of Children* (New York: Basic Books, 1985).

Zunz, O., *Making America Corporate* (Chicago, IL: University of Chicago Press, 1990).

INDEX

For Product Safety Concerns and Information please contact our EU
representative GPSR@taylorandfrancis.com Taylor & Francis Verlag GmbH,
Kaufingerstraße 24, 80331 München, Germany

Printed and bound by CPI Group (UK) Ltd, Croydon, CR0 4YY

08/05/2025

01864507-0001